Her Majesty The Queen

Her Majesty
THE QUEEN

Hugh Montgomery-Massingberd

WILLOW BOOKS · COLLINS/LONDON

Dedicated to the memory of the author's dear
uncle and fellow royalty-watcher the late Very
Reverend Monsignor Hugh Montgomery

Frontispiece: Billowing cloaks on the
steps of St George's Chapel, Windsor, following
the annual service of the Order of the Garter

Willow Books
William Collins Sons & Co Ltd
London/Glasgow/Sydney/Auckland/Toronto/
Johannesburg

First published in Great Britain 1985
© Antler Books 1985

Produced by John Stidolph, Antler Books Ltd
11 Rathbone Place, London W1P 1DE

Page design by Paul Watkins
Picture research by Tom Williams
Editorial assistant Susan Bilton
Index by Geraldine Christy

British Library Cataloguing in Publication Data
Montgomery-Massingberd, Hugh
    Her Majesty The Queen
    1. Elizabeth II Queen of Great Britain
    2. Great Britain – Kings and rulers – Biography
    I. Title
    941.085'092'4   DA590
    ISBN 0–00–218072–3

Typesetting by Falcon Graphic Art Ltd
Wallington, Surrey
Origination by BBE Colour Ltd
Chelmsford, Essex
Printed by Collins, Glasgow

Contents

Introduction/6

1 The Queen and Her Upbringing/10

2 The Queen and Prince Philip/32

3 The Queen and the New Elizabethan Age/46

4 The Queen and the Constitution/62

5 The Queen and Her Travels/74

6 The Queen and the Commonwealth/94

7 The Queen and the Royal Round/102

8 The Queen and the Royal Family/122

9 The Queen and Her Homes/172

10 The Queen and Her Court/196

11 The Queen and Her Sport/210

12 The Queen at Sixty/222

Chronology of the Queen's Reign/236

Acknowledgements/254

Index/255

Introduction

The Queen and her guards: Her Majesty inspecting the Queen's Company of the Grenadier Guards at Windsor Castle, April 1983. The Queen succeeded her godfather, the Duke of Connaught, as Colonel of the regiment in 1942

By the sudden death of my dear father I am called to assume the duties and responsibility of sovereignty", the Queen told her Privy Council in her typically simple and direct Accession Declaration on 8 February 1952, the day after her return from Kenya where she had (unknowingly for the first few hours of her reign) succeeded to the throne. "My heart is too full for me to say more to you today than that I shall always work, as my father did throughout his reign, to uphold constitutional government and to advance the happiness and prosperity of my peoples, spread as they are the world over." To those who can remember the vivid image of a strikingly youthful, solitary figure, dressed in black, coming down the gangway of the aircraft the day before to take up the immense burden of monarchy, it seems extraordinary to think that the Queen is now on the verge of being "a senior citizen". At her Accession Declaration her mere 25 years made, as Oliver Lyttelton (later Viscount Chandos) recalled, her Privy Councillors look "immeasurably old and gnarled and grey". Although the Queen has inevitably lost, if only quite recently, some of her remarkable bloom that no photograph has ever succeeded in capturing and which so startles those who see her for the first time in the flesh, nobody could call her old (the grey only discreetly apparent around the temples). It certainly gives one pause to realise that she celebrates her 60th birthday on 21 April 1986.

"Elizabeth The Second, By the Grace of God, of the United Kingdom of Great Britain and Northern Ireland and of Her Other Realms and Territories . . ." goes the sonorous roll-call and it is as well for those who complain of her harping on about the Commonwealth that she is indeed not only Head of the Commonwealth of some four-dozen countries but also, as it were, wears ten other crowns on her dignified brow. Despite often being thought of as just "the Queen of England", she is also Queen of Australia, Queen of the Bahamas, Queen of Barbados, Queen of Canada, Queen of Fiji, Queen of Grenada (*pace* Ronald Reagan), Queen of Jamaica, Queen of Mauritius, Queen of New Zealand and Queen of Papua New Guinea. Little Englanders tend to forget that she is not just "our Queen" but "theirs" too; she never does. For the development of her beloved "Commonwealth family" (as she describes it) is probably, in her eyes, the proudest achievement of her reign.

Whatever her official nomenclature, she is known the world over as "The Queen". When a Frenchman refers to "*La Reine*" he is not – with all due respect to, say, Margrethe of Denmark or Beatrix of the Netherlands or even the late lamented Queen Selote of Tonga – meaning anyone other than Queen Elizabeth II. And yet for all her worldwide celebrity the Queen remains a very private person. She has managed to remain aloof from the brash vulgarity of the modern age. She has adapted with the times but never too much. The Queen does not give interviews.

Her personality remains something of an enigma. She has inherited her grandmother Queen Mary's stiffness and shyness, and also her devastatingly haughty glower. What the royal household knows as the Queen's "acid-drop" look can speak tomes of Majestic displeasure. Once her rather stern features relax into a smile, the Queen is quite another person: warm, humorous (with a disarmingly unpompous laugh), surprisingly "easy" and unaffectedly natural. Emphatically a country person, passionately fond of racing (her virtually unrivalled knowledge of the Turf has become an absorbing, dedicated diversion from her official duties), the Queen might well prefer a life of horses, dogs, headscarves and gum-boots, watching television with her supper on a tray and so forth to all the panoply of monarchy. She is not an actress or an outgoing "performer" like the Queen Mother and the job obviously makes enormous demands on such a naturally withdrawn character. It is a job she takes very seriously indeed for "duty" is her watchword.

As Field-Marshal Smuts observed at her wedding, the Queen has always been "serious and wise beyond her years". By no means an intellectual, she is nevertheless sharply intelligent (quite a different matter) with an instinct for statecraft and a grasp of essentials. Politicians have testified to her knack of going straight to the core of a problem, cutting incisively through a cloud of waffle. She tackles a vast workload (the ubiquitous "Red Boxes") unseen and unappreciated by those who only associate her with pomp and pageantry or holidays in Scotland.

Part of the Elizabethan enigma is that the Queen's true worth is underestimated and undersold. Far from a cipher or a constitutional puppet, the Queen exercises a much more important and effective influence over affairs of state than is generally understood. She is, after all, the most experienced political figure in Britain and the Commonwealth, having already dealt with eight British Prime Ministers from Sir Winston Churchill to Margaret Thatcher (who did not even enter Parliament until the eighth year of the Queen's reign). She has never lacked for courage, consistently ignoring the pleas of her politicians to keep away from danger spots and braving a bizarre series of incidents (blank shots at the Birthday Parade, an unhinged intruder in her bedroom) with incredible calmness and cheerfulness.

As if to multiply the paradox, though we may not know the Queen or fully appreciate her statesmanlike qualities, many people somehow feel they know what she is really

Right: The Queen gratifies one of Princess Anne's dogs (Apollo by name) in the park at Windsor

like, what she thinks, what she stands for. The Queen is a sort of national conscience. She represents, in more than a symbolic way, what is best in Britain and the Commonwealth. She is the rock that links the past to the present and future. "In the year I was born", she recalled in one of her Christmas broadcasts, "radio communication was barely out of its infancy: there was no television: civil aviation had hardly started and space satellites were still in the realm of science fiction." Her reign has witnessed astonishing changes in travel and mass communication which have revolutionised the monarchy but she has never deviated from her course. For the Queen the monarchy is an hereditary office with a mystical, rational and lasting purpose, not a job from which she can – or would – retire at sixty or any other age.

I. The Queen and Her Upbringing

Her Royal Highness the Duchess of York was safely delivered of a Princess at 2.40 a.m. this morning, Wednesday, April 21st" (1926) announced the Home Office whose Secretary of State, Sir William Joynson-Hicks, had been officially "present" at the birth to make sure there was no baby-swapping. The birth took place in a first-floor room of the London house of the Duchess's parents, the Earl and Countess of Strathmore and Kinghorne, 17 Bruton Street. It was not a straightforward delivery; the medical bulletin from Mayfair reported that "a certain line of treatment was successfully adopted". In other words, a Caesarean section was performed to produce the infant Princess.

Just as at her Coronation 27 years later the weather was inclined to drizzle but this did not deter the crowds outside in Bruton Street, which runs from Bond Street to Berkeley Square. They were rewarded that April afternoon with the sight of the Princess's grandparents, King George V and Queen Mary, who had driven over from Windsor to see what the Queen described as "the little darling". The Princess was their first granddaughter (their daughter, Princess Mary, already had two sons, George and Gerald Lascelles) and became third in line of succession to the throne after her uncle, the Prince of Wales, and her father.

Royal births have a happy knack of coinciding with less agreeable events which are thus put into a proper perspective. At the time of the Princess's arrival on the scene, her grandfather the King was preoccupied with the problem of the miners' wage negotiations, the breakdown of which was to lead to the General Strike, called on 4 May by the Trades Union Congress. After the vision of a Bolshevist rising, similar to the one which had destroyed the Imperial House of Romanoff in Russia less than ten years before, had receded within a few days, it was noticeable that crowds were congregating in Bruton Street. On 14 May, the day after the General Strike was called off, there was such a gathering outside Number 17 that the Princess had to be spirited out of the back door for her daily constitutional with her nanny Clara Knight (always known as "Allah"). Mabell Countess of Airlie, the *confidante* and long-serving Lady of the Bedchamber to Queen Mary, who was among the first to see the Princess, commented that the reason for the crowds was that the people saw in this child "something of continuity and of hope in the future".

The popular newspapers took to referring to "The Empire's little Princess" but there was, at this stage, no earthly reason to suppose that her father and herself would not eventually be displaced in the line of succession by the children of her uncle, the Prince of Wales, then an extremely eligible bachelor approaching his 32nd birthday.

The Princess was christened "Elizabeth Alexandra Mary" in the private chapel at Buckingham Palace by the Archbishop of York (Cosmo Lang) on 29 May. Her formal style was thus "Her Royal Highness Princess Elizabeth of York".

The choice of Christian names reflected obvious close connexions. The previously mandatory "Victoria" was dispensed with as it was hardly likely that the Princess would ever succeed to the throne. "Elizabeth" was after her mother, the former Lady Elizabeth Bowes-Lyon; there had not, in fact, been an "Elizabeth" in the royal family "for such a long time" (as the Duke of York reminded his father) and George V was pleased to have the great Tudor Queen recalled. "Alexandra" was in memory of the Princess's great-grandmother, the melancholic and beautiful Danish widow of King Edward VII who had died at Sandringham during the previous winter. "Mary" was after the Queen herself, the formerly shy Princess May of Teck who had later blossomed into the superb queenly figure beside her endearingly gruff husband.

"Of course", observed Queen Mary of her first granddaughter's christening, "poor baby cried". Lady Airlie recalled in her memoirs *Thatched with Gold*:

She was a lovely baby although she cried so much all through the ceremony that immediately after it her old-fashioned nurse dosed her well from a bottle of dill water – to the surprise of the modern young mothers present, and the amusement of her uncle, the Prince of Wales.

The King and Queen stood sponsor to Princess Elizabeth and the other godparents were her maternal grandfather, Lord Strathmore, her aunts Princess Mary and Lady Elphinstone and her great-grand-uncle, the Duke of Connaught, whose own christening was captured in Winterhalter's famous picture "The First of May" (where he is shown in the arms of his mother, Queen Victoria, with his godfather, the venerable Duke of Wellington, bearing a gift). Lord Strathmore, then aged 71, was the head of one of the great families of Scotland, the Lyons of Glamis, an historic dynasty famous long before his youngest daughter, Lady Elizabeth Bowes-Lyon, had married the Duke of York. Princess Mary, later to be declared Princess Royal, was married to Viscount Lascelles, the heir of the 5th Earl of Harewood, whom she had married in 1922. Lady Elphinstone was the eldest surviving sister of the Duchess of York and nearly 17 years her senior; the Duchess and her brother David were so much younger than the other Bowes-Lyon children that they were known as "the two Benjamins".

As a child Lady Elizabeth Bowes-Lyon was also, prophetically, known as "Princess". Born in London in 1900 and largely brought up at St Paul's Walden Bury in Hertfordshire, she received what her biographer Elizabeth

Longford describes as "a quasi-royal training with the starch taken out of it" at Glamis, the Lyon stronghold in Angus. With its massive tower and cluster of pointed turrets, Glamis is everyone's idea of a Scotch castle, notorious for its "Monster" which is said to inhabit a secret room within. The castle incorporates fragments of a hunting lodge of the medieval Scots Kings, to whom it belonged until Robert II granted it to his son-in-law, Sir John Lyon, in 1372. The Lyons later became Lords Glamis and, in the 17th century, Earls of Strathmore. The family name became Bowes-Lyon after the Strathmores had inherited the estates of the immensely rich Durham family of Bowes whose heiress married the 9th Earl in the mid-18th century. Lady Elizabeth's father, the 14th Earl, had married Cecilia Cavendish-Bentinck, a cousin of the Duke of Portland and of his half-sister, the Bohemian Bloomsbury hostess Lady Ottoline Morrell.

It was Lady Strathmore who shrewdly remarked that King George V's second son, Bertie, would be "made or marred by his wife". Whatever their public virtues, parentage was not a calling sympathetic to King George and Queen Mary. As a father he indulged in the most distressing sort of Victorian authoritarianism (as if in reaction against his own "Edwardian" paternity), barking out orders like a martinet; while her Teutonic stiffness and reserve made for uneasy maternal relationships. Born in the cramped and uncongenial York Cottage on the Sandringham estate in 1895, Prince Albert Frederick Arthur George was a highly-strung boy who suffered from chronic ill health and a devastating stammer. At one time his bandy legs were encased in splints. His nervous, not to say hysterical, disposition, however, masked a quiet purposefulness and determination. This was to see him through some difficult years in the Navy (as Midshipman "Johnson" he saw action at the Battle of Jutland in 1915, discharging himself from the sick list on HMS *Collingwood* in order to take part) and also characterized his steadfast pursuit of Lady Elizabeth Bowes-Lyon. Although they had met as children and at dances, they were brought together by her friendship with his sister, Princess Mary, soon after he was created Duke of York in 1920. The canny Lady Airlie encouraged the match, but noticed that Lady Elizabeth was "frankly doubtful, uncertain of her feelings and afraid of the public life which would be asked of her as the King's daughter-in-law". She did indeed turn him down at first, but eventually on Sunday 13 January 1923, in the grounds of St Paul's Walden Bury, the Strathmores' country house near Hitchin, Lady Elizabeth agreed to become the Duchess of York. Using a pre-arranged code, the Duke telegraphed his delighted parents "ALL RIGHT. BERTIE".

The marriage marked a significant turning point in the history of the monarchy for since Tudor times it had been the practice for princes to marry foreign princesses. The last exception to the rule had been in the mid-17th century when an earlier Duke of York (later James II) married Lady Anne Hyde, daughter of the Earl of Clarendon (who considered her to be a "presumptuous strumpet"). The Hanoverians had married German princesses, Queen Alexandra was Danish and Queen Mary was another German. In the wake of the "Kaiser's War", during which the royal family had busily divested themselves of Teutonic trappings (substituting the made-up surname "Windsor" for "Wettin") the advent of a bride from the long-established Scottish aristocracy was particularly welcome to the German dynasty on the throne determined to be more British than the British. H.G. Wells's criticism of "an alien and uninspiring Court" had touched on an exposed nerve; "I may be uninspiring", commented George V, "but I'll be damned if I'm an alien". In addition to her remarkable personal attributes, which enchanted the old King, the diminutive and vivacious Lady Elizabeth Bowes-Lyon brought some much-needed British blood back into the royal family.

The wedding of the Duke and Duchess of York took place on 26 April 1923 at Westminster Abbey, where the bride placed her wedding bouquet on the tomb of the Unknown Warrior. Earlier she had set out in a landau with her father, Lord Strathmore, from the Bowes-Lyons' Mayfair house, 17 Bruton Street. It was here, almost exactly three years later, that the first child of the marriage, Princess Elizabeth of York, was born.

In the 1920s Bruton Street was still largely made up of aristocratic town houses. The Pakenhams, for instance, lived opposite the Strathmores, and the writer Lady Violet Powell (the present Earl of Longford's sister) remembers playing the great period game of "Beaver", across the street with Lady Elizabeth Bowes-Lyon and her future husband, the Duke of York. (The appearance of the Duke's father, the bearded George V, would, of course, have had a decisive effect on the game). In the 1930s, Number 17, a fine double-fronted Classical mid-18th century town house was, like so many other elegant Georgian buildings in that particularly philistine period, demolished to make way for a dreary office block. Today Bruton Street is an anonymous-looking West End thoroughfare, but a plaque marks the site of Princess Elizabeth's birthplace and it still enjoys a royal connexion through Her Majesty's dressmakers, Norman Hartnell Ltd, being based at Number 26 on the other side of the road.

In 1926 the Yorks were staying with the Duchess's parents, the Strathmores, as they were without a home of their own. On their marriage Queen Mary had done up

Princess Elizabeth, shortly after her first birthday, May 1927

her own childhood home, White Lodge in Richmond Park, for the young couple, but after they had duly moved in, they soon found that this Palladian villa was much too far from the centre of London to be practicable. They had still not found a more convenient alternative at the time of Princess Elizabeth's birth.

The Princess therefore spent her early months under the Strathmores' wing. Her redoubtable nanny, Clara Knight (accorded, as was the custom, the courtesy style of "Mrs", though a spinster) was the daughter of a tenant farmer on the family estate at St Paul's Walden Bury and had nursed the "two Benjamins" (David and Elizabeth Bowes-Lyon) in their infancy. The nursery gives rise to many nicknames and Mrs Knight's sobriquet of "Allah" was based on childish mispronunciations of "Clara" just as the Princess's affectionate family diminutive, "Lilibet", derives from her own early attempts at "Elizabeth".

The year of her birth saw the baby Princess already following an itinerary which was later to become the pattern of her life. To Scotland in August, and later to Sandringham at Christmas was the schedule. On her first visit north of the border, the Princess stayed not at Balmoral but at Glamis with her grandparents, the Strathmores. The now curly-headed Princess's first Christmas was spent with her other grandparents, George V and Queen Mary, at Sandringham in the "Big House" where they had now succeeded its original *châtelaine*, Queen Alexandra. Early in the New Year of 1927 Princess Elizabeth was subjected to another aspect of royal life when her parents were obliged to leave her behind for a six-month tour of the Antipodes. With the help of an Australian speech therapist in London and the devoted encouragement of his wife, the Duke of York had manfully struggled to master his stammer before setting off on this demanding ordeal.

Such a lengthy parting of parents and young child would now be regarded as quite unacceptable; the present Princess of Wales, for instance, took young Prince William with her on an Antipodean tour of only a few weeks in 1983. While bearing in mind that "privileged" children in those days saw little enough of their parents in any event, tending to live in the world of nanny and the nursery, it still seems unduly insensitive of the often unfeeling George V to have packed off the new parents to the other side of the globe for half 1927. The Duchess of York wrote to her mother-in-law, Queen Mary: "I felt very much leaving . . . and the baby was so sweet playing with the buttons on Bertie's uniform that it quite broke me up".

During their absence, Queen Mary belatedly indulged the maternal instinct that had been so suppressed in her dealings with her own children by taking a close interest in her first granddaughter, who came to stay at Buckingham

15

Palace in February 1927, following a brief spell with the Strathmores at St Paul's Walden Bury. Like many grandmothers, Queen Mary was able to form a closer, less complicated relationship with her grandchildren than with her own offspring. She and Princess Elizabeth were particularly attached to one another and many have rightly pointed out certain similarities in their looks, manner and characteristics – though the present Queen is not afflicted with shyness to quite the same degree as her grandmother.

Balcony appearances at Buckingham Palace could be considered a cure-all for shyness and the 14-month old Princess made her debut on the parapet outside the Centre Room on the Mall front on 27 June 1927, in front of the crowds gathered to welcome the Duke and Duchess of York back from their travels. As an *encore*, Princess Elizabeth was soon brought out again on another balcony, not far from the Palace, at 145 Piccadilly – the new home of the Yorks to where the young family had immediately repaired.

Opposite: Princess Elizabeth bucking up her convalescing grandfather at Bognor ("G. delighted to see her", recorded Queen Mary in her diary for 13 March 1929). The signed picture (below) is one of the photographs Queen Mary sent out to the Princess's parents, the Duke and Duchess of York, during their six-month tour of the Antipodes
This page: The Duke and Duchess of York leave 17 Bruton Street for their tour, January 1927

demolished at the end of the 1950s to make way for traffic improvements. It is an indication of the extent of the changes during the present Queen's life that much of the story reads like an archaeological survey; her birthplace is now an office block, the chapel where she was christened is now an art gallery, her childhood home a six-lane freeway and the tree-house where she succeeded to the throne razed.

The two nurseries (day and night) at 145 Piccadilly were situated at the top of the house. Here the tall figure of "Allah" Knight would hold sway, assisted by Margaret ("Bobo") MacDonald. Their young charge's toy cupboard bore witness to her parents' recent tour when numerous stuffed animals had been proffered for the Princess back home. For all the day nursery's appropriate red carpet, though, there was never any danger of Princess Elizabeth being spoilt. Apart from her parents' strong-minded views on the subject, there was soon visible something intrinsically serious, modest and tidy about the child herself.

In March 1929 Princess Elizabeth of York made her first signal contribution to the saga of the House of Windsor by cheering up her ailing grandfather, George V, during his recuperation from the removal of an abscess on the lung the previous winter. The King had been packed off to the seemly south coast resort of Bognor for a convalescence by the sea and, in the words of his official biographer, Sir Harold Nicolson, as "an emollient for jaded nerves" his soon to be three-years-old granddaughter was summoned to the side of his bath-chair. Again, as was the case with Queen Mary, George V found it easier to relax with his granddaughter than he had been able to with his own children. He had never played with them but he did play with his dear little "Lilibet".

The sentimental school of royalty watchers still like to believe that the "little Princesses" called their grandfather "Grandpapa England", though the younger "little Princess", Margaret, told the royal historian Elizabeth Longford that they "were much too frightened of him to call him anything but Grandpapa". However, like many myths, "Grandpapa England" has an attractive air of symbolism; George V's relationship with Princess Elizabeth of York can be seen in some way as reflecting that with his people. From being an almost "unknown" Prince of Wales, completely overshadowed by the outsize personality of King Edward VII, he gradually established himself as a much-loved "father figure", particularly through his attractively straightforward messages, delivered in his engagingly guttural tones, over the wireless. For all his philistinism and lack of imagination, George V was a worthy constitutional monarch who handled the innumerable crises of his reign with sound commonsense.

The Duke and Duchess of York had, in fact, settled on 145 Piccadilly as their first proper central base shortly before they left for Australasia but as the house had been empty for six years it needed a major overhaul which was carried out while they were away. The Yorks had taken out a lease on the house from the Crown Estate Commissioners. 145 Piccadilly was better known to an older generation as Northampton House, after its former occupancy as the town house of the Marquesses of Northampton. A large, tall terraced house at the Hyde Park Corner end of Piccadilly, backing on to the peaceful triangle of Hamilton Gardens, it was what estate agents would call "imposing", but the Duchess of York exercised her special talents to create a pleasantly domestic atmosphere within. It proved to be a happy home and later a haven from the crisis of 1936 which finally impelled the Yorks to move down Constitution Hill to Buckingham Palace. After 145 Piccadilly had received a direct hit in the Blitz of 1940, it lingered on in a derelict state until it was

A child's eye view of a grandfather is nicely expressed in another sentimental – and possibly apocryphal – anecdote told of Christmas at Sandringham in 1929. Hearing the words "Glad tidings of great joy to you and all mankind" in the carol "While Shepherds watched", Princess Elizabeth had no difficulty in identifying who "old mankind" was; it was, of course, Grandpapa. That Christmas was especially exciting for the three-and-a-half-year-old Princess as she was given her first pony. She had, in fact, already been in the saddle for over a year and was soon a highly proficient horsewoman with an assured seat, much to the satisfaction of her grandfather George V. The King had once admonished his eldest son, the Prince of Wales (who took a number of crashing falls point-to-pointing): "If you can't ride, you know, I am afraid people will call you a duffer".

The Duchess of York saw to it that nobody would call Princess Elizabeth a duffer, supervising her early education in person. The Duchess coached her young daughter in the elementary lessons of obedience to God, response to duty and thoughtfulness to others. It was her mother who taught the Princess to read and, in time, to speak French – her mastery of this language continues to put many of her politicians to shame. On the Princess's fourth birthday, celebrated on Easter Monday 1930 at Windsor, she received a typically educational present from Queen Mary in the shape of a set of building blocks made from 50 different woods from different parts of the Empire.

In the summer of 1930 the Yorks went north to stay with the Strathmores at Glamis for the Duchess was expecting another child or, to be precise, a Prince. On 21 August the Duchess was duly delivered of a child in the castle (the first royal birth in the direct line to take place in Scotland since the future Charles I's at Dunfermline in 1600). It was not, however, a Prince but, in the words of the attendant Home Secretary, "a fine chubby-faced little girl". This was the last occasion when a Government minister was required to be present at a royal birth; following the somewhat farcical to-ings and fro-ings of the wretched J.R. Clynes, the practice, which went back to the late 17th century, was thankfully discontinued. At least his sojourn in Scotland earned this otherwise forgotten Lancastrian Labour (no pun intended) politician a footnote in the history books.

The arrival of a Princess rather than the expected Prince threw the prepared nomenclature into disarray. The Duke and Duchess of York opted for "Ann Margaret" but George V did not care for "Ann". Eventually, as late as October 1930, the new Princess was registered as "Margaret Rose" – and was initially always known by both names. Princess Elizabeth told Lady Cynthia Asquith that she was going to call her new sister "Bud", explaining that she was not yet a real "Rose". (It is tempting to crush this old chestnut by adding that, as far as we know, Princess Margaret Rose was never called "Bud".)

To deal with the new addition to the York family, the nursery staff were redeployed. While Nanny Allah now concentrated her attentions upon Princess Margaret Rose, with assistance from Ruby MacDonald (Bobo's sister), Bobo herself looked after Princess Elizabeth. She has done so to this day. For nannies, like Field-Marshals, never retire. The octogenarian Bobo MacDonald has become to the present Queen rather what another Scot, John Brown, was to Queen Victoria: the sovereign's own Highland servant, not afraid to tell the mistress exactly where she stands without any loss of mutual respect.

The Duke of York was, in the words of his official biographer (and fellow-stammerer) Sir John Wheeler-Bennett, "determined that, come what might, Princess Elizabeth and Princess Margaret should look back upon their early years as a golden age." As a vital part of this process, the Duke and Duchess created a country retreat at Windsor from 1931 onwards by transforming the Royal Lodge, a former "grace and favour" residence in the Great Park, which had once been a *cottage orné* of the Prince Regent, into a delightful weekend home. In a most evocative painting by James Gunn entitled "Conversation Piece at the Royal Lodge", the house's one-time occupant, George IV, looks down from above the chimney-piece on a cosy domestic scene very different from his own raffish way of life. This picture of the family at tea – the mother preparing to pour from the pot, the tweed-clad father, the clean-cut daughters, the solitary fruit cake, the corgi snoozing on the carpet – perhaps expresses better than anything else the Duke of York's fond vision of "us four".

In the garden at Royal Lodge while the Duke was indulging his passion for rhododendrons, the Princesses would play in their tiny thatched cottage, *Y Bwthyn Bach*, a present from the people of Wales, installed in 1932. When Queen Mary came to visit her two granddaughters in this rural complement to the famous Dolls' House, designed by the greatest architect of the day, Sir Edwin Lutyens, in Windsor Castle, she found that she could not stand up inside. The Princesses' new nursery governess Marion Crawford, a strapping Scots lass (recommended by the Duchess of York's sister, Lady Rose Leveson-Gower, later Countess Granville), who arrived on a month's trial shortly before Princess Elizabeth's sixth birthday, managed to find one place inside the little Wendy House where she could remain vertical.

There are faint echoes in Marion Crawford's career which recall another Scottish teacher of romantic persuasion, Muriel Spark's Miss Jean Brodie. The prime of Miss Marion Crawford found her as a stimulating

companion to the "little Princesses" and as a teacher not lacking in certain inspiring qualities. Her fall from grace as the author of some highly imaginative, not to say deeply embarrassing, reminiscences after she had left the royal employ – without the honour she cherished (and, to be fair, fully deserved) – in the late 1940s, found her utterly cast out. She was never forgiven by the royal family for betraying their trust and, after an ill-fated career as a magazine columnist ("reporting" events which had unfortunately been cancelled by the time her gush appeared in print), emigrated to Canada. And yet, for all that, *The Little Princesses*, her first and best book, remains a uniquely valuable and entertaining (if admittedly far from punctiliously accurate) sketch of the present Queen and her sister's early life. Though high-minded librarians refuse to stock such "ephemera" and every royal hack has a jolly good sneer at the authoress before blithely proceeding to lift her material, *The Little Princesses* is still an indispensable source and should surely be reprinted.

Under the tutelage of "Crawfie", Princess Elizabeth began a regular timetable of lessons. Queen Mary always took a particular interest in the curriculum, sending the

governess her considered thoughts on the matter. Bible-reading, poetry ("wonderful memory-training"), history and geography (". . . the Dominions and India") found special favour with the old Queen; she also laid stress on the importance of "genealogies, historical and dynastic". History was a strongish suit of Crawfie who, as Princess Margaret has recalled, was "highly dramatic." It obviously took seed, for once when Princess Marie Louise (one of the numerous royal relics from the Victorian era) apologised to Princess Elizabeth for a lengthy digression into the past, the latter replied "But Cousin Louie, it's *history* and therefore so thrilling".

Princess Elizabeth was beginning to see history at first hand as she gradually emerged into public life. In November 1934 she was a bridesmaid to the beautiful Princess Marina of Greece and Denmark at her wedding in Westminster Abbey to the Duke of York's dashing and erratic youngest brother, Prince George, newly created Duke of Kent. "She played her part", recalled Lady Cynthia Colville, a Woman of the Bedchamber to Queen Mary, "with dignity and sang-froid". Shortly after her ninth birthday, Princess Elizabeth and her sister attended

the Thanksgiving Service at St Paul's Cathedral to celebrate George V's Silver Jubilee. The diarist Henry ("Chips") Channon spotted the "two tiny pink children" (the little Princesses always tended to be dressed alike). Later in 1935 Princess Elizabeth was a bridesmaid again, this time with Princess Margaret Rose, at the wedding of the more stolid Prince Henry, Duke of Gloucester; he followed his brother Bertie's example by marrying a Scottish noblewoman, Lady Alice Montagu-Douglas-Scott, a daughter of the 7th Duke of Buccleuch who had died a few weeks before the consequently quiet ceremony.

After George V's life had moved, in the words of the broadcast bulletin, "peacefully to its close" (whether or not with a last nautically-expressed message for Bognor), in January 1936 the conscientious nine-and-three-quarters-of-a-year-old Princess exclaimed to her governess "Oh Crawfie, ought we to play?" Dressed in black, she was taken by her parents to the Lying-in-State at Westminster Hall and, according to the obvious source, reported back to Crawfie that "Uncle David", who was standing vigil round the bier with his three surviving brothers, Bertie, Harry and George (John, an epileptic, had died virtually

incognito), had "never moved at all . . . not even an eyelid".

At the old King's funeral her favourite "Uncle David" (now King Edward VIII) moved much more than an eyelid when part of the Imperial Crown on top of the coffin fell off into the gutter. "Christ", exclaimed the new sovereign, "what's going to happen next?" The answer had already been predicted by his late father. "After I am gone", George V had told Cosmo Lang, now the Archbishop of Canterbury, the previous year, "the boy will ruin himself in twelve months". As the historian Alan Palmer has pointed out, it is significant that the King should still have thought of his heir, at 41, as "the boy". Of course, the Princess's dashing Uncle David had never grown up: he was Peter Pan – charming when young, now rather tiresome and still painfully immature in early middle-age.

All things considered, however, it will be a long time before a cool verdict can be pronounced on the Abdication saga. At present it is, quite understandably, overladen with sympathy for George VI and his family – virtual walk-on players, so to speak, who were thrust without any warning from the wings into centre-stage by an exiting star denied the chance of selfishly grafting an utterly miscast leading lady into the play. Edward VIII – as he now tends to be remembered rather than "Duke of Windsor" – is the apparently irredeemable villain of the piece; since his death in exile in 1972, his stock has continued to fall. Almost no insult is now considered too bad for him, or his wretched bedridden widow; senior courtiers have been heard to restrict their comments on Edward VIII to words of four letters. It is easy to forget that he was once possibly the most popular Prince of all time with more what is now called "charisma" than the rest of the House of Windsor put together. And yet the rather shallow qualities which made him a glamorous Prince of Wales were certainly not those fitting for a responsible constitutional monarch. One erstwhile "ghost" writer to the Duke and Duchess of Windsor says that a statue to the Duchess should be erected in the Mall as the saviour of the British Monarchy. He argues that if Edward VIII, alleged to have flirted uncomfortably with Fascism, had sat any longer on the throne it would have been catastrophic.

Another "ghost" writer, in the Duchess of Windsor's autobiography, *The Heart Has Its Reasons*, recorded something of the open animosity between – as they were then – the Duchess of York and Mrs Simpson, the twice-divorced American whom Britain and the Empire would not accept as their potential Queen Consort. Much more material concerning these two ladies will need to be published in the doubtlessly distant future before historians can attempt anything approaching a balanced judgement. *The Heart Has Its Reasons* contains a fairly catty description of Mrs Simpson's teatime visit to the Yorks at Royal

The scene on the balcony of Buckingham Palace after the Coronation, 12 May 1937: (left to right) Queen Elizabeth, Princess Elizabeth, Queen Mary, Viscount Lascelles (now the Earl of Harewood), Princess Margaret and King George VI. "They looked too sweet", wrote Queen Mary about her granddaughters, "in their lace dresses and robes, especially when they put on their coronets". The old Queen broke with precedent in attending her son's Coronation: she wanted to show her support for the new regime

Lodge in the spring of 1936. However, she could not fail to be impressed by the two little Princesses: "Princess Elizabeth . . . was then 10, and Princess Margaret Rose was nearly 6. They were both so blonde, so beautifully mannered, so brightly scrubbed, that they might have stepped from the pages of a picture book."

By the end of that Year of Three Kings (shades of 1483), Princess Elizabeth's reading matter was of a more earnest nature than picture books. "Abdication Day" (as she headed a sheet of paper) altered her destiny.

"Does that mean that you will have to be the next Queen?", Princess Margaret Rose asked her sister.

"Yes, some day", replied Princess Elizabeth.

"Poor you", said Princess Margaret Rose.

On 11 December 1936, at the age of 10½, she formally became heir presumptive to the throne now occupied by her father who assumed the style of George VI. She is said by the sentimentalists to have reacted to her new status by praying for a baby brother. Her father's reluctance to become King (there was a suggestion made of passing him over in favour of his youngest brother, the reformed Duke of Kent, who already had one son) was not through any lack of guts on his part – far from it – but because of his realization of the tremendous responsibility to which he was committing his elder daughter. From now on her life would be completely changed. When she married, her husband would have to be suitable to be her consort. When the King's reign was over she would become Queen with no respite from the red despatch boxes and endless engagements – and no hope of eventual retirement. "We must take what is coming", the Duchess of York (soon to be Queen Elizabeth) told Crawfie, "and make the best of it." The Princess herself said, in perfect truth, "I will be good".

And so the "golden age" was finally at an end. The new "royal family" moved into Buckingham Palace and King George VI made it his habit to spend some time each evening with Princess Elizabeth, helping to instruct her a little for her future reign. On 12 May 1937 the Princess and her sister were present at the Coronation in Westminster Abbey, wearing the robes of Princesses of the Blood Royal and specially designed coronets. They entered and left the Abbey side by side and behaved throughout the lengthy ceremony with remarkable dignity. The heir presumptive presented a lively account of the great day to her parents ("Every now and then we were hopping in and out of bed looking at the bands and soldiers . . .")

Princess Elizabeth was now very much a member of what her father came to call the "Royal Firm". She supported her father, as a keen Girl Guide, when he took the salute of the Scouts at Windsor and she displayed her excellent French – she was also learning German – in

Opposite: The two, not-so-little, Princesses out for a drive in a pony-and-trap at Windsor, August 1940. Corgis had been introduced into the royal family by their mother in 1933. Inset: Princess Elizabeth dressed as a Girl Guide (Kingfisher patrol) and Princess Margaret as a Brownie (Leprechaun six)

Below: The fateful meeting at the Royal Naval College, Dartmouth, 22 June 1939. The 13-year-old Princess Elizabeth is third from the left; the 18-year-old Prince Philip is seen chuckling in the back row next to his uncle, Lord Louis Mountbatten (in a double-breasted suit). Every picture, as they say, tells a story and Mountbatten's expression speaks volumes

conversation with President Lebrun of France. For all her mental maturity and dedication to the job in hand, the Princess was still attractively young for the teenager she became in April 1939. "At that age", wrote Crawfie, "When so many are gawky, she was an enchanting child with the loveliest hair and skin and a long, slim figure".

The key to the Princess's upbringing was her mother Queen Elizabeth's catechism of educational priorities: "To spend as long as possible in the open air, to enjoy to the full the pleasures of the country, to be able to dance and draw and appreciate music, to acquire good manners and perfect deportment, and to cultivate all the distinctively feminine graces".

Princess Elizabeth's grooming for her inevitable, inexorable role now received an imaginative boost. She was sent to the Vice-Provost of Eton, Henry Marten (later Sir Henry Marten and Provost of the College), the distinguished historian, for tutorials in constitutional history and law. From Marten she acquired, with her exceptionally retentive brain, a less colourful but more solid grounding in historical matters than that afforded her by Crawfie. Either at Eton or Windsor Castle, the Vice-Provost and the Princess covered a wide spectrum of knowledge. This proved a most successful and rewarding association, with Marten becoming rather a mentor.

In the last summer of peace, Princess Elizabeth met the eighteen-year-old Prince Philip of Greece and Denmark (described by the slightly disapproving Crawfie as "a fair-haired boy, rather like a Viking, with a sharp face and piercing blue eyes") during a visit with her father to the Royal Naval College, Dartmouth. Also of the party, and no doubt playing an all-too-prominent part in the proceedings, was Lord Louis ("Dickie") Mountbatten, who just happened to be Prince Philip's uncle. The Princess was much impressed by the good-looking cadet. ("She never took her eyes off him the whole time", wrote Crawfie later, adding that she herself thought "he showed off a good deal"). Indeed, the story is simply told: the Princess fell in love and, dear reader, married him when she came of age.

Meanwhile, there was the Second World War. The King and Queen stayed put at Buckingham Palace in the heart of

Right: "My sister is by my side . . ." The two Princesses' first broadcast (on Children's Hour, *13 October 1940) sent a cheery message of hope to the children of Britain and the Empire during a low point in the Second World War*

Below: Princess Elizabeth and Princess Margaret, dressed with wartime austerity, at Buckingham Palace, May 1942; and (opposite) with their parents

their people ("The King is still in London" went the popular song of the day) and provided inspiring leadership. There was no question about it: the monarchy had recovered from the shock of the Abdication and was stronger than ever. The Queen dismissed talk of evacuating the Princesses out of the country: "The children won't leave without me; I won't leave without the King; and the King will never leave". When Buckingham Palace was bombed in the Blitz of 1940, Queen Elizabeth remarked that she could now "look the East End in the face".

The two Princesses spent the War years mostly at Windsor, which they brightened by performing annual Christmas pantomimes. "I have never known Lilibet more animated", wrote Crawfie about the 1943 production of *Aladdin*. "There was a sparkle about her none of us had ever seen before". The reason was not hard to find: her third cousin, Prince Philip, was out front.

In the dark days of 1940 the two Princesses made their first broadcast, sending a cheering message across the airwaves on Derek McCulloch's (alias "Uncle Mac") show, *Children's Hour*. When she had done her bit (". . . in the end all will be well"), Princess Elizabeth memorably exhorted her sister ("Come on, Margaret") to add her own "Goodnight and good luck to you all". In her message, Princess Elizabeth had said that "We are trying . . . to bear our own share of the danger and sadness of War". Windsor was certainly not immune from air raids and the castle was considerably less than comfortable. In 1942 the Princesses' uncle, the Duke of Kent, was killed in a flying accident on active service.

Princess Elizabeth was now 16 and continuing to increase her activities in the public sphere. She often accompanied the King and Queen on their wartime tours of Britain. In 1942 she registered for pre-service training as a Sea Ranger and succeeded her godfather the old Duke of Connaught as Colonel of the Grenadier Guards, duly inspecting the regiment with meticulous thoroughness. This was also the year of her Confirmation.

Following instruction from Canon Crawley of St George's Chapel, the Princess had been confirmed shortly before her 16th birthday in the private chapel at Windsor Castle. Queen Mary, attended by the ever-faithful Lady Airlie, had driven up from Badminton in Gloucestershire, where she was spending an eventful war with her long-suffering niece, the Duchess of Beaufort, for the ceremony. It was such an intimate occasion that no pictures have ever been released of Princess Elizabeth on her confirmation day. Lady Airlie saw

a grave little face under a small white net veil, and a slender figure in a plain white woollen frock. The carriage of her head was unequalled, and there was about her that indescribable something which Queen Victoria had.

26

Opposite: In khaki at last in the closing stages of the Second World War, Second Subaltern E.A.M. Windsor of the ATS changes a wheel at Aldershot. Below: Band, eyes front! On her 18th birthday, in 1944, Princess Elizabeth inspected the Grenadier Guards at Windsor

Below: VE Day, 8 May 1945. Mr Churchill joins the "Royal Firm" on the Buckingham Palace balcony (note the barricaded, unglazed windows of the Centre Room behind)

Here we pause to take in Elizabeth Longford's acute interjection: "For 'indescribable something' read 'regality'". Back to Lady Airlie: "Although she was perfectly simple, modest and unselfconscious, she gave the impression of great personality".

A more prosaic description of the Princess was entered into the military records after she had finally persuaded her over-protective father to permit National Service shortly before her 19th birthday. Training with the Auxiliary Territorial Service at the No.1 Mechanical Transport Training Centre Aldershot, she was registered as "No.230873, Second Subaltern Elizabeth Alexandra Mary Windsor. Age: 18. Eyes: Blue. Hair: brown. Height: 5ft 3ins." Second Subaltern Windsor soon became adept at dismantling and reassembling engines, retiming valves and changing wheels. ("We had sparking plugs last night all the way through dinner", complained her proud mother.) Happily covered in oil and axle grease, the heir presumptive passed out a qualified driver. The Princess's involvement in the war effort certainly enhanced her popularity among those of her own generation.

Earlier in the war she had made her first public speech (as President of the National Society for the Prevention of Cruelty to Children at the Mansion House), acted as one of four Counsellors of State (in the King's absence inspecting troops in Italy), improved her French (with a new French tutor, Vicomtesse de Bellaigue), dazzled Cecil Beaton with "her mother's smile", impressed Noel Coward as "beautifully behaved" (during a visit to the set of the film *In Which We Serve*) and kept up a "cousinly" correspondence with the nephew of that film's idealized hero.

On the evening of 8 May 1945 the royal family gathered, with the Prime Minister Winston Churchill, on the balcony of Buckingham Palace to celebrate "Victory in Europe"; it was an emotional experience for the 19-year-old khaki-clad Princess Elizabeth. In his diary for VE Day, however, King George VI noted sympathetically of his two daughters: "Poor darlings, they have never had any fun yet". Crawfie observed that what the King and Queen wanted most for the Princesses was: "A really happy childhood, with lots of pleasant memories stored up against the days that might come and, later, happy marriages". The King was only too aware that "the days that might come" – Abdication Day and its aftermath – had come with a vengeance. As far as "marriages" were concerned, the later the better from his point of view.

Below: Sailing away to South Africa, February 1947, on HMS Vangaurd

Opposite: Princess Elizabeth in the full bloom of womanhood at Buckingham Palace

Princess Elizabeth actually became "unofficially" engaged to Prince Philip in 1946, but, at the insistence of the King, it was not officially announced until July 1947 after the "Royal Firm's" tour of South Africa. Queen Elizabeth the Queen Mother remembers the visit to South Africa as a particularly happy time. The war was over, the King and Queen were at the height of their popularity, the King was still in reasonable health – it was not until January 1948 that the first sign of his fatal illness, cramp in both legs, began to manifest itself – and the family were happy to be together on their first (and last) tour as a "firm". Field-Marshal Smuts, the veteran ex-Boer commando who ended up as a great favourite of the royal family, was still Prime Minister, and the political situation in South Africa was considerably more relaxed than it later became. The tour, though as remorselessly scheduled as all royal duties, now seems like time out between the hard knocks of George VI's reign.

They also left behind them an exceptionally appalling British winter, and the King was characteristically concerned about the welfare of his domestic subjects amid all the postwar privations. In April 1947, Princess Elizabeth celebrated her 21st birthday in Cape Town, from where she broadcast a message to the "British Commonwealth" (as the Empire was, somewhat prematurely, beginning to be called). She said that though she was 6,000 miles from the country where she was born, she was "certainly not 6,000 miles from home". Then came her famous dedication to duty:

I declare before you all that my whole life, whether it be long or short, shall be devoted to your service and the service of our great Imperial Commonwealth [*sic*] to which we all belong . . .

On a private level Princess Elizabeth had already made another major personal commitment. For her, the South African episode was a time of waiting – a time, she later agreed, to the relief of her doting father, that had been for the best. The heir presumptive to the throne was waiting to have her engagement announced.

30

2. The Queen and Prince Philip

Apart from the traditional firm denial from the Buckingham Palace press office that any engagement was in the offing, there were certain other preliminaries to be gone through before Princess Elizabeth's betrothal would be formally made public knowledge. One of the matters requiring attention was that the Princess's intended husband, though a serving officer in the British Navy, was not actually British. This basic fact, obvious as it may be, needs always to be borne in mind in any assessment of Prince Philip's character. Behind the brash, breezy, forthright, no-nonsense nautical manner lies a fundamentally serious philosophy and an earnestly progressive practicality that is essentially un-English. Prince Philip's aggressive "normality" disguises a more complex personality than many of his supporters – not to mention his critics – quite grasp. Without labouring the psychology, there is clearly an element of "over-compensation" for his background which was neither affluent nor stable.

Prince Philip of Greece was born in June 1921 on the dining-room table of a house called "Mon Repos" on the Island of Corfu. The name of his place of birth may conjure up images of suburbia that the architecture of the early 19th century neo-Classical villa (originally built as a summer retreat for the British High Commissioner on the island) certainly does not justify, but, as things turned out, the inference of genteel poverty would not be wholly amiss. Recalling his early years, Prince Philip has said that the family was "not well off".

In 1922, not many months after his birth, the infant Prince Philip was bundled away from Corfu in the British cruiser *Calypso* to experience a somewhat rootless childhood, mainly spent in Paris. His father, Prince Andrew of Greece, a brother of King Constantine I (who abdicated the throne in the same year), was among those unfairly blamed for a disastrous military adventure against the Turks. Narrowly escaping the death penalty at the hands of the turbulent Greek revolutionaries, Prince Andrew was banished into exile.

Prince Philip's nickname "Phil the Greek" is singularly inappropriate for, apart from his early exit from the country of his birth, there is no Balkan blood in his veins. The Greek royal family are of Danish extraction, being descended from Prince William of Glücksburg, a younger son of Christian IX of Denmark and brother of Queen Alexandra of Great Britain, whose first intimation that he had been elected King of Greece in 1863 was from the newspaper wrapping of a sardine sandwich in the lunch-packet which he took with him to the Naval Academy at Copenhagen. As Crawfie observed, when writing of Princess Elizabeth's encounter with Prince Philip at Dartmouth in 1939, the "fair-haired boy . . . with a sharp face and piercing blue eyes" was "rather like a Viking".

On his mother's side Prince Philip's ancestry is German and all his four sisters (whose seniority in age to him ranged from sixteen years to nearly seven) were to marry German princes. Princess Andrew was formerly Princess Alice of Battenberg, named after her maternal grandmother, the Grand Duchess of Hesse and by Rhine, who was herself the second daughter of Queen Victoria. Prince Louis of Battenberg, Princess Andrew's father, had a brilliant career in the British Navy which was cut short in 1914 when he was obliged to resign as First Sea Lord owing to anti-German feeling at the outbreak of the "Kaiser's War". Three years later when the British royal family thought it tactful to divest themselves of their Teutonic trappings, Prince Louis of Battenberg was transformed into Louis Mountbatten (a made-up name, loosely Anglicized from the original), 1st Marquess of Milford Haven. As his younger son, the late Lord

Mountbatten of Burma, recalled, Prince Louis was staying at the house of his elder son, George, in the summer of 1917 when he heard that the change of titles had been approved by King George V. He wrote in the visitors' book: "June 9th arrived Prince Hyde, June 19th departed Lord Jekyll".

The shabbily-treated Admiral died a few months after the birth of his new grandson, Prince Philip, and George, the 2nd Marquess of Milford Haven, became, to a certain extent, the young Prince's "guardian". During the dispiriting years of exile, Prince Philip's parents gradually went their separate ways. Prince Andrew, frustrated in his ambition to be of service to his country, became something of a *boulevardier* on the Riviera, dying virtually bankrupt in Monte Carlo in 1944. His estranged wife found consolation in religion, founding the Christian Sisterhood of Martha and Mary, whose grey garb became her customary attire. Unlike her husband, Princess Andrew did return to Greece, notably during the Second World War when she carried out sterling acts of charity in Athens. Mostly keeping out of the public gaze, Princess Andrew spent her last years at Buckingham Palace where she died in 1969.

Prince Philip's background and his eventual adoption of the surname "Mountbatten" when he finally became a naturalized British subject in 1947 have frequently been misunderstood, as Prince Philip himself pointed out in an interview with Basil Boothroyd for that writer's "informal biography":

I suppose they know I was born a Prince of Greece, but one impression that I think needs to be corrected is that the whole of my life has been spent here, and that I was brought up by Lord Mountbatten, neither of which is true. This impression that I've lived here all my life and that I'm a Mountbatten, which I'm not. I'm a Mountbatten in exactly the same way that everybody else is half-mother and half-father, but normally speaking you're concerned with the father's family. I don't think anybody thinks I have a father. Most people think that Dickie's my father anyway . . . I grew up very much more with my father's family than I did with my mother's.

Nonetheless, Prince Philip, an unsurprisingly boisterous boy according to his cousin Queen Alexandra of Yugoslavia, was taken in hand at the age of eight by his maternal uncle, George Milford Haven, who packed him off to an English preparatory school (Cheam in Surrey). He did not, however, proceed to a traditional public school but to Salem in Germany, the schloss of his brother-in-law, the Margrave of Baden, where the spartan Kurt Hahn had set up a pioneering educational establishment uncomfortably dedicated to the creation of an "aristocracy of accomplishment". Prince Philip's arrival at the school in 1933 was ill-timed, to say the least, because the Nazis were by then in the ascendant and Hahn, a Jew, had left Germany after a spell in prison. Following an uneasy year

at Salem, Prince Philip became one of the early pupils at Hahn's rugged new Scottish school started at Gordonstoun in Morayshire (once, incidentally, the home of the ostracised card-cheat Sir William Gordon Cumming) in 1934.

"I must confess that I enjoyed my days at Gordonstoun . . . I would like as many boys as possible to enjoy their school-days as much as I did", Prince Philip has said. His headmaster found him "often naughty, never nasty". According to Hahn, the Prince "felt the emotions of both joy and sadness deeply, the way he looked and the way he moved indicated what he felt". The visionary German became a mentor to Prince Philip, suggesting the germ of the idea of the Duke of Edinburgh's Award Scheme, and the Prince has remained a champion of the Hahn philosophy that education should develop character "and the whole man". He ended up as "Guardian", or head boy, showing "the greatest sense of service of all the boys in the school".

One of Prince Philip's celebrated sayings is: "I am one of those ignorant bums who never went to university and a fat lot of harm it did me". Instead, early in 1939 he passed into the Royal Naval College, Dartmouth. By this time the influence of his "Uncle Dickie", Lord Louis Mountbatten, was clearly beginning to make itself felt. George Milford Haven had died of cancer in 1938 and the mantle of "guardianship" had now fallen on his younger brother, then a Captain in the Navy. Prince Philip soon made his mark at Dartmouth, winning the King's Dirk for his all-round performance as a cadet.

This, then, was the eighteen-year-old Viking that so impressed the thirteen-year-old Princess Elizabeth, on her visit to Dartmouth at the end of July 1939 with her parents, George VI and Queen Elizabeth, and Princess Margaret. Also of the party was the King's personal Naval Aide-de-Camp, Lord Louis Mountbatten, who doubtless had a hand in deputing Prince Philip to entertain the two princesses and to keep them away from the risk of being infected by the chicken-pox and mumps that was currently rampant in the college. Whatever version of this fateful day one follows – and Crawfie's is the most detailed and compelling, with its account of Prince Philip showing off by jumping over the tennis net and guzzling "platefuls of shrimps, and a banana-split among other trifles" – there remains no question that Princess Elizabeth was now very much aware of the identity of her third cousin, previously only half-familiar from occasions such as Princess Marina's wedding to the Duke of Kent in 1934 and the Coronation of 1937. As the royal party departed in the *Victoria and Albert* yacht, some cadets sculled in its wake as a gesture of farewell; the story goes that Prince Philip alone did not obey the signals to turn back, only apparently doing so on his Uncle Dickie's command.

During the Second World War, which broke out that autumn and in which the now bearded Prince Philip distinguished himself in the Battle of Crete off Cape Matapan (being mentioned in despatches), he and Princess Elizabeth exchanged what Sir John Wheeler-Bennett describes as "cousinly letters". Gossips were already speculating on the possibilities of a closer relationship in the future. In January 1941 the Anglo-American socialite and minor politician "Chips" Channon went to a party in Athens with Lilia Ralli, a close friend of Prince Philip's first cousin, Prince Marina, and later noted in his diary:

Philip of Greece was there. He is extraordinarily handsome, and I recalled my afternoon's conversation with Princess Nicholas [*of Greece, mother of Princess Marina*]. He is to be our Prince Consort, and that is why he is serving in our Navy. He is charming, but I deplore such a marriage; he and Princess Elizabeth are too inter-related.

When confronted many years later with what appears to be a remarkably early piece of prophecy on Channon's part, Prince Philip was not unduly impressed. He observed to Basil Boothroyd:

Well. This is precisely the sort of language that they used. It had been mentioned, presumably, that "He is eligible, he's the sort of person she might marry". I mean, after all, if you spend ten minutes thinking about it – and a lot of these people spent a good deal more time thinking about it – how many obviously eligible young men, other than people living in this country, were available? Inevitably I must have been on the list, so to speak. But people only had to say that for somebody like Chips Channon to go one step further and say it's already decided, you see what I mean?

The inquisitive Channon continued to chart the progress of the putative romance in his diaries. As he signed the visitors' book in October 1944 at Coppins, the home of Princess Marina, the widowed Duchess of Kent, not far from Windsor, Chips "noticed 'Philip' written constantly", and added:

It is at Coppins that he sees Princess Elizabeth. I think she will marry him.

The previous Christmas Prince Philip had been among the audience for the Windsor Castle production of the pantomime *Aladdin*. "'Who *do* you think is coming to see us act, Crawfie? Philip'", is Miss Crawford's recollection of Princess Elizabeth's excitement on this occasion.

In the autumn of 1944 Prince Philip was among the guests at Balmoral and it could well have been around then that the cousinly friendship burgeoned into love. In January 1946 Queen Mary told her confidante Lady Airlie that Princess Elizabeth and Prince Philip had been in love for eighteen months:

But the King and Queen feel she is too young to be engaged yet. They want her to see more of the world before committing herself, and to meet more men. After all she's only nineteen, and one is very impressionable at that age . . . There's something very steadfast and determined in her – like her father. She won't give her heart lightly, but when she does it will be for always.

Queen Mary referred to the aristocratic young Guards officers drummed up at Windsor to divert Princess Elizabeth and her sister as the "Body Guard". Among them were the future Dukes of Grafton, Rutland and Marlborough and Mark Bonham-Carter. Of these the most strongly tipped runner was Hugh Euston (son and heir of the Duke of Grafton), until a posting to India removed him from the scene. Gossips maintained this was a manoeuvre of Lord Louis Mountbatten's to leave the stage empty for his nephew, but even if this were true it would not have been necessary. The race was, in short, a walkover for Prince Philip.

"I suppose one thing led to another", Prince Philip recollected to Basil Boothroyd in his deceptively jovial saloon-bar manner that sounds rather like a *Private Eye* parody:

I suppose I began to think about it seriously, oh, let me think now, when I got back in forty-six and went to Balmoral. It was probably then that we, that it became, you know, that we began to think about it seriously, and even talk about it . . .

In other words, Prince Philip would appear to have proposed to Princess Elizabeth at Balmoral in 1946 and to have been accepted, though the engagement was to be kept a family secret until the following year.

Prince Philip was anxious to renounce his foreign titles and become a naturalised British subject – apart from anything else this was a requisite of his converting his commission in the Royal Navy from temporary to permanent – but the Greek political climate of 1946 precluded such a move for the moment. However, after Prince Philip's exiled cousin, George II of the Hellenes, returned to Athens at the end of September following a plebiscite in favour of the restoration of the monarchy (always something of a shuttlecock in Greece), the coast was clear. The only question was: what should the new citizen be called? Schleswig-Holstein-Sonderburg-Glücksburg, his ancestral patronymic, would prove cumbersome even in a service used to such handles as Admiral the honourable Sir Reginald Plunkett-Ernle-Erle-Drax. The other family name of the royal house of Greece and Denmark was Oldenburg and the heralds wondered whether this would be acceptable in an anglicized version as "Oldcastle". The answer was in the negative and, in the event, Prince Philip's ubiquitous uncle, the newly created Viscount Mountbatten (he was to receive an earldom in 1947), pulled off one of his greatest coups in arranging, through the good offices of the Labour Home Secretary Chuter Ede, that the future progenitor of the royal dynasty should bear the equally confected surname of "Mountbatten".

In February 1947, almost thirty years after his maternal grandfather Prince Louis of Battenberg had become, at a

stroke, a Mountbatten and a Marquess, Prince Philip of Greece and Denmark was transformed into plain Lieutenant Philip Mountbatten, RN. This is how he was styled in the official announcement of the engagement of Princess Elizabeth from Buckingham Palace in June 1947; the day before the wedding that November, Lieutenant Mountbatten was granted the style of "Royal Highness" and on the day itself he was created Duke of Edinburgh. He did not receive the style of "Prince of the United Kingdom and Northern Ireland" until 1957; thus, strictly speaking, it is incorrect to refer to the Duke of Edinburgh as "Prince Philip" in relation to those intervening ten years. On the other hand, Lord Mountbatten was of the opinion that his nephew had been a British Prince all along, being a descendant of the Electress Sophia of Hanover (George I's mother). He based his view on the successful outcome of Prince Ernst August of Hanover's subsequent claim that all such descendants were British subjects – a case that rendered Prince Philip's "naturalization" unnecessary.

On the order of service for the wedding, which had gone to press before the bridegroom's elevation to the peerage, the new Duke of Edinburgh was billed for the last time as "Lieutenant Philip Mountbatten, RN". The wedding at Westminster Abbey on 20 November 1947 was the first major "royal event" since the war. Service dress, rather than ceremonial dress, was the order of the day while the choice of clothes for the women was severely restricted by rationing. Eager for some fairy tale romance to brighten up the postwar gloom, many loyal monarchists sent Princess Elizabeth their clothing coupons to add to her bridal dress allowance. These were duly returned, with thanks, though gifts of nylon stockings, also sent in, were gratefully accepted. Despite the privations and the matching austerity of the weather, the occasion exceeded all expectations in impressiveness as only royal weddings can. For the bridal gown Norman Hartnell managed to concoct a Botticelli-inspired creation of ivory satin with garlands of York roses entwined with stars, ears of corn and orange blossom picked out in raised pearls and crystal. To onlookers used to seeing the adolescent Princess Elizabeth in practical wartime outfits or uniforms, the sight of this stunning young woman blossoming before their eyes was a revelation.

"Oh, General", sighed her old cousin Princess Marie Louise to her neighbour Field-Marshal Smuts, "is she not beautiful? Are we not blessed to have such a Princess?"

Smuts' considered reply had an intuitive, prophetic ring to it. "She makes me very sad", he said. "Yes, sad because she is serious and wise beyond her years."

The bride's father was also watching the nuptials with mixed emotions. Always devotedly close to his beloved "Lilibet", George VI had been reluctant beyond all reasonable paternal caution to see her wed, delaying the inevitable match for as long as he could – he even hoped to postpone the wedding until the spring of 1948. In principle he had nothing against Princess Elizabeth's choice of husband ("I like Philip", he told George II of Greece. "He is intelligent, has a good sense of humour and thinks about things in the right way"), but in practice the fear of "losing" her proved agonizing. What with the shock of the Abdication and the horrors of war there had been so little time for "us four". Lilibet's youth had indeed been, in Noel Coward's phrase, "so terribly fleeting".

After the wedding George VI wrote to the new Duchess of Edinburgh, then honeymooning at Broadlands, the ancestral seat of Lord Mountbatten's wife Edwina Ashley:

I was so proud of you and thrilled at having you so close to me on our long walk in Westminster Abbey, but when I handed your hand to the Archbishop I felt that I had lost something very precious. You were so calm and composed during the Service and said your words with such conviction, that I knew it was all right . . . I am so glad you wrote and told Mummy that you think the long wait before your engagement and the long time before the wedding was for the best. I was rather afraid that you had thought I was being hard hearted about it. I was so anxious for you to come to South Africa as you knew.

Then came a touching outpouring of possessive parental passion:

Our family, us four, the "Royal Family" must remain together with additions of course at suitable moments!! I have watched you grow up all these years with pride under the skilful direction of Mummy, who as you know is the most marvellous person in the world in my eyes, and I can, I know, always count on you, and now Philip, to help us in our work . . . I can see that you are sublimely happy with Philip which is right but don't forget us is the wish of
Your ever loving and devoted
PAPA

There were not many suitable moments left to the already ailing George VI for additions to the royal family, but happily he lived long enough to see the arrivals of Prince Charles in 1948 and Princess Anne in 1950. The son and eventual heir was born at Buckingham Palace a week before his parents' first wedding anniversary, while the Duke of Edinburgh played a distracting game of squash with his equerry Michael Parker. Queen Mary expressed herself "delighted at being a great-grandmother!" and fancied that she detected a likeness between the baby and his great-great-great-grandfather, Prince Albert (not a name, surprisingly, to feature at his baptism, when he was christened "Charles Philip Arthur George"). The proud mother was particularly impressed by her son's hands: "Fine with long fingers – quite unlike mine and certainly unlike his father's. It will be interesting to see what they become."

The King, who was still in his early fifties, must have been counting on some peaceful years during which he could prepare his elder daughter for her reign and enable the Edinburghs to enjoy a relatively carefree period of "normal" family life. It was not to be. Shortly before the birth of Prince Charles, the pains in George VI's legs were diagnosed as the beginnings of arterio-sclerosis. Worries about her father's health clouded Princess Elizabeth's attempts to be an ordinary Navy wife to her serving officer husband. From time to time she was called on to deputize for the King or render close support on ceremonial occasions. At the Trooping the Colour in 1949, for instance, Princess Elizabeth rode beside George VI, who took the Birthday Parade from his carriage on Horse Guards Parade.

That winter, however, the Edinburghs were able to embark on what, with hindsight, seems to have been the great adventure of their married life – a straightforward service posting to Malta where they could experience more or less everyday pleasures away from the British royal round. Uncle Dickie was also out in the Mediterranean as Flag Officer commanding the First Cruiser Squadron and the Edinburghs had the run of his villa overlooking the spectacular Grand Harbour at Valletta. There were plenty of diversions and jollifications but the chief pleasure for the Princess was in the sort of things her fellow officers' wives took for granted – like shopping with her own money. In 1950 the Duke of Edinburgh, newly promoted Lieutenant-Commander, achieved every naval officer's ambition of his own ship, the *Magpie*, a frigate in the Mediterranean fleet. He escorted his wife, installed in HMS *Surprise*, on a goodwill tour to Greece, the land of his birth, where they were rapturously received in Athens. Basil Boothroyd's amiable biography of Prince Philip immortalizes some of the jolly signals that were transmitted over the waves between the two ships.

Surprise to *Magpie*: "Princess full of beans."

Magpie to *Surprise*: "Is that the best you can give her for breakfast?"

The Edinburghs' Maltese idyll was brought to a sudden end by increasing anxiety over George VI's illness. The King's haggard, drawn appearance was particularly noticeable when he opened the Festival of Britain, that pinchbeck cultural fun palace on London's south bank, in May 1951. People were beginning to fear the worst and lung cancer was duly confirmed (though not spelt out to the King himself) by a chest specialist. The Duke of Edinburgh was obliged to abandon his naval career – for good, as it turned out – and the family returned to their London home, Clarence House in the Mall.

They had first moved into Clarence House in 1949 after a spell renting Windlesham Moor near Ascot and shortly before leaving for Malta. Originally a sort of outbuilding to St James's Palace, the house takes its name from the time George III's somewhat eccentric, earthy son the Duke of Clarence lived here. It was rebuilt by John Nash in 1825

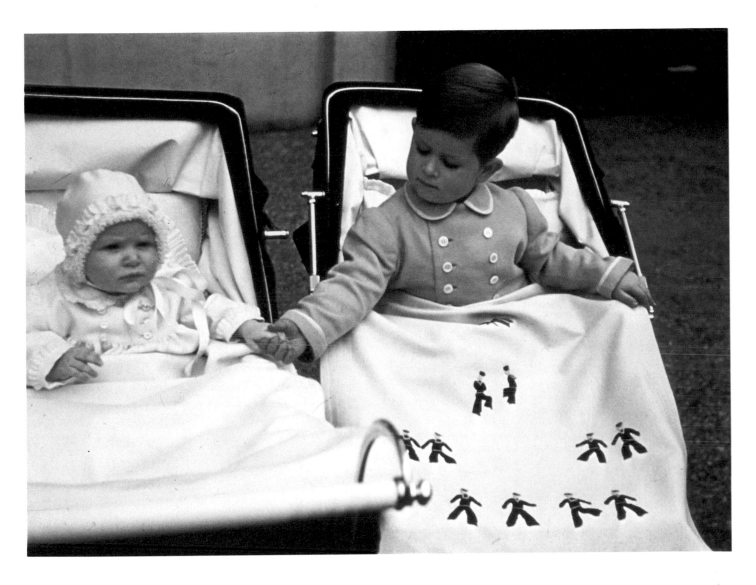

and when the Duke was on the throne as William IV, Clarence House briefly became the residence of a sovereign. After the death of the bluff "Sailor King", Clarence House reverted to its position as a lesser royal residence. Queen Victoria's formidable mother, the Duchess of Kent, lived here and in 1866 it was given to Victoria's second son, "Affie", the Duke of Edinburgh. The external appearance of the house today dates from this period.

Clarence House was remodelled and linked to St James's Palace by the addition of a wing on the south front, overlooking the Mall, which also acquired a Tuscan portico above the new entrance. Queen Victoria's third – and favourite – son, the Duke of Connaught, succeeded his brother, the Duke of Edinburgh, here in 1900, staying on until his death during the Second World War. Latterly it had been used as the headquarters of the Red Cross. The House of Commons voted £50,000 for Clarence House to

be renovated and redecorated in order to serve as the Edinburghs' first married home.

In August 1950, between sojourns in Malta, Princess Elizabeth gave birth at Clarence House to a daughter who was christened "Anne Elizabeth Alice Louise". Princess Elizabeth breast fed her children to begin with, as her mother had done, and installed two nannies in the nursery at Clarence House, Helen Lightbody and Mabel Anderson (the latter getting the job, much to her surprise, through an advertisement in a "Situations Wanted" column). One of Prince Charles's earliest memories is lying in his mother's old pram and feeling quite overwhelmed by this gigantic conveyance which had been pressed into service once more. The nursery regime at Clarence House went as follows. First, in the morning, the children would have breakfast and then play until nine o'clock. Next, they would see their mother for half-an-hour. After tea Princess

Elizabeth would join Charles and Anne in the nursery where she would entertain them until it was time for their bath. She would see to the bathing and putting to bed herself.

The growing responsibilities of being heir to a sick father left little enough time for the family life Princess Elizabeth so enjoyed. In September 1951 the King's left lung was removed and the following month the Edinburghs dutifully set off on a pre-arranged tour of North America, though Princess Elizabeth knew that she might never see her father again. As a melancholy reminder of this eventuality her constitutional baggage on the trip included a sealed envelope containing a draft Accession Declaration and a message to both Houses of Parliament.

Happily the King was still alive, indeed distinctly perkier, when the Edinburghs returned home in the middle of November 1951. The North America tour had gone well and George VI showed his appreciation by making both his elder daughter and his son-in-law members of the Privy Council. They had enthusiastically covered vast expanses of Canada, attracting enormous crowds; the only hitches were the Duke of Edinburgh's occasional gaffes. Never afraid to say bluntly what he thinks or to make a provocatively teasing remark that does not always read well in print, the Duke was already exhibiting a tendency to put his foot in his mouth. What he may have lacked in tact, however, the young couple made up for in glamour. The high spot of their tour of the United States was the visit to the plain-speaking President Truman in Washington.

"We've just had a visit from a lovely young lady and her personable husband". the President wrote to George VI. "They went to the hearts of all the citizens of the United States". In typically folksy vein, little Harry from Independence, Missouri, added: "As one father to another we can be very proud of our daughters. You have the better of me – because you have two!"

That Christmas the royal family were in cheerful spirits at Sandringham as they listened to the King's pre-recorded broadcast on the wireless. George VI and Queen Elizabeth were looking forward to a private holiday in South Africa in the spring while the Edinburghs were preparing to undertake the marathon royal tour of East Africa, Australia and New Zealand that the King was not strong enough to carry out himself. On the eve of the Edinburghs' departure, "us four", and, of course, Philip, shared the royal box at Drury Lane to see the Rogers and Hammerstein musical *South Pacific*.

The next morning at London Airport the façade of the King's supposed recovery was starkly exposed as the cameras filmed him waving goodbye. Oliver Lyttelton

The Queen (or Princess Elizabeth as she then was), the Duke of Edinburgh, Prince Charles and the infant Princess Anne at Clarence House in 1950

Opposite: Princess Elizabeth telephones her mother from the royal train at Montreal (above) after her arrival in Canada, October 1951, to enquire about her father's health. Wrapped up against a snowstorm (below left), the Princess (in mink) and the Duke (wearing a ten-gallon hat) watch the Calgary "Stampede". Wearing (below right) a dirndl skirt and peasant blouse, Princess Elizabeth takes a twirl in a barn dance at Ottawa

(later Viscount Chandos), who was there in his capacity as Secretary of State for the Colonies, recorded his impressions of the poignant event:

I was shocked by the King's appearance. I was familiar with his look and mien, but he seemed much altered and strained. I had the feeling of doom, which grew as the minutes before the time of departure ebbed away. The King went on to the roof of the building to wave good-bye. The high wind blew his hair into disorder. I felt with deep foreboding that this would be the last time he was to see his daughter, and that he thought so himself.

A week later, after an enjoyable "Keeper's Day" end of season shoot at Sandringham, the King died in his sleep during the night of 5/6 February 1952.

The death of George VI was for Princess Elizabeth the deepest emotional experience of her life. Anniversaries of her accession are not causes of celebration but reminders of the loss of a 56-year-old father. What made it even harder to bear was that he had been the King (a role brutally thrust upon him and which surely foreshortened his life); now at the age of only 25 the Princess not only had to cope with devastating grief but to face up to the awesome avalanche of responsibilities from which there would be no respite.

To help her learn to live with this appalling double tragedy, the Queen (as, of course, she immediately became) was fortunate in her husband, the Duke of Edinburgh, a man capable of filling the gap left by her father's death. One of the most perceptive passages written about the Queen's marriage to Prince Philip was Andrew Duncan's summing-up in *The Reality of Monarchy* (a book resulting from the royal family's fairly short-lived "open door" policy in the late 1960s):

Theirs was a relationship deepened by arguments, made lonely by his travels, scrutinized everywhere, derided by cynics, devalued by schmaltz. A relationship made more poignant because she had only loved once, only could love once. Like other women who have a deep affection for their father, this had all been transferred and heaped exclusively on one other man and, whatever her position, whatever her obligations, even if she had lived in a semi-detached in Pinner, it would have been no different.

Lord Mountbatten also used to say that the Queen would have been perfectly happy to be plain "Mrs Mountbatten".

Paradoxically, the man the Queen deeply admired and to whom she so ardently looks up (her marriage vows actually included the "obey" clause) is obliged, both metaphorically and literally, to walk several steps behind her. Just as the Queen had to make wholesale adjustments to her life upon the death of her father, so did the Duke of Edinburgh find himself in a seemingly impossible position. From being in command of his own ship he had to adapt to the thankless role of royal consort; Prince Philip has, incidentally, never shown any enthusiasm for taking the style of "Prince Consort" that was borne by his woefully misunderstood predecessor Prince Albert.

"Constitutionally," Prince Philip has reflected ruefully, "I do not exist". His only official role is indeed as husband of the Queen. He sees no State papers and though he is a member of the House of Lords he has never spoken in the Chamber (which seems an unnecessary pity). As William Hamilton, MP, has observed "the role of a Prince Consort has never been easy to assess".

Prince Philip once told an interviewer who asked him how a prince consort can be master in the Queen's house (not, perhaps, a question so likely to be put today in the modern feminist climate) that he began, on his marriage in 1947, with a normally authoritative position in his own home. Then, in 1952 when Princess Elizabeth became the Queen he had to work out new ways of serving her and leading a meaningful existence. "It's almost like being self-employed", he once said, "in the sense that you decide what to do".

The scene at London Airport a week later: the new Queen comes down the gangway into the goldfish bowl from which there is no escape. . . Of the venerable, black-coated and hatless figures waiting to greet her, Winston Churchill is on the right

In the early years of the reign Prince Philip was something of a gadabout. He could not settle down among what he called the "fundungus" of Court life and frequently resembled a bear with a sore head. Lord Mountbatten characteristically, and not very convincingly, put down some of the Duke's disenchantment to the way the illustrious name of Mountbatten was blocked from becoming the surname of the future royal dynasty by Sir Winston Churchill's intransigence. Whatever their cause, the Duke's prolonged absences abroad in the 1950s inevitably led to Fleet Street rumours. During one four-month trip that found him away from home at Christmas, the beleaguered Buckingham Palace press office even officially denied a rift between the Queen and the Duke.

Eventually the Duke seemed to come to terms with himself and his situation, carving out a hardworking and rewarding niche within the system. His principal

achievements have been in the field of helping deprived young people fulfil themselves in the outdoors through such schemes as the Duke of Edinburgh's Awards, the National Playing Fields Association and the Outward Bound Trust. Of the latter, he said that it

seeks, first, to show the boy the stuff he is made of, to find himself, to become even dimly aware of his own possibilities. It may seem ridiculous that this can be done in a month at a school near the sea or in the mountains, but that is the fact of the matter; it is being done. It may take a given time to acquire skill or to become physically fit; but that doesn't mean to say that you need a three-year syllabus to touch a man's soul.

In his principal role of supporting the Queen and serving the monarchy, Prince Philip has dedicated himself to being a modernist. "To survive", he has said, "the monarchy has to change." As Elizabeth Longford has pointed out Prince Philip's "vocation . . . has been to carry the monarchy forward into the second half of the twentieth century".

3. The Queen and the New Elizabethan Age

Queen Elizabeth I is said to have learnt of her accession to the throne in 1558 while under a tree in the park at Hatfield in Hertfordshire (where, as Alan Jay Lerner observed, "hurricanes hardly ever happen"). Nearly 400 years later, the so-called "New Elizabethan Age" began while the Queen, in the words of Harold Nicolson, was "perched in a tree in Africa, watching the rhinoceroses coming down to the pool to drink". Unusually in modern history, it is not known for certain exactly when Princess Elizabeth became Queen because her father had died in his sleep. It was not until the assistant royal valet, James Macdonald, arrived in the King's bedroom at Sandringham with the early morning tea on 6 February 1952 that the end of the reign was ascertained.

The Princess had spent the night in an observation outpost of the Outspan Hotel at Nyeri in Kenya, run by Captain Eric Sherbrooke Walker and his wife Lady Bettie (whose father, the 9th Earl of Denbigh, had been a long-serving courtier), known as Treetops. The simple "hide" of three bedrooms and a chemical lavatory was set 35 feet up a giant fig tree overlooking a waterhole. To reach Treetops the Princess had had to brave a close encounter with a herd of trumpeting elephants. During the night that was to change her life forever, the Princess spent several hours excitedly watching the wild animals below lit up by the floodlights. When she took her leave of the Walkers the following morning the Princess said that it had been her "most thrilling experience yet". Blissfully unaware, as they all were, of what had happened at Sandringham, Captain Walker said: "Ma'am, if you have the same courage in facing what the future sends you as you have in facing an elephant at eight paces, we are going to be very fortunate."

The Queen's courage has certainly been one of the great features of her reign. Another has been the revolution in communications, though the tardy process by which the news of her accession was relayed to the sovereign now seems to belong to the old Elizabethan age rather than the new. Princess Elizabeth was, in fact, virtually the last to know that she had become Queen. The official announcement of the King's death was made in London at 10.45 a.m. (1.45 p.m. in Kenya) and the Duke of Edinburgh broke it to Princess Elizabeth a full hour later after a desperate time spent obtaining definite confirmation of the message. The baton of tragedy was passed from a journalist on the *East African Standard*, who had picked up an unconfirmed agency newsflash from Reuter at about 1.30 p.m. (local time), to the Princess's private secretary, Martin Charteris, at the Outspan Hotel. Charteris then telephoned Michael Parker, the Duke of Edinburgh's private secretary, at Sagana Lodge (the comfortable "Happy Valley" retreat presented by the colony to the Edinburghs on their marriage) where the royal party had now returned from Treetops.

Commander Parker took the Duke of Edinburgh aside. "I'm afraid there's some awful news", he said. "The King is dead." The Commander later recalled: "I never felt so sorry for anyone in my life. He looked as if you'd dropped half the world on him."

For "the lady we must now call the Queen" (as Martin Charteris put it to a press conference at the Outspan Hotel) practical concerns diverted and delayed the shock. Displaying her extraordinary dedication to duty, the Queen dispatched the matters in hand. The rest of the royal tour, planned to take in Australia and New Zealand, had to be postponed indefinitely; arrangements for the immediate return to London had to be made. ("We got out of that place in an hour", said Commander Parker). The Accession documents were duly unsealed and engrossed by the Queen. When Charteris enquired by what name she wished to be styled as sovereign, the Queen replied decisively: "My own name, of course – what else?"

From Nanyuki in Kenya the Queen and her entourage flew to Entebbe Airport in Uganda (later notorious for the murderous behaviour of one of the Commonwealth's worst monsters, Idi Amin) and then home by way of Libya. In the gloom of a February afternoon, the aeroplane taxied to a halt at London Airport where it was boarded by the Queen's uncle, the Duke of Gloucester, together with the Mountbattens, whose daughter Lady Pamela had accompanied the Edinburghs to Africa. The Queen, who had changed in the aeroplane into the mourning clothes, packed against such an eventuality, prepared herself to face the ordeal of her public entrance. "Shall I go down alone?" she asked.

Only the week before – though it already seemed an aeon ago – she had managed a cheerful farewell wave to her father from the gangway at the same airport. Now she had to descend the steps that led to her inescapable destiny. With a terrible inexorability the pressures on the new Queen had begun. They would never relent so long as she lived.

First, she was greeted by Winston Churchill and her senior statesmen whose venerability contrasted poignantly with the youth and beauty of their sovereign. Then, the Queen drove to Clarence House (the royal standard flying from its flagpole) where shortly afterwards Queen Mary arrived to do obeisance. "Her old Grannie and subject" said the 84-year-old matriarch, "must be the first to kiss Her hand".

The following morning, Friday 8 February, the Queen made her Accession Declaration ("My heart is too full for

me to say more to you today than that I shall always work, as my father did . . .") to the Privy Council at St James's Palace. From the balcony of Henry VIII's Friary Court in the same palace, Garter Principal King of Arms, looking like a figure from a playing-card in his heraldic tabard, proclaimed the Queen "Elizabeth the Second, by the Grace of God of the United Kingdom of Great Britain and Northern Ireland and of her other Realms and Territories, Queen, Head of the Commonwealth, Defender of the Faith". Similar proclamations were read out at Temple Bar, the entrance to the City of London, and at other places all over those "Realms and Territories". It was the first time the expression "Head of the Commonwealth" had been used. Canada, Australia, New Zealand, South Africa, Pakistan and Ceylon all varied the wording slightly, each naming its own country.

That Friday afternoon the Queen and the Duke of Edinburgh drove down to Sandringham where she was reunited with her mother, a widow at the age of 51, and her sister, Princess Margaret. On the Sunday the Queen attended a brief service at St Mary Magdalene, in the park at Sandringham, where the King's coffin, made of oak from the estate, rested before the altar. On the Monday, the Queen accompanied her father's coffin back to London for the Lying-in-State. A haunting photograph was taken of the three Queens (the Queen, her mother, Queen Elizabeth, and her grandmother, Queen Mary), all veiled and in deep mourning, as they awaited the arrival of the bier at Westminster Abbey.

The Queen's relentless programme continued. On the Tuesday, the traditional day for the Prime Ministerial audience, Winston Churchill was received at Clarence House. The next day the Prime Minister reappeared at Buckingham Palace to present an Address from the House of Commons to the Queen. The Duke of Windsor, the Queen's favourite uncle when she was a little girl, returned from "exile" in Paris, without his wife, to pay homage to his niece. Other audiences followed on the Thursday with foreign monarchs and heads of state, high commissioners and other Commonwealth representatives over for the funeral. On the Friday the Queen took part in the King's funeral procession through London; at the burial in St George's Chapel, Windsor, she threw some earth from a silver bowl over the coffin at the moment of committal. A couple of days later, on 17 February, there was a private memorial service for the King in the private chapel at the royal family's retreat in Windsor Great Park, Royal Lodge, where George VI had planted out his beloved rhododendrons.

By the end of February the Queen had held her first meeting of the Privy Council and her first investiture, as well as receiving Dr Adenauer, the West German states-man, and approving the new wording of the prayers for the royal family. The pattern of constitutional monarchy had smoothly resumed its traditional groove. The Queen, faithfully following the teaching of her father and of her old constitutional mentor, Sir Henry Marten, displayed a remarkable maturity for a 25-year-old. With her deep sense of responsibility, she worked tirelessly at her "Red Boxes", full of Government reports and diplomatic telegrams, tackling a formidable workload under the initial guidance of her father's Private Secretary, Sir Alan ("Tommy") Lascelles.

Her first public engagement was the Maundy Service at Westminster Abbey, the day before Good Friday, when she distributed the "Royal Maundy" (alms consisting of specially-minted silver coins) to some worthy pensioners – 25 in all, the recipients numbering as many years as the sovereign's age. The ceremony is said to go back to medieval times; in the old days the monarch was expected to wash the pedal extremities of the poor before coming across with the cash. The ceremony in its present form was revived, without the feet-washing, by the Queen's grandfather, George V. Later in the Queen's reign, the Maundy Service was to take place away from Westminster Abbey in alternate years (beginning its tour of the provinces at St Albans Abbey in 1957). It was the first time the Maundy had been dispensed outside the capital since the days of Charles II. Recently it has become even less usual to have the service at Westminster.

Ceremonial and its precedents were to be much on everyone's minds at the beginning of the new Elizabethan age for, in June 1952, Court mourning came to an end and the Coronation was proclaimed for the following year. Arcane traditions were lovingly dusted down as elaborate plans were laid for an explosion of patriotic fervour, the intensity of which is both memorable and almost unreal over a generation later. Photographs of coroneted peers and peeresses clutching their robes out of the wet as they head for Westminster Abbey recall the chorus in Gilbert and Sullivan's *Iolanthe*; the cornucopia of foreign crowned heads seems to take one back to the golden days of Old Europe before 1914 rather than the aftermath of Hitler's War. And yet, paradoxically, the Coronation, although an orgy of pomp and circumstance, heralded a revolution in communications.

Dermot Morrah, the long-serving writer on royal matters thought that

when the sacring of Queen Elizabeth II was communicated by the revolutionary invention of television to a watching world, there were many who believed themselves aware of a quite new sense of corporate exaltation in the body of the people when they saw the Queen anointed as their supreme representative; it even seemed not altogether fanciful that the look of dedicated joy that shone in her eyes as she sat enthroned was in some way reflected in the hearts of the spectators far away.

Below: The Queen processes through the streets after the Coronation in Sir William Chambers's fairytale rococo State Coach. The stands are adorned with giant Tudor roses

Opposite above: The scene in Westminster Abbey after the Queen's sacred crowning with St Edward's Crown (made for Charles II). Below: A study of the Queen in her Garter Sash and Star by Baron, a friend of Prince Philip's who vied with Cecil Beaton to be the "royal photographer" in the 1950s

Below: The Queen processes through the streets after the Coronation in Sir William Chambers's fairytale rococo State Coach. The stands are adorned with giant Tudor roses

When that passage was published in a symposium, edited by the present writer, on the British Monarchy in the early 1970s, another contributor, of a cynical disposition, complained that it was unutterable guff, but there is no doubt Morrah captured the contemporary mood of the Coronation.

If television "made" the Coronation, the Coronation certainly made television. Hitherto rather an obscure medium of minority entertainment, the box was launched into its present significance by the coverage of the first great event of the Queen's reign. For the millions who huddled around the television sets of friends, neighbours and relations life would never be the same again after the seven hours' transmission. And yet if the Archbishop of Canterbury and the Royal Household had had their way the BBC cameras would not have been allowed into the Abbey at all for fear of vulgarizing such a sacred occasion. Thanks, however, to the Queen, Prince Philip and that beady master of ceremonies, the Duke of Norfolk, all save the most intimate moments of the ceremony were revealed to the public gaze. The unctuous Richard Dimbleby described the scene in the reverential tones that were to earn him, in Malcolm Muggeridge's phrase, the unofficial title of "Gold Microphone in Waiting" and the era of televised monarchy had begun.

"Vivat Regina Elizabeth! Vivat! Vivat! Vivat!" shouted the forty scholars of Westminster School as the Queen hove into view in the Abbey. After the "recognition" whereby the Archbishop of Canterbury presented "your undoubted Queen" to the congregation, she pledged the oath that ensures the sovereign governs according to law. Next, the Archbishop anointed the Queen's hands, breast and head with Holy oil under cover of a golden canopy held up by four Garter knights. Then, after the Queen had been given the emblems of sovereignty – the vestments, spurs, jewelled sword, the orb, ring, royal sceptre and the rod of equity and mercy – came the actual crowning. As she sat on the Coronation Chair, which Edward I made to display the Stone of Scone, the Archbishop of Canterbury placed St Edward's Crown on her head. "God Save the Queen", shouted the princes and princesses, peers and peeresses and kings of arms in somewhat ragged unison as they crowned themselves with their own coronets.

The last stage of the Coronation ceremony was the homage. Prince Philip, attired as an Admiral of the Fleet, duly knelt at her feet before kissing the Queen's left cheek, to be followed by her uncle the Duke of Gloucester, her cousin, the Duke of Kent, and the senior peers of each degree. It all went off with the smooth precision that the late Duke of Norfolk made his hallmark in his years as Earl Marshal. Even that acute observer Cecil Beaton only noticed a few hitches: "Princess Marie Louise, agonizingly old but still athletic, is obviously very angry with her fatuous lady-in-waiting for making such a balls-up with her train".

The gargantuan Queen Selote of Tonga stole the show in the procession through the pouring rain by gallantly inisting that the landau she was sharing with the comparatively diminutive Sultan of Kelantan be kept open. The Oceanic queen, a hefty 6-footer, beamed infectiously at the cheering crowds as she was soaked to the skin: "If the people could wait so long in the rain and cold, I quite willingly faced getting wet myself", she said later. History does not record what the wretched Malaysian sultan thought about it all. However, this upstaged passenger was noticed by a friend of Noel Coward's who inquired of the "Master": "Who's that sitting opposite the Queen of Tonga?"

"Her lunch", said Coward.

It was reckoned that some 20 million people in Britain (almost half the then population) saw the Coronation on television. The other revolutionary feature of the new Elizabethan age apart from television, was the ever-increasing advance in mobility. The *Comet* aircraft was the latest thing in travel and after the Duke of Edinburgh had given it a trial run in the Spring of 1952, his mother-in-law and sister-in-law buzzed around Europe in the new jet.

For Queen Elizabeth the Queen Mother (known by the first half of that style in court circles, the second in the wider world) widowhood was proving a much greater strain than many of her cheering admirers appreciated. The death of the husband she had nurtured into a strong king

was a shattering blow from which she took a considerable time to recover. On one occasion she even sought consolation in clairvoyance. A medium, one Lilian Bailey, was invited to Clarence House (where the Queen Mother had taken up residence from her elder daughter after the Queen had moved into Buckingham Palace in May 1952) to conduct a séance at which it was hoped to communicate with the dead King. This unconventional experiment was not repeated, though it is said that the Queen Mother's grandson, the Prince of Wales, who shares her leanings towards mysticism, tried similar ways of reaching his "honorary grandfather", Lord Mountbatten, following the latter's murder in Ireland.

Thanking Edith Sitwell for an anthology of poems that had comforted her, the Queen Mother referred to "a day when one felt engulfed by great black clouds of unhappiness and misery". Sorrow, she said, "bangs one about until one is senseless". But like the great trouper she is, the Queen Mother managed to find a new purpose in a supporting role to her elder daughter. Soon she was

undertaking major tours overseas as well as a ceaseless round of engagements at home. Flamboyantly dressed, smiling and giving her much-imitated wave, Queen Elizabeth was taken to the nation's bosom as "the Queen Mum".

The Queen Mother's younger daughter also needed plenty of support to help her through the traumas of her ill-fated romance with Group-Captain Peter Townsend. A hero of the Battle of Britain, Townsend had been an equerry to George VI, who regarded him as his protégé, almost like a son. The airman was a loyal and tactful member of the royal entourage, calmly coping with the King's occasional bouts of querulous irascibility. After the King's death the Queen Mother appointed Townsend to be the Comptroller of her household at Clarence House where Princess Margaret, who had admired the flying ace with the matinée idol looks since her girlhood, was also living. By the time of the Coronation, Peter Townsend and the Princess were clearly in love. There was, however, a snag. Despite his DFC and bar, DSO and all the rest of it,

*"Conscious of my duty to the Commonwealth. . .", said
Princess Margaret when announcing in 1955 that she was not
going to marry Group-Captain Peter Townsend. Her sister, the
Queen, is seen with her Commonwealth Ministers that same year*

despite his special intimacy with the royal family, Townsend bore a stigma. He had been through the divorce courts, having sued his wartime bride for adultery in 1951.

Princess Margaret and Peter Townsend were told, in effect, to wait and see. After the Coronation they separated for two years, the Group-Captain being tactfully posted away to a diplomatic job in Brussels. Matters finally came to a head after the Princess's 25th birthday in 1955. Constitutionally she now had the right to marry without the consent of the Sovereign or Parliament, should she choose to do so, on condition that she relinquished her royal status. But both the Princess and Townsend played straight down the line. Sir Anthony Eden, the new Prime Minister, was told by the Queen of her sister's wish for Parliament's consent to the marriage. Sniffing another "Abdication"-style sensation, the press staked out Clarence House for pictures of the troubled couple. Meanwhile, with their customary love of publicity, various clergymen obliged by supplying gratuitous remarks about the sanctity of marriage (or not, as the case might be)

and leader-writers invoked the Commonwealth. It had been "Commonwealth opinion" that had dished the twice-divorced Mrs Simpson's chances in 1936 and the Group-Captain was to fare no better in 1955. The voice of the diehard Marquess of Salisbury carried the day in the Cabinet discussion of the issue. He said he would resign as Lord President of the Council if the Cabinet gave its consent to the marriage ("Bobbety's" threats of resignation were a regular occurrence and he was not a little miffed when Harold Macmillan eventually decided to take him up on the idea). On the last day of October 1955 Princess Margaret put a stop to the circus by announcing that she had "decided not to marry Group-Captain Peter Townsend", being

mindful of the Church's teaching that Christian marriage is indissoluble, and conscious of my duty to the Commonwealth, I have resolved to put these considerations before others.

Looking back from a generation later, it is striking how extraordinarily badly the Townsend saga was handled. Hope was held out, wrongly and improperly, only to be

later denied. If such a union between a princess and a divorced man was considered unacceptable, then the position should have been made clear at the outset. The villain of the piece was "Tommy" Lascelles, the Queen's Private Secretary until 1953, who signally failed to grasp the nettle. Quite apart from the obvious issues involved, one suspects a contributory factor was that Lascelles (a cousin of the 6th Earl of Harewood who married George V's only daughter, Princess Mary, the Princess Royal) took a dim view of Townsend, a minor public school man who had arrived at Court by way of the RAF, getting ideas so far above his station.

Such a snobbish attitude would not have been out of place in the so-called New Elizabethan Age. Like the "New Look" it was, in essence, not "new" at all, but part of a general harking back in the first half of the 1950s to an idealized past. As a reaction to the drab informality and forced egalitarianism of the war years and the socialism of the Attlee regime, aristocratic habits and manners of former times were enthusiastically revived following the Tory resurgence at the 1951 Election. Visitors from war-ravaged Europe were dazzled by the dinners and balls of the London Season which were both brilliant and extremely formal. The apex of this 1950s traditionalism was, of course, the monarchy.

Thus the New Elizabethan Age dawned in an atmosphere of almost embarrassingly excessive euphoria. The young Queen was sentimentally cast as a symbolic "Gloriana", while the veteran hero Winston Churchill was portrayed – historical metaphors becoming somewhat confused – in a role analogous to that of Lord Melbourne guiding the young Queen Victoria. The fantastic mood manifested itself in the Coronation, the apotheosis of the prevailing optimism.

The trouble was that the hopes were not very well founded. Britain had won the war, Churchill was still Prime Minister and so forth but, in reality, the country had ceased to be a world power. This sad truth was not to be brought home to the "New Elizabethans" until the humiliating withdrawal from Suez fiasco in 1956 when the Americans were able to snap their fingers at Britain's depleted imperial might.

The reaction to Suez (castigated as an exercise in flag-wagging, wog-flogging by Kenneth Tynan) released a flood of protests against the "Establishment". Venerable institutions from the monarchy downwards came under attack. John Osborne, author of *Look Back in Anger* (first produced in the year of Suez), described the royal family as "a gold filling in a mouth full of decay". There was nothing new in the crown receiving some stick (in Queen Victoria's reign, for instance, the abuse heaped on the monarchy from some republican quarters makes present-

day sniping seem very tame), but in the hysterical climate of the New Elizabethan Age any breath of criticism seemed tantamount to treason.

In 1957 two articles appeared that provoked an amazing rumpus. The first by Lord Altrincham (who later disclaimed his peerage and is now better known as John Grigg) appeared in the *National and English Review* of which this 33-year-old peer was the editor. Distorted extracts from his article – especially phrases plucked out of their precise context like "pain in the neck" and "priggish schoolgirl" – were splashed all over the newspapers. Suddenly this moderate Tory peer became Public Enemy Number One. He was anathematized by the Archbishop of Canterbury, threatened with all manner of hideous deaths by staunch monarchists, slapped by an elderly "official" of the League of Empire Loyalists, challenged to a duel, even threatened with expulsion from his club. The Queen Mother's nephew, the Earl of Strathmore, was reported as saying that if he had a gun he would like to shoot his fellow peer, while the Duke of Argyll said that Altrincham should be hanged, drawn and quartered. The row encouraged the New York *Saturday Evening Post* to reprint a 1955 article on the monarchy by Malcolm Muggeridge. Originally entitled "The Royal Soap Opera" this had caused little stir when first published in the *New Statesman*, but now, when the usual garbled snippets were flashed back to London from New York, monarchical hysteria was redoubled. The League of Empire Loyalists sprang into violent action again. Excreta and razors were stuffed through Muggeridge's letterbox and among the hate mail was a letter rejoicing in the death of the journalist's son in a ski-ing accident.

Whether disgusting or ridiculous the over-reaction to the criticism indubitably did far more harm to the monarchy than the original articles (which, of course, hardly any of the outraged loyalists had actually seen). Re-reading Altrincham and Muggeridge's pieces nearly thirty years on, one is struck by their mildness and fundamentally sympathetic approach. Indeed Lord Altrincham's article appears to be a virtual blue-print (very pale blue, of the well-meaning "One Nation" range) for the "democratization" process of the monarchy.

Prince Charles's education, said Lord Altrincham, should be "very different" from the Queen's own and should ensure

that he mixes during his formative years with children who will one day be bus-drivers, dockers, engineers, etc. – not merely with future landowners or stockbrokers . . .

Presentation parties for debutantes are "a grotesque survival from the monarchy's 'hierarchical' past" which "pander to snobbishness" and should be scrapped. As for the Court, which "has remained a tight little enclave of

British 'ladies and gentlemen'", Lord Altrincham wanted the Queen to

be surrounded by advisers and companions with as many different backgrounds as possible. A truly classless and Commonwealth Court would not only bear eloquent witness to the transformed nature of the Monarchy, but would also give the Queen and her Family the advantage of daily contact with an interesting variety of personalities and points of view . . . over a period of time the composition of the Court would gradually become more catholic and more representative.

On the subject of broadcasting Lord Altrincham urged the royal family "to pay increasing attention" to television. The Queen was advised to improve "her present style of speaking, which is frankly a 'pain in the neck' ". (A Mr D. Durham Jones, writing in the *Daily Express*, observed: "Lord Altrincham would have had a 'pain in the neck' all right had Elizabeth I been on the Throne. He would have lost his head.") And if she had to read her speeches from a script could she not read them better? "The subject-matter", added Lord Altrincham, "must also be endowed with a more authentic quality". He complained (in the sentence that was, hardly surprisingly, the source of the most notorious selective quotation) that:

The personality conveyed by the utterances which are put into her mouth is that of a priggish schoolgirl, captain of the hockey team, a prefect and a recent candidate for Confirmation.

The monarchy, though, "need not descend to the petty bicycle-riding showmanship which some monarchs consider necessary to keep themselves in business". To fulfil their mission in the Commonwealth, Lord Alrincham did not think it necessary for the royal family to become a "tribe of nomads", but they must indeed reside more in countries other than the United Kingdom. By the end of Lord Altrincham's article one is even half-expecting to read a suggestion along the lines of a "walkabout".

While others were fuming at Lord Altrincham's impertinence (all the more infuriating coming from a peer of the realm), the Duke of Edinburgh, for one, would appear to have taken his words to heart. Certainly a number of the points adumbrated by Altrincham came to pass, but no doubt the Duke – the most potent force for change in the modern monarchy – had already been thinking along similar lines. Presentation parties, at which debutantes were paraded in full plumage before the Queen (having previously jammed the Mall) were duly abolished

after the 1958 "season". Garden party guest lists were broadened; informal luncheons for the Queen to meet a wider range of "achievers" were introduced at Buckingham Palace; and attempts were made to ginger up the Household with the occasional importation of new faces from Australia, New Zealand and Canada. The Christmas broadcasts, televised from 1957 onwards, gradually developed from the formal poses of the Queen sitting in front of an outsize microphone to include more relaxed family scenes, visual effects (one year the Queen tossed a pebble into the lake at the Palace to illustrate a point) and travelogues of her Commonwealth tours. As for the Queen's style of speaking, this too eventually became more relaxed, and the pitch descended a little.

At the time of Lord Altrincham's article, the nearly nine-year-old Prince Charles's education was already under way. "The Queen and I want Charles to go to school with other boys of his generation and learn to live with other children, and to absorb from childhood the discipline imposed by education with others", the Duke of Edinburgh had said during a visit to the United States of America in 1956. Although he may not have encountered

many future bus-drivers or dockers at Hill House, Cheam or Gordonstoun, by the time the Prince of Wales had completed his education (according to a pattern suggested by a committee), with stints in Australia, Cambridge, Aberystwyth, and all three services, he could be said to have covered a sizeable part of the waterfront.

As Elizabeth Longford remarks in *The Royal House of Windsor*, the "'new Elizabethans' quickly became old grousers". The disillusionment resulting from the Suez fiasco, which roughly coincided with the winding up of the Empire and the full-scale arrival on the scene of an articulate body of State-educated iconoclasts (categorized as "scum" by Somerset Maugham), showed up the heady days of the "New Elizabethan Age" to have been a false dawn. For the Queen, now in her early thirties, the honeymoon period of her reign was over. The style of monarchy she had inherited from her father was having to change with the times. And in the wake of Suez, she was faced with a constitutional crisis when Sir Anthony Eden, her second Prime Minister, tendered his resignation because of ill health. The royal prerogative was now to be put to the test for the first time in her reign.

4. The Queen and the Constitution

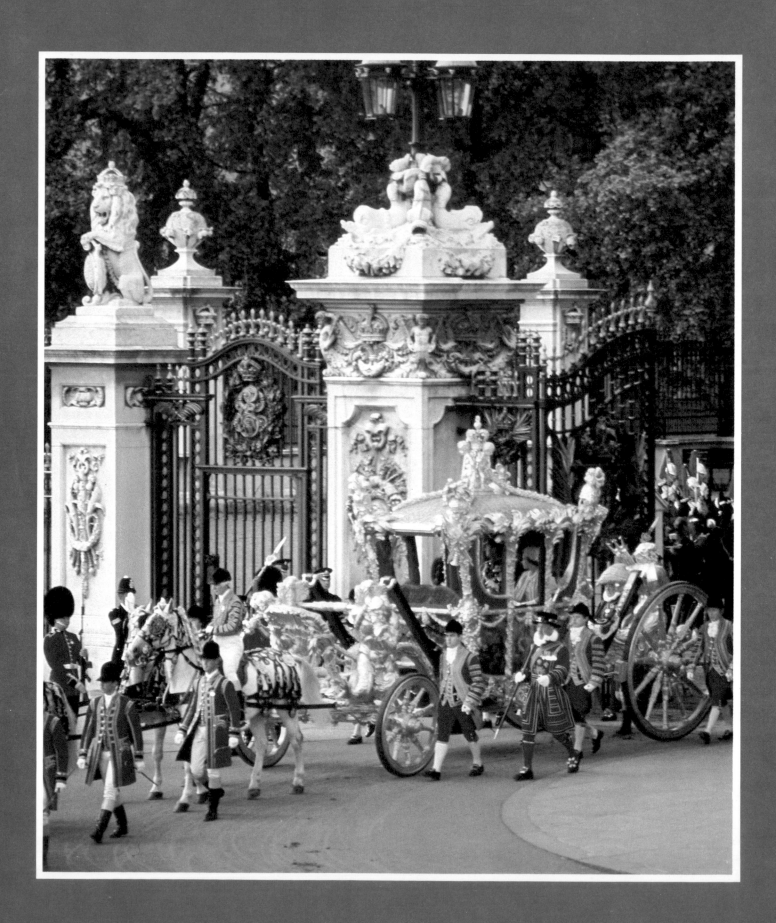

*The Gold State Coach, with the Queen and Duke of Edinburgh,
pulling out of the gates of Buckingham Palace on Jubilee Day
1977, epitomizes the majesty of the Head of State and guardian
of the British Constitution for the last third of a century*

Under the unwritten British Constitution the Queen is still a highly influential figure, exercising far more power than perhaps many who only associate the monarch with arcane pageantry quite realise. In his classic Victorian work on the *English Constitution*, Walter Bagehot defined the three rights of a constitutional monarch: "the right to be consulted, the right to encourage, the right to warn". He added that

a king of great sense and sagacity would want no others. He would find that his having no others would enable him to use these with singular effect. A wise king would gradually acquire a fund of knowledge and experience which few ministers could rival.

This has certainly been the case with the Queen. After 33 years on the throne she is without doubt the most experienced political figure around today, having dealt with eight Prime Ministers – from Sir Winston Churchill (over 50 years her senior in age), Sir Anthony Eden, Harold Macmillan, Sir Alec Douglas-Home, Sir Harold Wilson, Edward Heath, James Callaghan, to Margaret Thatcher (a mere six months older than the Queen). The Queen has impressed them all with her mastery of the crucial issues. What Lord Esher said of her great-grandfather, Edward VII, is strikingly apt for her too:

He had an instinct for statecraft which carried him straight to the core of a great problem without deep or profound knowledge of the subject. He had one supreme gift, and this was his unerring judgement of men and women.

The Queen's knack of going "straight to the core" has disconcerted several modern politicians.

"What did you think about that most interesting telegram from Baghdad?" the Queen once asked her first Prime Minister, Winston Churchill, who had to admit that he had not read the document in question. Harold Macmillan (later the Earl of Stockton) wrote of an audience which he had on his return from the United States in 1960: "I was astonished at Her Majesty's grasp of all the details set out in various messages and telegrams". In the following year, when for security reasons many voices were raised against her visit to Nkrumah's strife-torn Ghana, Macmillan commented that she "means to be a Queen and not a puppet". Harold Wilson, the first Labour Prime Minister of the Queen's reign, was equally impressed. At his farewell dinner in March 1976, he urged his successor James Callaghan, to read all the telegrams and Cabinet papers in good time before the Tuesday evening audience and not to leave them until the weekend.

Although the Queen officially "opens" Parliament every autumn, she has – unlike, say, the President of the United States – no veto over the legislature. In fact there has been no example of the use of the royal veto since the reign of Queen Anne. According to Bagehot, the Queen "must sign her own death warrant if the two Houses unanimously send it to her". The last monarch to dissolve Parliament without the advice of a Prime Minister was William IV who dismissed his radical Whig Government in 1834. He was constitutionally entitled to do so, though no sovereign since the "Sailor King" has put this right to the test. Certain other residual royal "prerogatives" do, however, still have some potency.

The most important is the choice of Prime Minister. If a party commands a clear majority in the Commons, then its leader is obviously an automatic choice for Prime Minister. But things have not always been so straightforward as that.

In the early part of the Queen's reign the Conservative Party did not have its own elective machinery to find a new leader – the right candidate "emerged" by a process of elimination and consultation within the hierarchy of the party. Matters have always been more clear-cut in the Labour Party; only the elected leader has ever been eligible for the Premiership. The Trollopian charade of the Tories may have worked well enough in another age but the system failed to survive the traumas of Eden's and Macmillan's resignations through ill health in 1957 and 1963 respectively. On both occasions "Rab" Butler appeared to be the obvious candidate but he was twice passed over after deliberations that certainly exercised the Queen's prerogative. The Queen consulted various prominent Conservative figures as to Eden's successor. Bobbety Salisbury had taken Cabinet soundings by asking each of its members whether they preferred "Wab" or "Hawold". "Hawold" it was. Sir Winston Churchill, whose own succession by Eden two years previously had been a smooth changeover to his long-serving deputy, later boasted that his "advice was acted on" by the Queen with regard to the Macmillan appointment.

If Macmillan's "emergence" was a surprise, that of the 14th Earl of Home in 1963, when Macmillan himself was incapacitated by a prostrate operation, caused a sensation. Determined to prevent Butler from succeeding him, Macmillan initially encouraged the candidature of Lord Hailsham. After this flamboyant character had launched his campaign in a somewhat over-emotional speech amid the highly-charged atmosphere of the Party Conference at Blackpool, the outgoing Prime Minister decided to opt for a compromise dark horse "unity" candidate in Lord Home, the Foreign Secretary. When the Queen broke with precedent and came to visit Macmillan in the King Edward VII Hospital for Officers in Marylebone where he was recuperating, he recommended that she send for Home despite the fact, which he virtually discounted, that seven or eight members of the Cabinet were backing Butler.

The Queen has been criticised for allowing one wily old

man – who had, in fact, already ceased to be her Prime Minister earlier that morning – to choose his own successor. Some say that she should have taken other advice before inviting a peer to form an administration with the "speed" urged on her by Macmillan. But one of Butler's main supporters, Iain Macleod, in his celebrated article in the *Spectator* about the "magic circle" of Old Etonian grandees manipulating the succession, exonerated the Queen. "There is no criticism whatever that can be made of the part played by the Crown", he wrote. Referring to the more than a little loaded pro-Home memorandum Macmillan had put forward, Macleod continued: "Presented with such a document it was unthinkable even to consider asking for a second opinion." Macmillan's manoeuvring, though, could be said to have harmed the royal prerogative; his sovereign was treated not so much as a queen but as a pawn.

The upshot of this extraordinary episode was the introduction by Sir Alec Douglas-Home (as he had become after renouncing his earldom) of elective machinery whereby the Conservative Members of the House of Commons decided through ballots as to who their leader should be in future. In 1965 Edward Heath became the first leader of the Conservative Party to be elected under this new system and ten years later he was replaced after a party poll by Margaret Thatcher. Both these changes of leadership took place while the Conservatives were in Opposition so there was no issue of the royal prerogative involved.

The most interesting aspect of the royal prerogative as it affects the choice of Prime Minister concerns the eventuality where no party commands a clear majority in the House of Commons. After the General Election of 1974, Labour had a tiny majority over the Tories but not over the other parties. The defeated Prime Minister, Edward Heath sat it out for four days at 10 Downing Street seeking a coalition with the Liberals which Jeremy Thorpe, their leader, apparently wanted though his colleagues did not. Finally, Heath resigned and the Queen sent for Harold Wilson. With a "minority" Government there was always the risk of the royal prerogative having to be brought into play. What would happen, for instance, if Wilson asked for a dissolution, that is to say another General Election, almost immediately? Might the Queen turn down such a request and invite some other statesman with enough broad appeal to form a coalition administration in the national interest? The General Election that did eventually take place that autumn was only a little more decisive (Labour winning an overall majority of four) and such questions were still valid. As it happened, the Queen was spared any further constitutional crises – at least in Britain – but the advent of the Social Democratic Party/Liberal Alliance in 1981 created a new political climate in which the Queen could well have a decisive role to play.

The possibility of a "hung Parliament" is now more real than ever. Should the Alliance's beloved proportional representation ever come to pass a fragmented system of government could be a racing certainty, making life extremely difficult for the Queen as the only disinterested authority involved. As the British Constitution is unwritten further speculation as to the possible outcome would be idle.

That the power of the crown is not entirely nominal was demonstrated by the workings of the Australian constitution in 1975. Acting in the Queen's name (though she herself took no part in the decision), the Governor-General of Australia, Sir John Kerr, dismissed the intransigent Labour Prime Minister, Gough Whitlam, during the stalemate over a Budget that Australia's upper house, the Senate, had refused to pass. Amid much outraged obloquy for his allegedly autocratic behaviour, the Governor-General then asked Malcolm Fraser to form a caretaker administration until an election could be held. Some half-a-century previously, in the wake of a Canadian brouhaha, an Imperial Conference resolution maintained that the Governor-General's functions were "similar in all essentials" to those of the sovereign. The definition of the "essentials", however, remains elusive.

To advise the Queen on the workings of constitutional monarchy, there is that key, if largely unsung, figure, the Private Secretary. Although the job can be traced back to poor George III's time (when Lieutenant-General Sir Herbert Taylor was called in to facilitate dealings with the increasingly blind and mad king), it really took on its present importance with the appointment of that great Victorian *éminence grise*, Sir Henry Ponsonby. The official Court duties of the Private Secretary (arranging tours at home and abroad, drafting the Queen's speeches, administering the royal archives, the Palace secretariat and the press office) give little clue as to the vital significance of his part in the proceedings. Professor Harold Laski, a doctrinaire Socialist, outlined the ideal incumbent:

He is the confidant of all ministers, but he must never leave the impression that he is anybody's man. He must intrude without seeming to intrude. He must be able to carry the burden of the sovereign's mistakes. The royal secretary walks on a tight-rope below which he is never unaware that an abyss is yawning. I do not think it is beyond the mark to say that a bad Private Secretary, one who was rash, or indiscreet, or untrustworthy, might easily make the system of constitutional monarchy unworkable unless the monarch himself was a person of extraordinary wisdom.

Sir Alan ("Tommy") Lascelles, who was Private Secretary to George VI and, briefly, to the Queen, said that the job was not "by any means beer and skittles". He continued:

Lord Mountbatten seated between the Queen and the Prince of Wales at Smith's Lawn Polo Ground, Windsor. This "Polonius" of the Queen's Court campaigned behind the scenes for the new "House of Mountbatten"

The Private Secretary's work, both in volume and responsibility, is continually increasing. In my office at present we compare unfavourably with our relative opposite numbers in the Civil Service, as regards man-hours per day, as regards pay, and as regards leave. We serve, I may remind you, one of the very few men in this world who never gets a holiday at all and who, unlike the rest of us, can look forward to no period of retirement at the end of his service for his service never ends.

Lascelles was succeeded in 1953 by Michael Adeane (later knighted and, on retirement in 1972, made a life peer), a grandson of Lord Stamfordham, who had served Queen Victoria and George V in a similar capacity. Lord Adeane's memorial is the lapidary memorandum he wrote about the Queen's activities for the Select Committee on the Civil List in 1971. When Sir Martin Charteris, a younger brother of the Earl of Wemyss, took over from Lord Adeane, it was noticeable that the Queen's speeches took on a more relaxed, even occasionally humorous vein. Philip Howard of *The Times* commented that it was engaging to watch Sir Martin laughing immodestly at his own jokes as spoken by the Queen. ("I think everybody will concede that on this of all days I should begin my speech with the words 'My husband and I'", quipped the Queen at the Silver Wedding celebrations the year Charteris took office).

The present Private Secretary, Sir Philip Moore, who succeeded Sir Martin Charteris (now Lord Charteris of Amisfield, Provost of Eton and the first Chairman of the National Heritage Memorial Fund) in the year of the Queen's Silver Jubilee is not, unlike his predecessors, from a landed background but the son of an "Indian civilian" (a member of the crack Indian Civil Service). Educated at Cheltenham, Sir Philip won Oxford Blues at rugby and hockey, representing England at the former game. A diplomatist and sometime Civil Servant, he joined the Royal Household in 1966 from the Ministry of Defence where he had been Chief of Public Relations. Sir Philip has carefully avoided becoming a well-known public figure, though his responsibilities are hardly short of the highest Government rank.

In Sir Michael Adeane's important memorandum on "The Queen's own duties in her capacity as Sovereign of the United Kingdom, and of the ten other self-governing Commonwealth Monarchies and the remaining colonial Territories, and as Supreme Governor of the Church of England and with her special responsibility to the Established Church of Scotland", the first category of her work was lucidly defined as that

arising from the normal operations of Government in the form of information she receives both from Ministers at home and representatives abroad, and submissions which she has to approve and sign. The Queen receives copies of all Government papers – reports from Ambassadors and Ministers abroad, instructions or replies from the Foreign Office, copies of Parliamentary papers, copies of memoranda and minutes of all important conferences such as meetings of Commonwealth Ministers. There is therefore a continuing burden of unseen work involving some hours' reading of papers each day in addition to Her Majesty's more public duties . . .

In his memoirs, Edward VIII (who described kingship as "an occupation of considerable drudgery") has left us a picture of his father, King George V, "doing his boxes" as "the relentless grind of the King's daily routine". What are known as the "Red Boxes" arrive every day (wherever she is) for the Queen to read, and contain the cream of the official information, not only of all the UK Government departments, but also all the Commonwealth ones. Thus the Queen's information is as good as any statesman's and, as her reign progresses, she becomes increasingly knowledgeable. With her retentive brain, this means that her political contribution, bounded by Bagehot's constitutional maxim about consulting, encouraging and warning, grows ever more important.

The relationship between the Queen and her Prime Minister is the cornerstone of the constitution. When the Queen is in London, the Prime Minister turns up every Tuesday evening for an hour or so's audience when their discussions can embrace any topic. Many people wrongly assume that because the Queen seems conservative (with a small "c") she must be a dyed-in-the-wool Tory. Hard as it may be to grasp, she is in fact genuinely apolitical; she was brought up not to favour any political party. "The Queen doesn't make fine distinctions between politicians of different parties", said Sir Godfrey Agnew, sometime Clerk of the Privy Council, in a nicely double-edged observation. "They all roughly belong to the same category in her view."

Much as the Queen enjoyed certain aspects of her audiences with her first Prime Minister, Sir Winston Churchill – particularly their chats about racing – the relationship was certainly not in the Queen Victoria and "dear Lord M." mould. Another Lord M., the late Earl Mountbatten of Burma, claimed that there was even some sort of constitutional showdown between the two over the question of the royal surname. When Princess Elizabeth married Lieutenant Philip Mountbatten she had, according to Lord Mountbatten (and his view of the matter was bound to be more than somewhat partial), been very happy at the idea of bearing the surname of Mountbatten. In common law, a Queen Regnant is the last of her line. Her son inherits his father's name and founds a new dynasty. That is what happened in the case of Queen Victoria and Edward VII; the former was the last ruler of the House of Wettin, the latter the first of the House of Saxe-Coburg and Gotha. Thus Prince Charles seemed destined to become the first of the House of Mountbatten.

On the accession of the Queen in 1952, however, one of the first declarations of the new reign established that the "House of Windsor" (the English name substituted for Saxe-Coburg and Gotha in 1917 by George V), would continue under that name. Churchill had apparently recommended that the surname of Mountbatten (made-up, Germanic, etc) be dropped. The Queen demurred, feeling this to be a grave insult to her husband. Churchill, speaking as her "constitutional Prime Minister", stubbornly insisted. Lord Mountbatten seemed to believe that the Queen was so upset to think her children Prince Charles and Princess Anne were not to be allowed to bear their paternal name that this actually had some effect on her not adding to her family for some years (until, indeed, the matter was resolved). According to another source, Prince Philip bitterly protested that the stripping of his surname from its rightful status made him "an amoeba – a bloody amoeba", though in Basil Boothroyd's informal biography the matter is carefully played down. In all fairness, as Dermot Morrah observed, the Declaration of April 1952 "did less than justice to her husband as the progenitor of the dynasty to come".

Lord Mountbatten said that Churchill's insensitively "British" attitude to the affair was heavily influenced by Lord Beaverbrook, who virtually "kept" the famous statesman. "The Beaver" and Dickie were, of course, old enemies. (Their feud is supposed to have dated from a baseless squabble over a girl back in the 1920s; it was fanned during the war by the press baron's notion that Mountbatten had wasted Canadian lives on the disastrous Dieppe raid, and by a provocative frame in Noel Coward's film *In Which We Serve*, showing a newspaper floating on the water amid the wreckage of the fictional vessel portraying Mountbatten's ill-fated HMS *Kelly*. It was Beaverbrook's *Daily Express* showing the banner headline "THERE WILL BE NO WAR THIS YEAR".)

In one of the many correctives to modern royal mythology that Elizabeth Longford includes in her excellent biography of *Elizabeth R*, she quotes an anonymous "messenger" who gives a somewhat different version to the one outlined by Lord Mountbatten to the present writer. In this story Dickie features not as a sadder but wiser wronged innocent in the wings but bragging centre stage. On learning that Lord Mountbatten had been joyfully drawing attention to the presence of a Mountbatten on the throne, an infuriated Queen Mary, the matriarch of the House of Windsor (which her husband had founded), sent this messenger round to see the Prime Minister. Churchill, encouraged indeed by Beaverbrook, promptly put the kibosh on the "House of Mountbatten".

In view of the rather haphazard way Prince Philip chose his new surname the objections to "Mountbatten" might seem valid enough, though the name of "Windsor" was of no greater authenticity.

The saga did not, however, end there. When Macmillan became Prime Minister, the Queen asked him whether the decision on the "House of Mountbatten" could be reversed. He came up with a compromise solution and the hyphenated surname of "Mountbatten-Windsor"; thus a few days before the birth of Prince Andrew in February 1960 (the propinquity of the two events, needless to say, emphasised by Lord Mountbatten) another Declaration was promulgated. Unfortunately this ambiguously worded statement only served to confuse the issue still further by its less than accurate assumption that "Royal Highnesses" do not have surnames; the name Mountbatten-Windsor seemed, as far as one could tell, to be destined for non-royal descendants as yet unborn. Basil Boothroyd tells us that Prince Philip was not the originator of the latest change and tactfully suggests that "the ins and outs of it all are better left to constitutional historians". The *Daily Express* had no such reservations: "One spectre has always confronted Earl Mountbatten of Burma: that his family name should die out."

In an attempt to clear up the muddle Lord Mountbatten, that latter-day Polonius of the Court, plotted behind the arras, enlisting various royalty watchers (the present writer, to his bafflement, among them) in the cause. The vulnerable point was the alleged absence of surnames for "Royal Highnesses". Surely there was at least one place where you had to have a surname – in a certificate of civil registration? The marriage certificates of Princess Anne and Prince Charles were to be the battleground. Sure enough, when Princess Anne married Captain Mark Phillips in November 1973, although she signed herself (in

the manner of princesses), "Anne" her name on the register was shown as: "Anne Elizabeth Alice Louise Mountbatten-Windsor".

So far so good, now for the clincher – the wedding of the Prince of Wales, the heir to the throne. If his marriage certificate also said "Mountbatten-Windsor" then that would put the matter beyond doubt: the next ruling dynasty would be the "House of Mountbatten-Windsor" (or, who knows, even plain "Mountbatten"?). Sadly, Lord Mountbatten did not live to see his "honorary grandson's" nuptials, being assassinated by the IRA in 1979. But when the wedding day finally dawned in July 1981, the loyal royalty watchers were confidently predicting, nay categorically stating (as the present writer did in broadcasts too humorous to mention), that the St Paul's Cathedral marriage register would set a new constitutional precedent, and so forth and so on. However, anti-climax ensued when it was discovered that under "Name and Surname" in the register was merely "His Royal Highness Prince Charles Philip Arthur George The Prince of Wales". No mention of "Mountbatten-Windsor". Curiouser and curiouser . . .

Whatever her relations with her Tory Prime Ministers (Heath no doubt earning the wooden-spoon as the least looked-forward-to Tuesday caller), the Queen seems to have enjoyed particularly cordial dealings with the wise-cracking Harold Wilson (now Lord Wilson of Rievaulx). When he resigned in 1976 Wilson not only advised James Callaghan to do his homework but expressed the hope that his successor would enjoy, as he had, the Queen's "manifold kindness, understanding and trust". Callaghan also apparently established a rapport with the Queen which is said to have been considerably warmer than that with, say, the trim Margaret Thatcher. (Princess Anne's aside to some photographer who was pestering her – "I am not *Mrs Thatcher*" – may perhaps reveal something or other.) Callaghan has shrewdly observed of the Queen's attitude to her politicians: "What one gets is friendliness but not friendship."

Diverting revelations as to the Queen's style in dealing with her ministers are given in the diaries of two more Socialist politicians, the late Richard Crossman and Barbara Castle. The former found the meetings of the Privy Council, which fell within his province as Lord President of the Council, "the best example of pure mumbo-jumbo you can find". The Privy Council, "The Queen's Most Excellent Majesty in Council", is the formal institution of Government for performing prerogative powers – the remains of once royal powers that do not depend on Parliamentary statute. Crossman resented that four busy Ministers all had to take a day and night off to travel to Balmoral for the two-and-a-half-minute business of a Privy Council meeting during which time some fifty or sixty "Titles of the Orders in Council" were approved by the Queen. Later he conceded that if this was necessary to the magic of monarchy, fair enough.

On one occasion, Crossman related, Sir Edward Bridges was introducing four politician Privy Councillors. They knelt on the wrong side of the room and Sir Edward had to indicate their mistake. They proceeded to crawl across the room on their hands and knees. "In the process", wrote Crossman, "they knocked a book off the table and it had to be rescued by the Queen, who looked blackly furious". As so often, Dick Crossman had got it wrong: later she revealed that she had been trying desperately not to laugh.

Crossman appreciated the problems faced by the Queen when they watched Wilson's devaluation speech together at Windsor Castle. The Queen was constitutionally forbidden to make a political comment after it, but if she said nothing, even that could have been interpreted wrongly. Eventually she said: "Of course, it's extraordinarily difficult to make that kind of speech". Another time, the Queen asked the Lord President how the morning sittings in the House of Commons were progressing. He looked surprised and she quickly said: "Oh! I'm sorry, I wasn't criticizing".

When Crossman put it about that he was not going to bother to turn up at the State Opening of Parliament, there was such a stir in what are known as "Court circles" that he felt obliged to go to see the Private Secretary, Sir Michael Adeane. Sir Michael explained that if he did not wish to be there, all he need do was to write to the Queen and ask to be excused without explaining why. The wise constitutionalist added. "Of course, the Queen has as strong a dislike of public ceremonies as you do. I don't disguise from you the fact that it will certainly occur to her to ask herself why you should be excused when she has to go, since you're both officials." (Note that last word.) The repentant Wykehamist duly trooped off to the Brothers Moss.

The fiery Barbara Castle found the Queen "much more relaxed and natural than her pictures show". The Transport Minister enjoyed a moment at the royal opening of the Severn Bridge in 1966:

Kerensky (the planner) was explaining the model with great pride – "The first of its kind in Europe" – and telling her all about the landscaping. "There is a mental home just here and the road will be completely hidden from it." The Queen turned to the Lord Lieutenant and chuckled: "They'll need that mental home to accommodate the people who go mad trying to find their way through this."

When staying at Windsor Castle in 1968, Barbara Castle observed that:

When the Queen arrived, she went round seriously shaking hands and then stood talking to Princess Anne with an air of almost glum indifference. So I joined in one of my hearty conversations with Philip who is always easy to talk to . . .
At this point the Queen came over and, as usual, as she talked to me her face relaxed into what can be her very charming smile. I can only conclude that she is either naturally shy or has inherited Queen Mary's glower without knowing it. She always gets animated when she talks about the children and one remark she made brought home to me vividly the basic horror of the royal life. Talking of Anne and Charles and how much they were enjoying school and university, she recalled that the first time she had ever joined in any collective activity was when she joined the ATS, during the war. "One had no idea how one compared with other people," she said simply. "And of course there were a lot of mechanical things one had to master." "Did you enjoy it?" I asked. "Oh yes, enormously." And I really felt sorry for her when she went on to say she had received a large number of critical letters because of something I had said in Parliament about mothers not taking children on their knees in the front of cars.
Apparently she had been in the estate car in Windsor Park with Andrew in the back and had taken Edward on her knee in the front seat. Some photographer had snapped her and she had been flooded with a hostile mail, saying Barbara Castle said she oughtn't to do that. Poor woman! I don't know which of us is more under the spotlight!

Barbara Castle salves her Socialist conscience by half-bowing to the Queen rather than dropping a curtsey. In her diary she makes a less flattering reference to the Queen during a diatribe against the "Honours System",

The most outrageous thing about it was that it reflected the system of social stratification and snobbery in this country. One of my most embarrassing jobs as a Minister was to present the BEMs (British Empire Medals) to railwaymen and other members of the lower orders with whom the Queen did not think it was worth her while to shake hands.

The creation of peers – such as "Mrs" Castle's late husband, Lord Castle – is the fourth prerogative (the choice of Prime Minister, the appointment and dismissal of Ministers and the dissolution of Parliament being, at least notionally, the other three) in which the personal wishes of the sovereign may play a part. The main innovations of the Queen's reign as far as peerages are concerned have been the Peerage Acts of 1958 and 1963. The former introduced the modern form of life peerage, of which hundreds have been handed out to nonentities and political time-servers (a much narrower sphere than originally envisaged). The 1963 Act allowed hereditary peeresses in their own right and peers holding only Scottish titles to sit in the House of Lords, as well as giving mavericks like the erstwhile 2nd Viscount Stansgate (now styled "Tony Benn") the chance to rid themselves of their titles for life. Various suggestions for radical reform of the House of Lords have been put forward during the Queen's reign, but none have proceeded very far; one was blocked in the House of Commons by the improbable combination of Michael

Foot and Enoch Powell. Although it is now fashionable to pretend otherwise, the Queen is at the head of the aristocracy; the decline of that class, which many fervent monarchists view with equanimity, does not augur well for the future of the monarchy. When the Queen once announced that "her" Government were planning to eradicate the hereditary element from the House of Lords, the excruciating irony seemed lost on almost everyone.

No new hereditary peerages or baronetcies were created between 1965 and 1983 and it seemed unlikely that any more hereditary titles would be created. The Queen's first grandson, Peter Phillips, had the indignity of being born without even a courtesy title which, for a few reactionaries at least, made a sad ending to the Queen's Silver Jubilee year. In keeping with the spuriously egalitarian climate of the age his parents, Princess Anne, the absurdly styled "Mrs Mark Phillips" (incorrect on at least two counts, if not three), and her husband Captain Mark Phillips had apparently spurned peerages. Happily disproving Evelyn Waugh's dictum that the Conservative Party never turns the clock back a single second, Margaret Thatcher recommended hereditary viscountcies for William Whitelaw and George Thomas, the outgoing Speaker of the House of Commons, following the General Election of 1983; and went on to recommend an earldom for the nonagenarian politician, Harold Macmillan, whose reluctance to be ennobled twenty years previously had helped to usher in the anti-historical attitude to titles. The harmless baronetcy, which confers no legislative power, still awaits revival. The Queen has created no titles in the two highest ranks of the peerage during her reign – no dukes or marquesses – though she did ask Winston Churchill (the heir presumptive to the Dukedom of Marlborough until he was nearly 23) if he would "like a Dukedom or something". The Prince of Wales's Dukedom of Cornwall was not specifically created (the title goes automatically to the heir apparent under its charter of 1337), but, before long, it now seems likely once more that Prince Andrew will be created Duke of York (a title traditionally associated with second sons, several of whom like Georges V and VI, later became King) and Prince Edward, say, Duke of Sussex.

As part of her personal prerogative, the Queen is the "fount of honour", but honours with a few exceptions – the Garter, the Thistle, the Order of Merit and the Royal Victorian Order – are conferred on the advice of the Prime Minister. With an increasing number of recent exceptions – such as Sir Winston Churchill, Sir Anthony Eden, Sir Harold Wilson and several lesser-known figures – Knights of the Garter have tended to be peers, or else members of the royal family or foreign royalties. In fact, until very recently, the Garter resembled some of the more exclusive foreign Orders in that admission to it depended more on who a person was than on what he had done; certain families among the dukes, marquesses and earls were known as "Garter Families" and their successive heads received the Garter almost automatically. This is what Lord Melbourne meant when he said that there was 'no damned nonsense of merit' in the Garter; a phrase which has since found its way into almost every letter acknowledging congratulations on receiving the honour – so that one feels that etiquette books might print a standard letter for use in such circumstances, incorporating this well-worn piece of false modesty. Now, however, it seems that there is more "damned nonsense of merit" in the Garter than there used to be. One is now likely to see a sprinkling of meritocrats, or Labour life peers, in the colourful procession down the hill at Windsor Castle on the Monday of Ascot week which mysteriously did not take place in 1984 for the first time for many years. When Sir Harold Wilson was installed as a Knight in 1976 the congregation included the journalist Bernard Levin, who was heard to observe that he would have been prepared to come a long way to see Wilson wearing a floppy hat.

"No damned nonsense of merit" applied until recently to Scotland's equivalent of the Garter, the Order of the Thistle; and it applied to the now-defunct Irish counterpart, the Order of St Patrick. Although suggestions have been made about a Most Noble Welsh Order (the Leek?), the idea has not been adopted. The most-quoted remark concerning the Thistle is not one which any recipient of the honour who is a self-respecting Scot would be likely to use when writing to acknowledge congratulations; it is attributed to another Prime Minister, who, when someone suggested that he recommend the Queen to give the Thistle to a certain notoriously stolid Scottish peer, replied, "What's the use? He'd only eat it".

Apart from a very few Knights of the Garter and the Thistle outside the peerage, those knights who belong to the Orders of Knighthood – as distinct from peers – belong to one or more of six other Orders: the Bath, the Star of India, the St Michael and St George, the Order of the Indian Empire, the Royal Victorian Order or the Order of the British Empire. These Orders are mostly given for distinguished service in an official or military capacity; the two Indian Orders, which ceased to be conferred after the end of the British Raj, for service in India; the St Michael and St George, for service overseas, particularly in diplomacy; the Royal Victorian Order, for service to the Crown, as distinct from service to the State. The newest of the Orders, the Order of the British Empire, is the one most freely given at the present time; though its name is now somewhat anachronistic, not to say misleading, since it is largely given for services within the United Kingdom.

The Queen, Princess Anne and plain (that is to say, untitled) Peter Phillips at Badminton

All these Orders – with the exception of the Garter, the Thistle and the Patrick, when it existed – have ranks lower than knighthood such as that of Companion or Commander, Officer, Lieutenant or Member. These are decorations, conferring no title or prefix, but initials after their holder's name.

Invoking a legendary figure from the Age of Chivalry, G.K. Chesterton once lamented:

Prince, Bayard would have smashed his sword
To see the sort of Knights you dub

At the sight of some recent Honours Lists (generally issued on New Year's Day, on the Queen's official birthday and on the dissolution of a Parliament), many have echoed his words.

One of the most imaginative honours awarded in the Queen's reign was the issue of a Silver Jubilee Medal in 1977 to her most vociferous and persistent critic, Willie Hamilton, Scottish Labour MP. In his own provocative way the well-known republican has done more than most for the Queen; above all, he has jolted her notional supporters out of the apathy wherein lies the real danger to the survival of the monarchy. Willie Hamilton was a member of the Select Committee on the Civil List whose report (published in November 1971) constitutes what one of its members, the constitutional historian and editor of Bagehot's works, Norman St John-Stevas has rightly called "a unique and valuable document on the workings of the monarchy in the second half of the 20th century". Hamilton, needless to say the dissenting voice on the Select Committee, wanted the Queen to have an annual salary of £100,000, to reduce, or abolish, the payments to the other members of the royal family and, for good measure, to confiscate the revenues of the Duchies of Lancaster and Cornwall.

At the beginning of each reign the monarch surrenders the hereditary revenues from the Crown Estates for the duration of the reign and, in return, is granted a fixed sum of money. This procedure (the "Civil List") has been followed since the accession of George III in 1760. By the Civil List Act of 1952, on the accession of the Queen, Parliament provided a sum of £475,000 a year for the support of the Queen together with annuities for certain members of the royal family. It was optimistically anticipated that this sum would suffice for the whole reign.

However, thanks to galloping inflation, the money of course proved inadequate and by 1970 total Civil List expenditure had reached £745,000. This meant there was a deficit of £240,000 which had to be met by the Privy Purse. In the words of Prince Philip the monarchy was "in the red". Thus, in 1971, the Queen was obliged to send a message to the House of Commons asking for additional financial provision for the royal family.

A Select Committee was accordingly appointed and considered a wide range of evidence, including Sir Michael Adeane's masterly memorandum about the Queen's duties. In the event, the Committee approved by majority an increase in the Civil List of £980,000 a year for the Queen and her household and increased annuities for other members of the royal family.

The committee also recommended that the royal trustees should report from time to time ("not less frequently than once every ten years") and that following

receipt of such reports the sums charged on the Consolidated Fund should be increasable by Treasury order. In this way the committee provided for a means of reviewing the royal finances but sought to avoid the embarrassment of annual inquiries into royal expenditure. The proposals were subsequently incorporated in the Civil List Act of 1972. In the highly inflationary period since then there have needed to be fairly frequent increases. To circumvent the wearisome political row every time an increase is necessary due to inflation, it was intimated that the Civil List allowances might have become "index-linked" but when the 1984 increases of 4 per cent were announced by the royal trustees (the Prime Minister, the Chancellor of the Exchequer and the Keeper of the Privy Purse) they proved slightly below the expected rate of inflation. The trustees said that the latest increase "may just be adequate to maintain existing standards". Any lesser increase would lead to a significant reduction in the scale or style of royal occasions.

The trustees, who are required to keep under review yearly amounts of Civil List expenditure and last reported in December 1974, said that they were satisfied that "every effort has been made to secure continuing economies in the administration of the Royal Household". The trustees noted that about 70 per cent of the Civil List is disbursed on salaries of staff in the Royal Household, the majority of which are directly linked to comparable grades in the Civil Service. Other costs of the royal family, including travel on official duties, the Royal Yacht *Britannia*, the Queen's Flight and maintenance of palaces and other residences, falls on Government departments.

The 1985 figures were as follows:-

	£
The Queen's Civil List	3,976,000
The Queen Mother	345,300
The Duke of Edinburgh	192,600
Princess Anne	120,000
Prince Andrew	20,000
Prince Edward	20,000
Princess Margaret	116,800
Princess Alice, Duchess of Gloucester	47,300
Duke of Gloucester	54,000
Duke of Kent	127,000
Princess Alexandra	120,900
	5,179,900
Refunded by The Queen	389,200
	4,790,700

Mr Hamilton and a few other Labour MPs never miss the opportunity for a whine about royal finance. The principal points of controversy have always been the annuities payable to other members of the royal family – Mr Hamilton has a particular down on poor Princess Margaret ("that wayward woman") – and the tax exemption of the Queen. Although the Queen pays no income tax, surtax, capital gains or transfer tax and can recover tax, taken away at source, on such things as investments, she does pay local rates, customs and excise and indirect taxes. In fact, the Queen pays a higher proportion of her income to the Exchequer than any other individual in Great Britain, handing over the net revenue of the Crown Lands and a decent contribution of her own money to the Civil List and it only takes a few elementary sums to establish that the Queen puts in more than she takes out.

The Queen's own private fortune, managed by Baring Brothers in the City, remains an unknown quantity, though this does not stop gossip columnists describing her as "the richest woman in the world" with a fortune estimated – or rather guessed – in terms of long-distance telephone numbers. A radical solution to the running sore of "royal money" would be to give to the Queen a direct share of her own revenues from the Crown Estates (some 300 acres of property in London and over 3 million acres in the rest of the country) and thereby remove the Civil List from the annual limelight of controversy. The Prince and Princess of Wales and their staff do not cost the public a penny. They live on the income of the Prince's own revenues from the Duchy of Cornwall. Like the Queen, the Prince of Wales does not pay income tax, but when he became entitled to the Duchy income (now over half-a-million pounds a year) at the age of 21, the Prince offered half to the Treasury – subject to review by the Consolidated Fund administered by the Exchequer. Faced with rising running expenses after his marriage, the Prince has now revised this to a quarter.

If the Queen's finances need any sort of crude justification, the value of her and her family in terms of tourism can hardly be overestimated. After all, people do not come to Britain for the weather or the food, they come to lap up the "heritage", of which the Queen is indeed the jewel in the crown. Seen against this background, the cost of running the monarchy (and the Civil List is merely the "expenses" and overheads for a job almost everyone wants the Queen and her family to do) is negligible. For instance, the Queen receives about half what a democratic head of state like, say, the President of West Germany, is granted to carry out his duties. With due respect, the name of this gentleman is not exactly a household word outside his own country (or, perhaps, even in it); whereas the Queen has additional duties in the countries of the Commonwealth all over the globe – for which, incidentally, she receives no extra pay.

Her Majesty is directly involved both in State Visits to this country of the Heads of Foreign and Commonwealth States . . .", Sir Michael Adeane told the Select Committee on the Civil List in 1971. (The list of the Queen's visitors – ranging from Krushchev and Bulganin, President de Gaulle, Emperor Haile Selassie of Ethiopia to Emperor Hirohito of Japan gives an indication of the breadth of her experience.) Sir Michael went on: "and in tours and visits overseas to Commonwealth countries and in State Visits to foreign countries. In particular, Her Majesty's programme has increasingly included visits for specific occasions to monarchical countries of the Commonwealth." This dry statement disguises the fact that the Queen's travels have made royal history. The jet age has made an enormous difference to the scope of her travelling. Together with television, this revolutionized mobility has been the major contrast between the Queen's reign and those of her predecessors.

Her father, George VI, had hoped to undertake a major tour of the Commonwealth to show his appreciation for its efforts in the Second World War but his fragile health had precluded this. The Queen was determined to complete the mission to Australasia she had begun on his behalf in February 1952 which was cut short in Kenya by her father's death. Once the Coronation was over, ambitious plans were put into motion for the great tour that was to make her the first monarch of any nationality to circumnavigate the globe, a voyage during which she was scarcely to set foot on any soil not part of the Commonwealth, taking in Bermuda, Jamaica, Fiji, Tonga, New Zealand, Australia, Ceylon (later Sri Lanka), Uganda, Libya, Malta and Gibraltar.

The Queen and the Duke of Edinburgh left on their great journey from London Airport in November 1953. They embarked on the Shaw Savill liner *Gothic* in Bermuda and sailed to Jamaica where the Queen, despite the overwhelming heat, travelled in an open car to give the islanders their first sight of a reigning sovereign. Next stop, via the Panama Canal, was Suva in Fiji. The Fijian islands, ceded to Queen Victoria in 1874, had also never seen their monarch and the Queen was greeted with formal homage from the colourfully attired native chiefs, one of whom presented the prized *tabua* (a whale's tooth). The Fijians regard silence as a mark of respect so – apart from a spontaneous initial outburst – there was no wild cheering as the royal party drove to Suva's Albert Park where the loyal toast was drunk in *yaqona*, a local brew served in coconut shells. Among those presented to the Queen on her visit to Fiji was John Christian who had travelled across the Pacific from Pitcairn Island, where his ancestor

Fletcher Christian had sailed in the *Bounty* after depositing his commanding officer in a long boat.

The *Gothic* steamed on to Tonga, the "Friendly Islands", where the Queen was greeted by the magnificent, beaming figure of Queen Selote, whose insistence on travelling in an open carriage at the Queen's Coronation had made such an indelible impression on the watching millions. Appropriately enough, the rain came down again as the two Queens settled into their carriage, only to stop the moment umbrellas were raised, causing hearty royal laughter. Next in the procession came the Duke of Edinburgh travelling in an improbable Polynesian conveyance, a London taxi. Queen Selote had ordered the vehicle as a souvenir of her triumphant visit to England. By the sight of her, the Tongan Queen did not look one to stint herself at the table and the royal party was duly served with two gargantuan feasts: "pyramids of roast pig, shiploads of yams, coconuts and fruit", drooled the reporters after the first of those blow-outs on the lawns of Queen Selote's palace. The following day, "sucking pigs by the dozen, cooked fish, raw fish, chickens in every state of dismemberment, tropical fruits . . ." were laid out in a clearing outside the Tongan palm thatch-and-post rural retreat. Not on the menu, but a memorable sight of the visit, was a venerable tortoise (who has since finally handed in his dinner pail) first brought to Tonga two centuries previously by Captain Cook.

Emulating the famous 18th-century explorer, *Gothic* proceeded to New Zealand. Undaunted by the pouring rain, which seemed to be becoming a traditional feature of her ceremonial life, the Queen rose to speak outside Auckland Town Hall without the benefit of any protection from the elements. "Give her an umbrella!" Antipodean voices barracked from the crowd. The deputy mayor, a Mr Buttle, rose to the occasion by divesting himself of his mackintosh. "Thank you very much Sir Walter Raleigh", the Queen responded in an aside that was picked up over the microphones to general Kiwi delight. Of such jolly, trivial incidents are royal tours made.

The following day, Christmas Eve, 1953, the happy atmosphere evaporated when a train fell into a river, killing 166 people. The Queen's first Christmas broadcast, made in Auckland, included a message of sympathy to the bereaved as well as an affirmation of her belief in the Commonwealth. She said

it bears no resemblance to the empires of the past. It is an entirely new conception built on the highest qualities of the spirit of man: friendship, loyalty and the desire for freedom and peace . . .

In keeping with these sentiments the Maoris swallowed any lingering bitterness towards the British Crown, to whom their lands had been ceded in 1840, in a ceremony at Waitangi. "Just as your great ancestress, Queen Victoria,

Right: The Queen after opening the South Australian House of Parliament at Adelaide, April 1954

Opposite above: The Royal Yacht Britannia *at anchor in the lagoon at Venice during the Queen's State Visit to Italy in May 1961; and below: the Queen Mother, Princess Margaret, Prince Charles and Princess Anne on the* Britannia's *return to London after the Queen's great circumnavigation of 1953/4*

offered us her royal protection," said a descendant of the Maori chief who had expressed his feelings at the time by chopping down a flagpole symbolizing the Great White Queen, "so do we now unfold ourselves under your mantle of love. We thank God for a century and more of British rule."

In another downpour the Queen, wearing her Coronation gown and a tiara, went to open the New Zealand Parliament in Wellington in January 1954; only at her father's State Opening of Parliament in South Africa had this ceremony been performed in person in the Southern Hemisphere. The following day she held a Privy Council Meeting which was, of course, another "first". Flying to the South Island, the Queen undertook an early forerunner of the "royal walkabout" at Nelson, walking along the main street through crowds up to fifty deep. Following an investiture at Christchurch, the Queen was at last permitted a few days rest from her heavy public programme at the Longbeach sheep station of the Grigg family (no apparent relation to her future critic, John Grigg, Lord Altrincham).

"It is impossible to calculate the benefits of this remarkable tour", the New Zealand Prime Minister Mr Holland told the Queen and the Duke at the end of their five-week tour. "New Zealand has seen nothing like it before." The Queen replied: "We have enjoyed every minute of our stay . . ."

Arriving in Sydney Harbour, the Queen wasted no time in getting the point across to the Australians that she was not a visiting sovereign from the old country but their own national Queen. "I have always looked forward to my first visit to this country," she said, "but now there is the added satisfaction to me that I am able to meet my Australian people as their Queen. I am proud indeed to be at the head of a nation that has achieved so much."

Her first official act on Australian soil was to lay a wreath in memory of those who had died in the Allied cause in the Second World War. The Queen opened the Australian and Tasmanian Parliaments, went west to Perth and as far north as Cairns, Queensland on the Great Barrier Reef. Unlike her Uncle David (Edward VIII), whose tour of Australia as Prince of Wales was marred by the occasional unfortunate misunderstanding, the Queen charmed the Australians into uncharacteristic fulsomeness. Little incidents like the Queen tipping off a military commandant at a parade in Canberra that a drummerboy was about to faint endeared her to the Aussies, while the Duke of Edinburgh's abrasive temperament clearly marked him as a man after their own hearts.

To illustrate the arduousness of her travels, statistics are sometime quoted as to the number of speeches the Queen has made (said to be 102 on the 1953/4 tour), the number

of other worthies' speeches she has had to sit through, the number of times she has endured the national anthem and so forth. Towards the end of her Australian tour, however, the incidence of handshaking declined as there was a polio scare. This should be borne in mind when faced with the information that the Queen is supposed to have made 13,213 handshakes on her global progress.

After her month in Australia, the Queen visited the Cocos Islands, opened the Ceylon Parliament in Colombo and witnessed the rare '*Raja Perehera*' procession up in the hill city of Kandy, with its lavishly decorated elephants and exquisite dancers; she celebrated her 28th birthday, 21 April 1954, on board *Gothic* as she sailed across the Indian Ocean to Aden, where the Duke of Edinburgh took a prescient interest in the new oil refinery. The royal party then flew to Entebbe (the airport where the new Queen had been in transit during the first few hours of her reign a couple of years before) in Uganda, where the Queen opened the Owen Falls Dam on the Nile.

At the beginning of May the Queen and the Duke of Ediburgh were reunited with their children, Prince Charles and Princess Anne, at Tobruk of Second World War fame in North Africa. On their first foreign trip, the five-year-old Prince and his three-year-old sister had sailed from Portsmouth on the maiden voyage of the Royal Yacht *Britannia*. Built at John Brown's shipyard on the Clyde at the cost of £2.1 million, *Britannia* was a belated replacement for the long unseaworthy *Victoria & Albert*. The new Royal Yacht, constructed rather like a cruise-ship, was designed so that it could be converted for use as a hospital ship in time of war; even in peacetime it has sometimes resembled a hospital owing to the number of passengers, not least the Queen herself, feeling the effects of its heavy "roll" in rough weather. None the less, after several extensive refits, *Britannia* is still very much in

service, transporting the Queen on various state visits and acting as a convenient floating base in which to repay her hosts' hospitality.

Before they saw their parents again, Prince Charles and Princess Anne stayed with Lord and Lady Mountbatten in Malta where Uncle Dickie was now Commander-in-Chief Mediterranean. Together again, the Queen, her husband and their children (the new royal version of "us four") sailed home in *Britannia* by way of Gibraltar. Here the Duke of Edinburgh is supposed to have thrown some peanuts to photographers, affecting to mistake them for the barbary apes capering on the Rock. This sort of behaviour (politely described as "practical joking" or "horseplay") finds the royal family at their most disobliging. The disagreeable tradition, faithfully followed by the Duke's second son, Prince Andrew, goes back long before the Mountbattens arrived on the scene. In his diary the lyricist of *Land of Hope and Glory,* A. C. Benson notes royalty's "odd fondness for 'ragging' other people and laughing at their discomfiture when they are sure they will never be made to look foolish themselves."

Notwithstanding the Duke's occasional run-in with the press, the epic Commonwealth journey of 1953/4 was rightly hailed as the most successful royal tour ever undertaken when the Queen came back after 173 days away. At the Guildhall luncheon held to celebrate the Queen's return, she said that she had "received visible and audible proof" that the monarchy was "living in the hearts of the people".

Understandably there was no more official travelling for the Queen in 1954 but she made her first State Visit in the following year to Norway. For all the formality of State it was very much a family occasion as the Norwegian royal family is the closest in blood to the present British dynasty. When the country became independent (for the first time in five centuries) in 1905 it chose as its King, Prince Carl of Denmark, a son-in-law of Edward VII of Great Britain and also nephew of his Danish wife Queen Alexandra. Prince Carl was transformed into King Haakon VII who was now, as Europe's oldest monarch, celebrating his Golden Jubilee on the Norwegian throne. The Queen and the Duke of Edinburgh sailed across the North Sea from Rosyth to Oslo where they were greeted with a warmth that made nonsense of protocol by the spry old Sea King and his heir, Crown Prince Olav.

At the State Banquet King Haakon spoke movingly of the hospitality he had received in Britain during the war when the German occupation drove him out. Among the houses King Haakon visited during his stay in Britain was the family home of the present writer; he is warmly remembered as a splendid figure of a man, tall, spare and erect with deep-set eyes and an aristocratic nose. He had

integrity, great charm and kindliness. He lived simply and was extremely hard working, following events closely. His presence in Britain became a rallying-point for the Free Norwegians and when he returned at the moment of liberation in 1945 he was welcomed as the living symbol of Norway's will to resist the Nazi oppression. The Queen's State Visit had a sad aftermath for, a few days after the departure of his great-niece, King Haakon slipped and broke his thigh, which never properly healed. He died aged 87 two years later.

In 1956 the Queen and the Duke of Edinburgh made a three week tour of Nigeria. It is an illustration of the change in mobility that when the Queen's cousin Princess Marie Louise went to that country thirty years previously it took her as long as three weeks to reach there by sea. The Queen flew there in seventeen hours. Thirty years on, even that seems an absurdly long time. To help her prepare for the visit to Nigeria (a country undergoing the transfer to independence within the Commonwealth), the Queen

*The Queen and the Duke of Edinburgh on route to open
Parliament in Nigeria, 1956*

had acquired a new temporary equerry, Major Aguiyi-Ironso of the Nigeria Regiment – the first non-white to join the Household since Queen Victoria's unsavoury Munshi, notorious for his "nephews".

After four days in Lagos, the Queen headed north for Kaduna where she held a Durbar. An English journalist compared the scene to the "Field of the Cloth of Gold":

As the movement of forming-up began, the morning sun caught the glitter of thousands of spears and sword-blades, and picked out the brocaded garments . . . an unreal procession of horses and men which might have emerged from the mists of African history . . . Emirs and great chieftains, spearsmen and archers, clowns and tumblers and half-naked pagans gathered in all their barbarous magnificence . . .

The most spectacular, not to say alarming, feature of the Durbar was when squadrons of horsemen, armed to the teeth and giving tongue to blood-curdling yells, charged at the royal dais, pulling up their steeds within a few yards of the Great White Mother.

In Eastern Nigeria the Queen and the Duke of Edinburgh braved the leper settlement on the Oji river. "The Queen's visit", said the supervisor, "will do more to conquer man's fear and hate of the disease than any other single act I can think of. People all over the world will read that the Queen and the Duke penetrated a leper settlement, and this will convince them as nothing else could that most of their fears of the disease are groundless." The Queen and the Duke were seen shaking hands with sufferers from leprosy. The Queen "adopted" eight leper patients and she and the Duke have continued to support the British Leprosy Relief Association (LEPRA).

In the summer of 1956 the Queen and the Duke sailed in *Britannia* to Stockholm for their State Visit to Sweden. Here, as in Norway, it was essentially a family occasion for Prince Philip's aunt Louise, a sister of Lord Mountbatten, was the second wife of King Gustaf Adolf. The archaeologist King's first wife Margaret had been a daughter of Queen Victoria's youngest son, the Duke of Connaught. Another Margaret, the Queen's sister – now

The royal tour of Nigeria, 1956. Left: The Queen receives the loyal address from the Speaker of the House of Representatives at Lagos. Above: Adeniji Adele II, Oba of Lagos, is presented to the Queen by the Governor-General of Nigeria, Sir James Robertson. Below: The Queen inspects the guard of honour formed by the Nigerian Regiment at Lagos Airport. Right: The Queen and the Duke of Edinburgh arrive at the Emir's Palace at Kano, the old capital of Northern Nigeria

having to come to terms with a life in which Group Captain Townsend could play no part – joined the royal party in Stockholm for the extension of the visit which had been planned to coincide with the equestrian events of the Olympic Games. The Queen's horse *Countryman* helped Britain win the gold medal for the three-day event.

The number of State Visits by the Queen increased significantly in 1957. Reunited with Prince Philip (as he had now become) after his lengthy absence on a round-the-world trip which took in the Olympic Games at Melbourne and a voyage to the Antarctic, the Queen made her first two State Visits to non-monarchical countries. With the cries of "*Viva la Rainha!*" and "*Vive la Reine!*" emanating lustily from republican throats the visits to Portugal and France proved another triumph for the Queen. In full bloom as she approached her 31st birthday, the Queen's magnetism when seen in the flesh (flesh being the operative word for her skin is of an exceptional quality) quite bowled over those who had only seen her in still photographs. Just as it was to be with her daughter-in-law, the Princess of Wales, sheer physical attractiveness was a vital factor in the Queen's appeal. In Paris, the centre of *chic*, the Queen threw down the gauntlet with a new hairstyle and a wardrobe by Hartnell that cocked a snook at the French couturiers.

The third State Visit of 1957 was to the more homely Denmark, another monarchy in the "royal family of Europe". For Prince Philip, of course, it was a return to his ancestral roots, while the Queen is a cousin of Queen Ingrid (a daughter of Princess Margaret of Connaught by her marriage to King Gustaf Adolf of Sweden). King Frederik was unfortunately unable to enjoy the occasion as much as he would have wished. As is often the way with "keep-fit" enthusiasts, violent exercise had resulted in unnecessary pain – in this case, a strained back brought on by weight-lifting. The sailor King's other recreation involved lifting nothing heavier than a baton; a talented musician, he would sometimes conduct, in private, the Danish State Orchestra.

In the autumn of 1957 the Queen donned her Coronation dress once again for the State Opening of Parliament in Ottawa on her first visit as "Queen of Canada". The night before she made her solo debut on television, speaking in both French and English to her Canadian subjects. The story is told that seeing the "expression of congealed terror" in the Queen's eyes before the transmission, the producer reminded her of Prince Philip's saying (an obscure private joke between them) about "the wailing and gnashing of teeth". The Queen relaxed a little, though nearly thirty years later

talking to camera is still an awkward experience for this essentially "unactressy" lady.

From Canada, the Queen flew to the United States of America where her first call was to what could be called her ancestral state of Virginia. At the heavily nostalgic town of Williamsburg she was presented with a picture of Colonel Augustine Warner, who settled in Virginia about eight years after the *Mayflower* had docked in New England. The Colonel's descendants include George Washington, Robert E. Lee and the Queen Mother – thus the Queen is a second cousin seven times removed of the great truth-telling founding father and a third cousin twice removed of the Civil War general. Judging by the success of the Queen's visits to America over the years the presumption that the Americans are royalists at heart seem to be well founded. An aspect of this is their obsession with George III (doubtless on account of the fact that he was the last King they ever had) whom the Queen jokily emphasised in her speech at Williamsburg as being commemorated by a county in Virginia. Also in Virginia the Queen and Prince Philip attended the Jamestown

Festival celebrating the 350th anniversary of the first British settlement in the company of a bewigged party of neo-Elizabethans.

President Eisenhower greeted the Queen in Washington DC where she was obliged to undertake no less than 36 public engagements within the space of two and a half days, including – fortunately as a spectator – a game of American football between the Terrapins and the Tarheels. In New York the Queen received a standing ovation on addressing that modern Tower of Babel, the United Nations, and a full scale ticker-tape welcome ("WELCOME PHIL AND LIZ" shouted the banners). All told the visit had helped heal the rift caused between Britain and the USA by the behaviour of President Eisenhower and his Secretary of State, Mr Dulles, who ensured that what might otherwise have been a successful operation at Suez became a fiasco.

The Queen's next State Visit was to the Netherlands in the spring of 1958, where she gave Queen Juliana the Order of the Garter. She returned to North America in the baking summer of 1959. Although by now expecting her third child (a fact which she confided to the Canadian

premier, John Diefenbaker), the Queen insisted on going through with the usual demanding programme of public engagements. Together with President Eisenhower she opened, as Queen of Canada, the joint Canadian-American venture of the St Lawrence Seaway up which they then sailed in *Britannia*. After visiting the International Fair in the "windy city" of Chicago (where she was hailed with yells of "Attagirl!"), the Queen and Prince Philip returned north to Canada, but finally the effects of the heat took their toll on the expectant mother and it was decided to abandon the planned tour of the North-Western Territories.

Following the birth of Prince Andrew at Buckingham Palace in February 1960 (the first child to be born to a reigning sovereign for over a hundred years), the Queen resumed her official travels in 1961 with a six-week tour of Cyprus, India (where she saw the Taj Mahal and laid a wreath on Mahatma Gandhi's monument), Pakistan, Nepal, Iran and Turkey. In the spring she paid a State Visit to Italy and the Vatican, spending 25 minutes with the beaming Pope John.

Later in 1961 there was considerable unease among the Queen's advisers – not least the Prime Minister, Harold Macmillan – about her tour of West Africa which was due to take in Ghana, the former Gold Coast. The country was in the grip of the corrupt regime of Kwame Nkrumah, a Marxist dictator prone to spend money sent in from Oxfam on swimming pools and other personal fripperies. Ghana seemed likely to break away from the Commonwealth but the Queen wanted it to stay part of the post-Imperial family. "How silly I should look if I was scared to visit Ghana and then Krushchev went a few weeks later and had a good reception", she said. Only five days before her visit Accra was hit with bombs but she remained resolute in her determination to go. Although there were some bizarre happenings – such as the top table at the State Banquet having several empty places due to the expected guests languishing in gaol – the Queen succeeded in her mission. The evil Nkrumah was later discredited and Ghana still recognises the Queen as Head of the Commonwealth today.

In 1962 the Queen and Prince Philip attended the silver wedding celebrations of Queen Juliana of the Netherlands

and Prince Bernhard. When the latter, the "Businessman Prince", disgraced himself in the Lockheed bribery scandal, some of Prince Philip's less ardent admirers came to appreciate his qualities rather more.

On her two-month Commonwealth tour of 1963, the Queen made her first venture into the Australian outback, addressing her subjects over the "Flying Doctor" network in Alice Springs. In 1964, following the birth of her fourth child, Prince Edward, the Queen received a distinctly coolish reception from the separatist French-Canadians in Quebec. There was also anxiety over the Queen's State Visit to the unruly Sudan, sandwiched between a tour of the then comparatively peaceful Ethiopia (as a guest of the venerable Emperor Haile Selassie of Ethiopia), but a truce between the warring factions was declared for the brief duration of her stay.

In the spring of 1965 the Queen became the first British sovereign to set foot on German soil since the days before the First World War. *Private Eye* featured a picture of the Queen (who is, of course, half-German by descent) inspecting the guard of honour with a bubble coming out of her mouth saying: "Hello Uncle Otto, Cousin Karl, Auntie Eva, Uncle Fritz, Cousin Ludwig etc. etc. . . ." The Queen was welcomed with tremendous and indeed slightly embarrassing fervour ("YOUR MAJESTY, GERMANY BELONGS TO YOU" trumpeted one headline). Twenty years after the Second World War the breach had been healed at last.

Later in the 1960s, the Queen's travels included a month's Caribbean tour, a sight of Expo'67 in Montreal and State Visits to Belgium, Brazil, Chile and Austria. Among the highlights of the early 1970s was the first so-called "walkabout" on the tour of New Zealand and Australia during which the Queen and Prince Philip were joined by their two elder children, by now firmly in the limelight, Prince Charles and Princess Anne. The tour was to celebrate the bicentenary of Captain Cook's landing in Australasia.

The four were together again in Canada later in 1970 for the centenary celebrations of the North-Western Territories and Manitoba which the Queen had been particularly keen to visit having had to cross them off her itinerary shortly before the birth of Prince Andrew. From Canada Prince Charles and Princess Anne went down to stay at the White House, a visit marred by President Nixon's clumsy attempts to encourage a friendship between the Prince and his daughter Tricia.

In 1972 the Queen embarked on a strenuous 25,000 mile South-East Asian tour taking in Thailand, Singapore, Malaysia (including a landing in long boats at Kuching in Sarawak where half the royal escort sank in a storm), the Maldive Islands, the Seychelles and Mauritius with a stopover to see President Jomo Kenyatta and his rose garden in Kenya. In the same year, during her second State Visit to France, the Queen saw her Uncle David for the last time. Dying of cancer at his house in the Bois de Boulogne, the Duke of Windsor was unable to come downstairs, as he had hoped, in order to welcome his niece who went up to his bedroom. Ten days later his coffin was on its way back to England to lie in State.

As Britain's long-awaited entry into the Common Market, denied by General de Gaulle, became a reality at last, the Queen's concern for the Commonwealth redoubled. In 1973, at the invitation of Pierre Trudeau, himself a French-Canadian, she attended the Commonwealth Conference in Ottawa and exhaustively plugged the message that she was "Queen of Canada and of *all* Canadians", not merely of "one or two ancestral strains". In Australia in the same year she formally approved her new title "Queen of Australia". The other reason for her tour down under was, as she laconically put it at a speech in Canberra: "There was the opening of an opera house somewhere in New South Wales." As "Queen of New Zealand" she opened that country's Parliament in Wellington the following year on a Commonwealth tour that embraced Norfolk Island, the New Hebrides (where Prince Philip is worshipped as a Messiah and expected to gird his loins in a *namba*), the British Solomon Islands, and Papua New Guinea, which was soon to be given independence within the Commonwealth.

One of the most colourful State Visits of the Queen's reign to date was made in Mexico in 1975. "La Reina Isabel" was received with wild enthusiasm everywhere she went, especially in Veracruz where she was serenaded on her balcony. In the same year the Queen and Prince Philip went to the crown colony of Hong Kong; there are plans for them to visit China itself to whom the island reverts in 1997. After Hong Kong the Queen notched up another historic "first" with her State Visit to Japan, where she was obliged to remove her shoes to enter a vernacular residence furnished with grass mats. At the tea ceremony held in the Palace of Katsura the Queen's comment upon her first sip of the frothy green beverage was: "Surprising".

To celebrate the American Bicentennial in 1976 the Queen presented a new Liberty Bell (the old one was cracked) to Philadelphia where she began her second State Visit to the United States. She told the guests at the luncheon on Capitol Hill in Washington DC that the founding fathers of the USA had behaved in a "typically British fashion" when they broke away from the mother country in 1776.

In an age of increasing terrorism, fear was expressed for the safety of the Queen in attending the Olympic Games at Montreal where, as Queen of Canada, she was due to

Below: The Queen with "His Hungriness" King Taufa'ahau Tupou IV of Tonga during her Silver Jubilee tour of the Commonwealth, 1977

Opposite: "The Rare White Heron" in her cloak of Kiwi feathers in New Zealand, 1977

perform the opening ceremony. True to form she insisted on going through with it and remained standing, a stationary target in the open Royal Box, for over an hour while all the competitors paraded past. Among them was her daughter, Princess Anne, a member of the British Three-Day Event team. Unfortunately the Princess on *Goodwill* came a cropper at the 19th fence on the cross-country course, eventually finishing sixth from bottom.

For her Silver Jubilee year of 1977 the Queen determined to visit as much of the Commonwealth as she possibly could, including places like Western Samoa which she had not visited before. In Tonga, Queen Selote's even larger son and successor, King Taufa'ahau Tupou IV, had slimmed down from 33 stone to a sylph-like 28 stone in honour of the Queen's Silver Jubilee visit, causing him to be known as "His Hungriness" among the Tongans. Happily the royal diet was jettisoned for the feast of lobsters, prawns, sucking pigs, turkey and tropical fruit, though the Queen does not share her host's taste for shellfish. In Fiji the rain gods ignored the pleas of the Waimaro tribe for fine weather and the Queen had to shelter from the downpour under the Prime Ministerial

umbrella, sipping her potion of *kava*, a root beverage which causes the mouth to go numb.

In New Zealand the Queen, known to the Maoris as the "Rare White Heron", wore a cloak of Kiwi feathers to receive her Silver Jubilee homage from a thousand-strong contingent of Maori warriors at Gisborne. In Wellington the Queen opened the new Parliament buildings (designed by the ubiquitous "Modernist" the late Sir Basil Spence) and there was a wry smile on her face when the curtains veiling the ceremonial plaque failed to budge. The Queen is said to derive a certain enjoyment from things like this going slightly wrong.

Unlike many of her loyal Australian subjects she was apparently mildly amused by Gough Whitlam's crack on hearing that the style of "Queen of the Solomon Islands" had been proposed. "What next?" said the former Labour Prime Minister, "Queen of Sheba?" Sir John Kerr's dismissal of Whitlam somewhat overshadowed the Queen's Silver Jubilee tour of Australia and there were various "demonstrations" (one banner bore the legend "A QUEEN IS QUAINT, A GOVERNOR-GENERAL AIN'T"). At the Centenary Test on Melbourne Cricket Ground, the fast

bowler Dennis Lillee asked the Queen for an autograph – something the Queen does not do – and his appeal was turned down. Nevertheless he was later sent a large signed photograph of the Queen. Earlier in the 1970s, a better mannered player, the great all-rounder Sir Garfield Sobers received the accolade of knighthood from the Queen, at a special ceremony in the cricket-mad island of Barbados.

It was in the West Indies that the Queen ended her second Silver Jubilee tour, having gone on there from Canada in the autumn. French separatism cast another slight cloud over the Canadian visit (Silver Jubilee badges, for instance, being tactfully withdrawn at the last moment when it was discovered that they were only printed in English), but the premier of Quebec, René Levesque, the leader of the separatists, deigned to meet the Queen at a lunch given at Mr Trudeau's house. The only sensation of the visit, however, was caused by the sight – not as novel as many people seemed to think – of the Queen wearing a pair of spectacles ("supra half-eyes" to be precise) to read the speech opening the Canadian Parliament in Ottawa.

Since the Silver Jubilee, one of the most successful royal tours has been the Queen's State Visit to the Gulf States in the Middle East in 1979. "I am delighted to be setting foot on Arab soil for the first time", the Queen told the Emir of Kuwait when she arrived by Concorde. The Queen and Prince Philip went on to Bahrain, Saudi Arabia (where she wore full-length dresses in front of the King), Qatar, Abu Dhabi and the United Arab Emirates. In Dubai the Queen made a stately progress up the Creek (the name of the river, that is) in a golden barge, enthroned on an elaborate armchair among Persian carpets and all manner of exotic foodstuffs.

The Queen's State Visit to Morocco in 1980 was a less agreeable experience owing to King Hassan's somewhat erratic behaviour, particularly in matters of timekeeping. On one notorious occasion the Queen was kept waiting for what seemed like an eternity outside in the blazing sun while the King of Morocco was apparently languishing within his cool caravan. "QUEEN IN RAGE OVER ROYAL SNUB" and "BRING OUR QUEEN HOME FROM THIS FLY-BLOWN DESERT KINGDOM" screamed the headlines of the British popular press, but, whatever she was really feeling, the Queen managed to see it through with her usual mixture of dignity and determination.

Below left: Attired in an exotic scarf and pillbox hat, the Queen arrives in Kuwait on Concorde *for the first stage of her three-week tour of the Middle East, 1979; and (right) the Queen at Al Ain University, Abu Dhabi, largest of the United Arab Emirates.*
Bottom: A study in contrasting attitudes during the Queen's visit to Bahrain

In 1983 on the Queen's tour of the Americas, the plans to sail along the coast of California in *Britannia* went awry due to the appalling weather conditions which drove her into a hotel inland. Here again one suspects that the Queen rather relishes such occasional upsets to the carefully organised royal schedules. (In the blizzards of 1982 at home she was obliged to shelter in a Cotswold pub but is said to have enjoyed the experience.) At a dinner during the visit to President Reagan's home state of California, the Queen observed that although she knew Britain had exported many things to America she had not been aware the weather was among them. The thespian President duly reacted as if he had just been pumped full of laughing gas.

Later that year, the Queen and Prince Philip returned to Treetops in Kenya where she had succeeded to the throne. The original hide had long since been burnt down and the visit proved a disappointment. The occasion turned into a distasteful media circus, with the Queen reluctantly posing beside a now treeless pool.

From Kenya, the Queen went on to Bangladesh and India where the Commonwealth Conference – or Heads of Government meeting as it is now called – was being held. The Queen's remarkably relaxed television chat in the garden with the Indian Prime Minister, Mrs Gandhi, was a feature of the 1983 Christmas broadcast. The most touching moment of the Queen's tour of India was her bestowing the insignia of an honorary member of the Order of Merit on Mother Teresa who travelled from her base in the slums of Calcutta to receive this highest honour in the sovereign's gift at Lutyens's magnificent Delhi palace.

In 1984 the Queen took another of her many brave decisions in going ahead with a State Visit to Jordan in the wake of bomb attacks in Amman against King Husain's moderate Arab regime by Syrian supported terrorists. *The Times* described the tour as "the most dangerous and diplomatically sensitive" of her reign. Under unprecedented security – with no "walkabouts" or

Above and below: The Queen and Prince Philip in Fiji and Tuvalu during the South Pacific Tour, 1982

Above: The Queen afloat in Stockholm on her 1983 visit to Sweden; and below: on a walkabout in Canada, 1984

*The Queen and Prince Philip are borne ashore in canoes at
Tuvalu, one of the smallest islands in the Commonwealth, 1982.
The islanders greeted Her Majesty as 'Mrs Gwin'*

Two brave monarchs: The Queen and King Hussein during her dangerous visit to Jordan, 1984

anything of that sort – the visit went off peacefully. "We have greatly admired the way in which you have guided your country through so many difficulties", the Queen told the Old Harrovian King at the State Banquet. "In an area of turbulence and of almost continuous and tragic conflict, you have made Jordan a beacon of stability and orderly progress." On the Queen's return from Jordan, the Israeli Government promptly suggested a State Visit. The invitation has been accepted for some future date.

The Queen's Canadian tour later in the year had its awkward moments. One local politician (later charged with drug offences) behaved somewhat strangely towards the Queen – touching, virtually pushing Her Majesty in a gratuitous manner – and another rumpus revolved around criticism that "the Monarch's dress sense is dowdy". Although the Queen had proclaimed a new constitution for Canada in 1982 (a ceremony boycotted by Monsieur Levesque) the political climate remained unsettled. Over the years, however, the Queen has faced the Commonwealth in all political weathers.

6. The Queen and the Commonwealth

In her 21st birthday broadcast, transmitted — ironically, as it turned out – from South Africa in 1947 the then Princess Elizabeth referred to our "great Imperial Commonwealth". Long before the Queen's 1984 Christmas broadcast the key phrase had become what she now referred to as "the Commonwealth family". This transition from the old Empire to the new Commonwealth has been one of the central themes of the Queen's reign. In her own words:

One of the more encouraging developments since the war has been the birth of the Commonwealth. Like a child, it has grown, matured and strengthened, until today the vision of its future is one of increasing understanding and co-operation between its members.
Notwithstanding the strains and stresses of nationalism, different cultures and religions and its growing membership, the Commonwealth family has still managed to hold together and to make a real contribution to the prevention of violence and discord.

In a very valid sense the mother of that child has been the Queen herself. She is patently the only unifying factor that has kept the unruly "family" from breaking up completely (the black sheep that have gone astray being Ireland, Burma, South Africa and Pakistan). As Margaret Thatcher has said: "I do not think the Commonwealth could be held together without the Queen".

Before the Second World War the idea of the "Commonwealth of Nations . . . united by a common allegiance to the Crown" replacing the great British Empire was little more than a pious hope. The contraction of the Empire had begun with the setting up of the Irish Free State in 1921. And though the postwar Labour Government gave India its independence in 1947 (with Lord Mountbatten, the last Viceroy, becoming the new partitioned Dominion's first Governor-General), it was really not until after the Suez fiasco that imperialism came to an end with Macmillan's "wind of change".

The phrase "Head of the Commonwealth", which was incorporated for the first time in the proclamation of the Queen's accession, goes back only to 1945 when India became a republic. Strictly speaking, the relation of the Head of the Commonwealth to its republican member states (which form a comfortable majority over monarchical members) is solely with the Governments. But, of course, the Queen's symbolic role means much more than that cold legal definition. "The strongest bonds of all", said the Queen on her first visit to Jamaica, "are those which are not recorded in documents but in the hearts of the people who share the same beliefs and the same aims".

To celebrate her 21st birthday in the Commonwealth signified something more than a coincidence for its future Head. The dedication to the Commonwealth ideal made in that 21st birthday speech was to be the lodestar of her life:

I declare before you that my whole life, whether it be long or short, shall be devoted to your service and the service of our great Imperial Commonwealth to which we all belong.

Thirty years later in her Silver Jubilee speech at the Guildhall in the City of London the Queen looked back at that broadcast:

Although that vow was made in my salad days when I was green in judgement I do not regret nor retract one word of it.

The Queen established her Commonwealth persona at the start of her reign with the marathon tour taking in Bermuda, Jamaica, Fiji, Tonga, New Zealand, Australia, Ceylon, Uganda, Libya, Malta and Gibraltar from November 1953 to May 1954. The excitement and the romance of that journey clearly made a deep impression on the Queen. As Auberon Waugh has satirically pointed out "She is never so happy as when she is being welcomed by a crowd of tribal dancers in grass skirts." One of the most extraordinary paintings of the Queen, *The Crown*, a consummately *kitsch* work by Grace Wheatley (formerly owned by the late Sir Emile Littler) expresses the allegory perfectly. It shows the lovely sovereign, dressed in full Coronation robes in the middle of a jungle, radiantly acknowledging the salute of sundry natives with various exotic wildlife in attendance.

Rather in the manner of Martin Luther King, the Queen has had a dream, a post-Imperial dream. Whatever the setbacks, the Queen has kept faith in her commitment to the Commonwealth. It is an ideal that has certainly taken some knocks over the years.

At the beginning of the reign there was a state of emergency in Kenya (the country where she had become Queen) caused by the bloody "Mau Mau" terrorists of the Kikuyu. After the Suez affair, Britain's last Imperial adventure, came the rushed "decolonization" of Africa. This was to lead, in 1960, to South Africa, a country with such happy memories for the Queen and the rest of "us four", voting (or at least its white population doing so) to become a republic. The following year it was made clear to Dr Verwoerd, the Prime Minister, that South Africa could not remain in the Commonwealth unless the "multi-racialism" that had been promulgated in the most recent Commonwealth Prime Ministers' Conference held at Windsor was adopted in the new republic.

The model democratic constitutions bequeathed by the British Empire were proving no less adhesive in the emergent black nations. Ghana (formerly the Gold Coast), which had become a republic within the Commonwealth in 1957, was in the grip of the Marxist dictator Kwame Nkrumah. Despite bomb explosions in Accra a few days before her departure, the Queen bravely insisted upon going ahead with a visit to Ghana in the summer of 1961. Her main concern was to ensure that the country did not pull out of the Commonwealth. Notwithstanding the odd incident, the Queen's tour proved successful – the success being that Ghana stayed part of the Commonwealth family.

Nor have the old Dominions always exemplified the harmonious Commonwealth ideal. From the early 1960s onwards Canada was becoming increasingly divided by the rise of French separatism. The Queen's 1964 visit to the hotbed of the separatists, the Province of Quebec, was overshadowed by death threats from terrorist gangs. Even the "moderate" French-Canadians were determined to show that the Queen was not welcome. In certain parts of the Commonwealth, such as Fiji, quiet may be a mark of respect but in Quebec in the autumn of 1964 the silence was deafening. "CHEZ VOUS!" read the banners.

Up until 1973 the Queen did indeed stay at home as far as the Commonwealth Conferences were concerned, only attending those meetings of the leading politicians from the Commonwealth when they were held in London. In an imaginative gesture Pierre Trudeau, the Canadian premier who is himself of French ancestry, invited the Queen to attend the Commonwealth Conference held in Ottawa that year. Since then the Queen has been a regular attender at the Conferences, wherever they are held, wearing, as it were, not the crown of any particular country but the mantle of the figurehead of the whole organization. At the Conferences, or "Heads of Government Meetings" as they are called, the Queen maintains a low profile. She does not formally open the proceedings (that is left to the host country) or attend the sessions.

The Rhodesian problem long remained a topic on the agenda. In 1965 the Queen had worked behind the scenes with Harold Wilson in an attempt to persuade Ian Smith against his Unilateral Declaration of Independence; she sent the Rhodesian Prime Minister a letter in her own handwriting making it clear that she did not accept Smith's line that he was a loyal servant of the Crown mistreated by the Labour Government. After Wilson's "weeks rather

than months" needed to settle the problem turned into years and even decades, matters finally came to a head at the Commonwealth Heads of Government meeting held in Zambia in 1979. By this time Black Africa's dissatisfaction with the Rhodesia/Zimbabwe goings-on, and in particular with the idea of Bishop Muzorewa being installed as a compromise leader of the new state, had reached a critical stage. The Commonwealth was looking distinctly shaky but the Queen set out to use her considerable influence with the African leaders in order to save the structure from breaking up. Before arriving in Lusaka for the Conference she went on a goodwill tour of Kenya, Tanzania, Malawi and Botswana. During the Conference hosted by Kenneth Kaunda of Zambia, the Queen received a steady stream of Commonwealth Heads of Government in audience in her bungalow office, doubtless conducting the conversations along the classical constitutional lines of consulting, encouraging and the occasional gentle warning. Sir Shridath ("Sonny")

Ramphal, the voluble Secretary-General of the Commonwealth, later spoke of how "the Queen brought to Lusaka a healing touch of rather special significance".

By the Queen's tactful but determined arbitration the way was paved for the Lancaster House talks on the future of Zimbabwe in 1980. Whatever credit accrued to Dr David Owen and Lord Carrington, the two Foreign Secretaries principally involved in the saga, no politician could have achieved the Queen's diplomatic triumph in Lusaka. Her ability to keep the ball in play was not only due to her detached role as "referee", but also owed much to the remarkable rapport she enjoys with African leaders such as Kaunda, Nyerere and Banda. Where others may see Pan-African Marxist demagogues as dictatorial tyrants the Queen sees old friends to whom, like her – if not to many of her British subjects – the Commonwealth still means something.

No shade of rose in the spectacles, however, could obscure either the horror of the Nigerian Civil War, in

The Queen with teachers from the Commonwealth at an educational conference at Lancaster House, 1972

The Queen with Mrs Gandhi in India, 1983

The Queen in the Peradeniya Gardens, Sri Lanka

The Queen in India with Mother Teresa

The Queen inspecting the guard of honour on arrival in Fiji

99

which Britain supported the strong, rich forces of federalism in committing genocide against breakaway Biafrans, or the barbarities in Uganda of "Field-Marshal" Idi Amin, who chose his predecessor's absence at the Commonwealth Conference at Singapore as the moment to seize power in 1971. Amin's expulsion of Uganda's Asian citizens made the Commonwealth idea of "multi-racialism" seem singularly hollow. There was even a war between two member countries, India and Pakistan, before the latter resigned its membership in 1972.

Concerned about the effect of Britain's entry into the European Economic Community on the Commonwealth, the Queen sought to reassure her listeners in the 1972 Christmas broadcast:

The new links with Europe will not replace those with the Commonwealth. They cannot alter our historical and personal attachments with kinsmen and friends overseas. Old friends will not be lost; Britain will take her Commonwealth links into Europe with her.

But inevitably the Common Market was bound to weaken the relationship between the "old country" and the old Dominions. The Queen has worked hard to counteract this – some would say too hard in that she has concentrated on the Commonwealth to the exclusion of Europe – by stepping up the number of visits to Australia, New Zealand and Canada. Thus, for example, in 1980 the Queen flew to Australia for a mere four days in order to open the new High Court in Canberra, spend a day each in Sydney and Melbourne, and then flew straight back to London. In Australia the Queen has had to weather the republican wash in the wake of the Whitlam affair; in Canada to put a brave face on the proclamation of the country's new Constitution in April 1982. The then Canadian Prime Minister Pierre Trudeau described this as the severing of the "last colonial link with Britain".

The Queen's recent Christmas broadcasts have thrown the delicacy of her role as "Head of the Commonwealth" into sharp relief. In 1983 her message included the statement that

the greatest problem in the world today remains the gap between rich and poor countries and we shall not begin to close this gap until we hear less about nationalism and more about inter-dependence.
One of the main aims of the Commonwealth is to make an effective contribution towards redressing the economic balance between nations.

These rather bland observations provoked an outburst from the maverick politician Enoch Powell ostensibly attacking the Queen's "Ministers" for

permitting themselves to place in the sovereign's mouth speeches which suggest that she has the interests and affairs of other countries in other continents as much or more at heart than those of her own people . . . They have seemed afraid for her to speak as a Christian Monarch to a Christian people, or as the British Monarch to the British nation.

Mr Powell's remarks struck a chord with those who had found the Queen's broadcast a sorry affair, full of platitudes about Commonwealth "communication" and containing no message of any comfort for the people of Britain. Many British viewers found the pictures of the Commonwealth conference in Delhi and of the Queen chatting with Mrs Gandhi somewhat disappointing.

Although Mr Powell was not referring specifically to the Queen's Christmas Broadcast, he missed the important point that such a speech is not put into the Queen's mouth by her "Ministers" but is a personal message from the "Head of the Commonwealth". Indeed that title, strictly speaking, has no constitutional character nor is it endowed with any repository of ministerial advice. As a leader in *The Times* put it, "in making her Christmas broadcast the Queen always has to bear in mind that she is on her own. There is no safety net of ministerial advice beneath her should she stray into contentious matters." *The Times* found the Queen's Commonwealth generalities "very arguable and thus quite legitimately open to direct criticism rather than the circuitous method pursued by Mr Powell".

The Queen, in *The Times's* view, was "falling victim to an insidious kind of global egalitarianism which suggests that the redistribution of income from better-off to worse-off is an end in itself to which we should all be working." That said, *The Times*, "begs too many questions to be included in a Christmas broadcast, even from the Head of the Commonwealth".

During the grand global tour at the beginning of her reign the Queen defined her function as Head of the Commonwealth. "The Crown" she said "is a human link between all peoples who owe allegiance to me – an allegiance of mutual love and respect and never of compulsion." Thirty years on, the Queen's faith in the system remains undimmed. Blithely ignoring the criticisms of her previous effort, the Queen included another paean to the Commonwealth in the 1984 Christmas broadcast:

Notwithstanding the strains and stresses of nationalism, different cultures and religions and its growing membership, the Commonwealth family has still managed to hold together and to make a real contribution to the prevention of violence and discord.

The Queen, unlike many of her British subjects, never forgets that she is also Queen of seventeen other realms and Head of a Commonwealth that includes 47 countries. The very name of the "Commonwealth" (not to mention the claptrap that often emanates from its secretariat at Marlborough House) may provoke widespread yawns in the United Kingdom. But to the Queen it is something to which, as she said in Nigeria in 1981, she *"personally"* (her emphasis) attaches "great importance".

7. The Queen and the Royal Round

One year in the life of the Queen is not so unlike another. Abroad there might be a visit to Canada or Australia, or a State Visit to a country outside the Commonwealth. At home there are the hardy annuals in the royal diary: New Year at Sandringham, the round of public engagements, investitures, Maundy Service, the Queen's birthday in April, the Chelsea Flower Show in May, the Derby, Prince Philip's birthday and the Queen's official birthday in June, Trooping the Colour, the Garter service, Royal Ascot, Garden Parties at Buckingham Palace and Holyroodhouse, the Queen Mother's birthday in August, holidays at Balmoral, State Opening of Parliament, Festival of Remembrance and the Cenotaph ceremony, the Prince of Wales's birthday in November, Christmas at Windsor. A regular pattern emerges.

In the early years of the Queen's reign Christmas was always at Sandringham, the royal retreat in Norfolk. "There is nothing quite like the family gathering in familiar surroundings centred on the children . . . when it is night and the wind and the rain beat upon the window . . . the family is most truly conscious of the warmth and peacefulness that surrounds the pleasant fireside", was the Queen's cosy message from Sandringham in her first Christmas broadcast transmitted in 1952. Twelve years later the "familiar surroundings" switched to Windsor because with four new additions to the royal family in 1964 (Prince Edward, Lady Sarah Armstrong-Jones, Lady Helen Windsor and James Ogilvy) it was considered more practicable than "dear old Sandringham".

The royal family assemble at Windsor on Christmas Eve and attend morning service the next day at St George's Chapel in the Lower Ward of the castle. In the age of televised monarchy this "royal" matins has become as much part of Christmas as the Queen's message traditionally transmitted at three o'clock in the afternoon. In the morning viewers can inspect the royal family spreadeagled on the west steps of St George's after the service – noting, say, the growth of Lord St Andrews's beard or how much some other half-familiar royal cousin has grown since last year. The Queen's broadcast in the afternoon now attracts an audience of some 120 million people all over the world. For the first five years of her reign the Christmas message was transmitted on the wireless, the television cameras being introduced in 1957. Initially the Queen sat formally in front of a forbidding-looking microphone facing the camera but a significant change in the style of presentation came about after the revolutionary *Royal Family* film of 1969.

Around the time of the investiture of Prince Charles as Prince of Wales at Caernarvon Castle (an event very much staged with the television coverage in mind) in that year, Buckingham Palace was besieged by television companies wanting to make biographical films about the royal family. The Queen decided that rather than various bits-and-pieces being cobbled together it would be best to have one authoritative – and authorized – television documentary. Richard Cawston, then head of documentaries for BBC Television, was accordingly invited to make the film which ended up as a 105-minute documentary. Approved by the Queen before it was broadcast, the *Royal Family* film changed the "royal image" overnight. Suddenly television viewers could see what went on behind the Palace walls – and, if they were fortunate, in colour. All the regular events of the royal year were shown, often from behind the scenes, interspersed with intimate shots of the Queen and Prince Philip in an aeroplane or the royal family together at the lunch table (with Princess Anne apparently reading a book). Viewers learnt that Lord Snowdon called his mother-in-law "Ma'am", that Prince Philip really did paint; that, in short, the figures they saw on public occasions had private opinions and senses of humour of their own. They sprang to life as never before. The mechanical media had made a sensational new contribution to the royal iconography. As Sir Roy Strong, then Director of the National Portrait Gallery, observed: "In a hundred years' time the recent television film of Her Majesty the Queen may be more highly rated as a portrait than a painting by, for example, Sir William Hutchinson."

Looking back at the *Royal Family* film fifteen years later, its producer recalls:

The big thing about it is not merely that we were allowed to film things that we had never filmed before – like the Queen in audience with Commonwealth Prime Ministers, or the Privy Councillors, or a royal picnic – but the fact that we had a microphone there, and the audience heard the Queen and Prince Philip talking informally. I think that before I began no member of the royal family had ever been heard on a public medium uttering anything other than a prepared speech.

The risk was whether the film would damage the "mystique" of monarchy, whether – to adapt Bagehot's phrase – it would let too much daylight in on the magic. If this exposure had revealed a group of morons with little purpose in life, the monarchy might not have been able to survive. Happily, though, it showed a success story. The Queen and Duke of Edinburgh emerged as conscientious and extremely hard-working, Prince Charles and Princess Anne as spirited personalities blossoming in their own rights, Lord Snowdon as a photographer with a social conscience, and so on. Significantly though, there has not been a sequel to *Royal Family* and royal television appearances have tended to be restricted to at least semi-scripted programmes about the heritage or conservation or other fairly "safe" topics. There have been no further "fly on the wall" documentaries.

None the less, Richard Cawston's remarkable achievement on the *Royal Family* documentary led to him being invited to take on the presentation of the Queen's Christmas broadcasts. Since 1970 these short (ten-to-twelve minute) films have become much more intimate views of the Queen and her "family firm". Using several of the same technicians that worked with him on the *Royal Family* documentary, Cawston prepares the broadcasts (irreverently known as "Corgi and Bess" at the BBC) on and off through the year in conjunction with Buckingham Palace. "Whatever we film for Christmas is always done specially, and secretly, and it is always kept in confidence until Christmas Day", says Cawston. Thus, on the day of Princess Anne's wedding to Captain Mark Phillips in November 1973, Cawston and his crew were inside the Centre (or Balcony) Room on the Mall front of Buckingham Palace. "When Princess Anne and Captain

Mark Phillips went out on to the balcony in front of that huge crowd we were behind them, and we showed them going back into the room, and the whole family with them. Nobody knew we had that material until Christmas Day." Responding to the urgings of the royal family for her to put in another appearance on the balcony, Princess Anne was heard to say on the soundtrack: "All right then", adding, specifically to Prince Edward: "but get off my dress first."

Contrary to what many people think, the film included in the Queen's Christmas broadcasts is not made up of old clips from newsreels. As Cawston explains: "We have material in the broadcast at Christmas which no newsreel would ever be allowed to have, and which is not repeated anywhere else." Despite many requests, the footage of the relaxed conversation between the Queen and Indira Gandhi, the highlight of the controversial 1983 Christmas

104

*The Queen and King Mahendra of Nepal on route for
Buckingam Palace from Victoria Station during his State Visit to
Britain, 1960*

broadcast, was not released at the time of the Indian Prime Minister's assassination the following year. The Christmas broadcast remains the copyright of the Queen. Even in the television age the monarch likes to preserve a certain distance. The Queen still does not give interviews.

After a month or so of the New Year at Sandringham – which, despite the shooting and country pursuits, is not a holiday for the Queen as she is never free of the daily grind of the "Red Boxes" – it is back to the routine of Buckingham Palace in the week and Windsor at weekends. The Queen's day is dominated by a formidable amount of reading. In addition to the Red Boxes, containing piles of official documents, the Queen receives *Hansard* and a wide selection of newspapers and magazines – even if she is said always to turn first to the *Sporting Life*. Then there is the enormous daily correspondence to be attended to, assisted by her Private Secretary with whom the Queen will discuss the business of the day; the administration of numerous matters concerning the running of the Household from menus to the choice of her wardrobe for official engagements; and somehow there has to be fitted into all this a walk with the corgis in the Palace gardens.

In addition to what Sir Michael Adeane described in his masterly memorandum about the Queen's actions, duties and responsibilities as this "continuing burden of unseen work", there are Her Majesty's more public duties:

The Queen receives a large number of important people in audience. These include those about to be appointed to, or retire from, senior public posts and discussions with the Prime Minister and other Ministers. She also holds meetings of the Privy Council and some fourteen investitures each year at which she personally bestows over two thousand orders, decorations and medals . . .

At an audience the Queen is invariably alone. She must appear to be, and assuredly is, knowledgeable and interested in the particular subject of the person being received, who may be an Ambassador, a High Court Judge, a Bishop, the Director of Royal Artillery or her stud groom. During a Commonwealth Prime Minister's Conference, she will see each Prime Minister separately. She must, and will, be up to date on the latest developments in each one's country.

During a State Visit from a foreign head of state to the United Kingdom the Queen's already arduous schedule has to be organised to accommodate a flurry of extra official engagements including a State Banquet in the ballroom at Buckingham Palace – not to mention the extra briefing required. There tend to be two or three State Visits to Britain each year. The visitors only come once, officially, though a new sovereign or president can come from the same country. Thus France has already sent three Presidents (de Gaulle, Giscard d'Estaing and Mitterand); King Gustaf VI Adolf of Sweden came in 1954 and his grandson King Carl XVI Gustaf in 1975; King Mahendra

of Nepal came in 1960, his son King Birendra 20 years later; Queen Juliana of the Netherlands in 1972, Queen Beatrix ten years later. In an imaginative gesture it was arranged that Queen Beatrix and her husband should give a banquet in honour of the Queen and Prince Philip at Hampton Court, the palace where the horse of "Dutch" William III stumbled on a molehill.

Among the memorable visitors received by the Queen has been the Emperor Haile Selassie on whom she bestowed the Order of the Garter in 1954. The Rastafarian "Lion of Judah" was no stranger to England as he had found refuge here in the late 1930s when Mussolini overran his country. In the course of their ice-breaking visit to Britain during the so-called "Cold War", the Russian leaders Bulganin and Krushchev were entertained to tea at Windsor the day after the Queen's 30th birthday in 1956. In 1958, when the Queen had to cancel a number of official engagements (including her attendance at the Empire Games in Cardiff to declare her son Charles "Prince of Wales") owing to persistent chills and colds, there were State Visits from the heads of two of Britain's Second World War opponents, Italy and Germany. Theodor Heuss, President of the Federal German Republic, was the first German head of state to have come on an official visit since the flashy figure of the Kaiser had stayed with his uncle, Edward VII, in 1907. Dr Heuss, an elderly academic, brought £5,000 from the German people as a welcome contribution towards the new building of Coventry Cathedral that had been destroyed by the Luftwaffe in the war, but he was generally received with less than rapturous warmth.

There was sharper controversy over the State Visit thirteen years later, in the autumn of 1971, of the Emperor Hirohito of Japan and his Empress Nagako. During the

Below: The scene on the west steps of St George's Chapel, Windsor, after Christmas Mattins, 1983

Bottom: Reeling at the Royal Company of Archers (The Queen's Bodyguard for Scotland) Ball. The Queen wears the green sash of the Order of the Thistle

The Queen in the Music Room at Buckingham Palace before the State Banquet for the Emperor of Japan, 1971. She is seen with Emperor Hirohito (wearing his recently restored Garter sash and star) and Empress Nagako

war the Emperor's Garter banner had been removed in disgrace from St George's Chapel, Windsor; now it had to be tactfully reinstated. *Private Eye* summed up the feelings of many whose relations had suffered abominably at the hands of the Japanese in the war with a cover proclaiming: "THERE'S A NASTY NIP IN THE AIR". Lord Mountbatten, the former Supreme Allied Commander in the Far East, could not bring himself to attend the State Banquet in honour of his old foe. "We cannot pretend that the relations between our two peoples have always been peaceful and friendly. However, it is precisely this experience which should make us all the more determined never to let it happen again," said the Queen in her speech. Whatever the diplomatic – or in other words commercial – pressures in favour of such a visit some felt it would have been wiser to have waited until the Emperor himself had been gathered to the Sun, or wherever, before issuing the invitation. After the horticulturist Hirohito had planted a symbolic tree in Kew Gardens, an ex-prisoner of the Japanese proceeded to cut it down, equally symbolically.

During the 1967 visit of Alexei Kosygin, who had succeeded Krushchev as Soviet supremo, the Queen relaxed the formal dress rules of the State Banquet at Buckingham Palace, permitting what are unfortunately described as "lounge suits" and short dresses to be worn. General de Gaulle had, however, refused to stand for any of this nonsense; at a similar banquet for Kosygin in Paris, the Russian had been obliged to don white tie and tails. In his speech and apparently somewhat persistently in conversation with the Queen, Kosygin pressed an invitation on her "to come to the Soviet Union". Nearly twenty years later, the Queen is still to take up this invitation to a regime which butchered her cousins in 1918 – though a visit to the People's Republic of China is now on the agenda for 1986.

Apart from State Banquets for visiting heads of State, the Buckingham Palace ballroom is used for investitures, which must constitute one of the most physically exhausting of the Queen's duties. An investiture involves the Queen standing for over an hour and a quarter during which time she must concentrate continually and maintain a friendly supply of appropriate comments as she invests some 200 worthies with their doubtless hard-earned honours. The dignity of the occasion is frequently offset by the incongruous tunes, drawn from deserved-to-be-forgotten Broadway musicals, emanating from the Guards band in the minstrels' gallery.

The small private luncheon party at Buckingham Palace for distinguished and seemingly ill-assorted guests from varying walks of life has become a regular feature of the Queen's routine over the last thirty years. The first one, held in May 1956, was attended by among others, the

Bishop of London, the Editor of *The Times*, the Director-General of the Boy Scouts International Bureau, a banker and a civil servant. There tend to be a dozen sitting down: eight guests, the Queen and Prince Philip, with the balance being drawn from other members of the royal family or the royal household. The idea is for the Queen and Prince Philip to meet informally people they might not otherwise come across in the normal royal round. Auberon Waugh has nicely categorized the guests as "the Arthur Askey sort of person". One editor who attended such a lunch was quite bowled over by how captivatingly attractive the Queen is in the flesh and how effervescent her conversation seemed to be – though he found it difficult to recall anything of particular note in its content beneath the unexpected bubbles.

The afternoon of the Queen's day may well be taken up with some sort of official engagement. The Queen's programme is planned months in advance and therefore her life is ruled by endless minor commitments. She cannot, like so many of her subjects, suddenly decide to take a holiday or a day off.

"There are many engagements both public and private involving visits to local universities, hospitals, factories and units of the Armed Forces . . ." noted Sir Michael Adeane in his memorandum to the Select Committee on the Civil List in 1971. These engagements are often in connexion with an organization of which the Queen is Patron or President. The Queen may be visiting a school, opening a hospital, or whatever, and will frequently carry out a series of engagements in one particular town or county.

On the "royal roadshow", as it is sometimes called, the Queen has somehow to maintain an unflagging interest in what she sees. When she drives through a city it is impossible for her to smile the entire time; she would suffer from lockjaw in the endeavour. Yet that one glimpse of her is perhaps the only time one of her subjects will see her in real life. If she looks cross, then he will always remember her as cross. The Queen also has the tricky problem of putting the people she meets at their ease; those presented to the sovereign are seldom at their best – either mute with fright or blurting out some inane remark in a

nervous attempt to make some sort of impression. In short, it is a tremendously difficult job for a not naturally outgoing person. Unlike her flamboyant mother and despite her own stirring performances in those wartime Windsor Pantomimes, the Queen is emphatically not an actress. Duty remains the watchword and the Queen performs all hers with a dedication rare in late-20th century Britain. A royalty watcher once aptly described "that level gaze, so calm in its consciousness of duty fulfilled".

The Queen's Flight which ferries her around is based at RAF Benson in Oxfordshire and consists of some Andovers and Westland helicopters. She does not normally use the latter herself, though an exception was made for her historic visit to Northern Ireland in Silver Jubilee year. Despite the fears for her safety, the Queen had been characteristically determined to go through with the promised visit: "We said we'd do it and it would be a pity if we didn't". In August she flew by helicopter from HMS *Fife* in Belfast Lough to Hillsborough Castle (the old "Government House"), amidst intense security arrangements. After being greeted by 200 children and

The Queen with Queen Juliana of the Netherlands and their respective consorts, Princes Philip and Bernhard

The glitter and gold of the State Banquet for President Reagan at Windsor Castle, 1982

The " garden party classes" assemble at Buckingam Palace

The Queen, with the traditional Maundy Thursday posies, prepares to distribute the Royal Maundy at Nottingham

invited guests, she then held an investiture and a garden party. In the evening the Queen received the leaders of the Ulster Peace Movement on board *Britannia*. The following day she visited the New University of Ulster at Coleraine and, in a televised speech, appealed to the people of Northern Ireland to forget the past and work together in a spirit of friendship and forgiveness: "People everywhere recognise that violence is senseless and wrong and that they do not want it. Their clear message is that it must stop and that is my prayer too".

The rest of the royal family – the "family firm" as Prince Philip calls it – act as the back-up team, carrying out their royal duties throughout the year on the Queen's behalf. "These functions, you're doing it for the Queen", pointed out the late Princess Alice, Countess of Athlone. "The Queen can't go and open every little bazaar. Therefore you do it for her as her family". Actually Princess Alice was talking about her grandmother, Queen Victoria, but this oldest ever member of the British royal family was still doing her bit for the present Queen as late as 1978 when she made these remarks in a television interview.

Every year Timothy O'Donovan, a leading light in the Windsor Festival and a steward of St George's Chapel, makes his own signal contribution to the recording of

modern monarchy in a letter to *The Times* containing a survey of the duties performed by the royal family as reported in that newspaper's "Court Circular" column. His letter in the New Year of 1985 read as follows:

Sir, I have again carried out a survey of the engagements carried out by the Royal Family during 1984, as reported in your Court Circular.

	1	2	3	4	5
The Queen	115	72	10	149	26
Duke of Edinburgh	146	111	30	11	82
The Queen Mother	74	29	3	6	5
Prince of Wales	125	38	17	24	36
Princess of Wales	59	12	–	1	2
Prince Andrew	10	4	1	–	15
Prince Edward	2	1	–	–	–
Princess Anne	188	67	9	4	64
Princess Margaret	117	36	4	4	8
Princess Alice	32	6	3	7	2
Duke of Gloucester	73	31	6	11	32
Duchess of Gloucester	58	15	3	1	14
Duke of Kent	68	22	14	6	31
Duchess of Kent	92	19	2	6	13
Princess Alexandra	85	21	1	7	22

1. Official visits, opening ceremonies and other appearances.
2. Receptions, lunches, dinners and banquets.
3. Meetings, including the Privy Council.
4. Audiences given.
5. Number of days spent travelling abroad on official tours.

Opposite: At the head of her soldiers, the Queen (riding the police grey, Doctor) returns to Buckingham Palace after the Birthday Parade, 1963

Below: The Queen presents her sister Princess Margaret to the eager Emir of Bahrain during his State Visit to Britain, 1984. The Prince and Princess of Wales look on

On offical tours abroad the Queen carried out 121 engagements, the Duke of Edinburgh 238, the Queen Mother 9, the Prince of Wales 112, the Princess of Wales 5, Prince Andrew 44, Princess Anne 233 and Princess Margaret 25.

In addition the Queen held 45 investitures and the Queen Mother 3. As in previous years, I have not included the weekly audiences given by the Queen to the Prime Minister.

The confinement and the birth of Prince Henry considerably reduced the number of engagements the Princess of Wales was able to carry out.

The statistics, for once, speak eloquently for themselves and repay careful digestion. As Mr O'Donovan said in an appendix to an earlier survey: "All this information again confirms the hard work undertaken by members of the Royal Family and hopefully it will be remembered by those politicians and members of the public who always criticise the annual review of the Civil List."

On the whole the Queen prefers not to go out in the evening, especially after a full day. Prince Philip will often attend evening engagements on his own. However, those who portray the Queen as a poignantly lonely figure eating her supper off a tray in front of the television set miss the point that such a way of spending the evening is a relaxing treat for her. Particular favourites among the Queen's viewing over the years have been *Dad's Army, Kojak, The Good Life* and anything with Dudley Moore.

The busiest time of the Queen's year is what used to be known as the London "Season". On a chosen Saturday (switched from Thursday in 1959) in the middle of June, the Queen celebrates her official birthday. An honours list is published and at 10.45 a.m. she rides down the Mall from Buckingham Palace to Horse Guards Parade where the Household Division is gathered for the colour of one of the five regiments of foot guards (Grenadier, Coldstream, Scots, Irish and Welsh) to be trooped. First performed on the sovereign's birthday for George III in the 18th century, the "Birthday Parade" became a regular feature of the royal year in Queen Victoria's reign on her actual birthday, 24 May, and it has continued to be held around that date ever since. The Queen, riding side-saddle, wears the uniform of whichever Guards regiment it is whose colour is being trooped. Over her red tunic she wears the Garter riband (unless it is the Scots Guards when she wears the dark green riband of the Thistle).

Traditionally envisaged as taking place on a golden summer's day, the Birthday Parade and Trooping the Colour has occasionally been marred by sudden cloudbursts which have drenched the Queen. In 1981 it was not the Queen's lack of protection from the elements that caused alarm. As the Queen rounded the corner of the

The gallimaufry of Garter Day: The Queen processes down the Lower Ward of Windsor Castle in the early years of her reign

Scenes of the Birthday Parade, one of the great ceremonial occasions of the monarchy. Below: The Queen and members of the royal family on the balcony after the parade. Bottom: The Queen takes the salute outside Buckingham Palace

A canter down the course at Ascot on the morning of the Royal Meeting. With the Queen are her Master of the Horse, the late Duke of Beaufort, Angus Ogilvy, the Countess of Lichfield and the Prince of Wales. The content of the Queen's house party for Ascot is always a subject of special interest for students of the more esoteric elements of the monarchy

Mall into Horse Guards, an adolescent armed with a replica pistol containing six blank shots loosed them off in her direction. Later the Queen typically made light of the incident, saying that her startled black mare, Burmese, had not been frightened by the shots but by the mounts of the two Household cavalry officers who had advanced afterwards to protect their sovereign. None the less when she saw that gun pointed at her out of the crowd the danger must have seemed real enough at the time. Although observers said the Queen went pale, the calmness with which she managed to control and reassure her prancing mare and then carry on with the parade as if nothing had happened showed extraordinary strength of character. The Queen's great courage had been revealed to the full. Both this incident, which resulted in the youth being imprisoned for five years under the Treason Act of 1842, and the intrusion of another deranged individual, Michael Fagan, into the Queen's bedroom at Buckingham Palace hardly more than a year later, exposed the terrible vulnerability of the Queen to attack. Even after the tightening of security following the latter lamentable lapse, there remains little that can be done to protect the Queen within the "open" style of monarchy to which she has dedicated herself. It is a contemporary truism, exemplified by all too many outrages in the modern world, that if some lunatic is determined to kill a public figure there is, in the event, no guarantee against him succeeding.

On the Monday following the shooting incident in the Mall, the cheers for the Queen in the Garter procession down the hill into the Lower Ward of Windsor Castle were especially and deservedly loud. The Queen looks her best in the magnificent blue velvet robes of the Most Noble Order of the Garter which has its annual service at St George's Chapel. As John Brooke-Little, the ebullient Norroy and Ulster King of Arms has observed, "Garter Day is a great and joyous day and particularly so because so many people are able to crowd into the castle precincts to witness it. It can be said to be England's official birthday". Any new knights are invested in the Throne Room at Windsor Castle, after which there is a lunch in the Waterloo Chamber from which in Norroy's words the Knights "emerge . . . in a haze of cigar smoke and general euphoria". The procession, consisting of the Military Knights of Windsor (formerly known as the "Poor Knights", who attend services at St George's in the absence of the Knights of the Garter) in their splendid scarlet uniforms, the Yeomen of the Guard in their equally colourful Tudor garb, the heralds in the tabards, and the officers and members of the Most Noble Order, winds its way down to St George's Chapel. New knights are conducted by Garter Principal King of Arms to their stalls, above which will be placed their armorial banners.

Garter Day falls at the beginning of Ascot Week. The Queen always entertains a house party for the Royal Meeting held on the celebrated racecourse laid out by Queen Anne on the fringes of Windsor Great Park and every afternoon before racing she and her guests drive down the course in landaus drawn by Windsor Greys to the entrance to the royal box. This tradition of driving down the course was begun by George IV. The Queen and the more equestrian-minded members of the royal party have also sometimes staged a private race of their own down the course in the early mornings, well in advance of the official card.

Back at Buckingham Palace the main events of the summer season are the garden parties. These large-scale gatherings on the expanse of lawn facing the Palace's honey-coloured garden front have come to represent a

more "democratic" way for the Queen to meet her subjects than the somewhat pompous old-style garden parties instituted by Queen Victoria or the presentation parties for debutantes (which were scrapped in 1958 to the dismay of many an old snob). Although genuine efforts are made to furnish invitations to what are known as "guests from all walks of life", the great majority of those worthies attending seem to belong to what Philip Howard nicely categorized as the "garden party classes". As many as 35,000 people descend on Buckingham Palace and Holyroodhouse every summer for these afternoon revels.

Apart from the Holyroodhouse garden party another annual Edinburgh event for the Queen is the Service of the Most Noble Order of the Thistle in St Giles's Cathedral. Dressed in the dark green velvet robes of the Order the Queen drives up into the City to the Thistle Chapel in St

Giles's Cathedral. The colour of the scene is enhanced by the picturesque green uniforms of the Queen's Bodyguard for Scotland (the Royal Company of Archers).

On the Queen's return from her Scottish holiday at Balmoral in the autumn, the royal round begins again with the State Opening of Parliament. After the Yeomen of the Guard report that their search of the vaults of the Houses of Parliament has revealed nothing untoward (a procedure dating from the time of the Gunpowder Plot), the Queen sets out in the Irish State Coach for the Royal Entrance to the Palace of Westminster. The Queen puts on the Robe of State and the Imperial Crown of State (which is only worn for this ceremony) in the Robing Room. Then, to a fanfare of trumpets, the royal procession advances through the Royal Gallery – the Earl Marshal and Lord Great Chamberlain walking backwards before the Queen – into the House of Lords. As the Queen enters the chamber, the dim lights are dramatically turned up. "My Lords, pray be seated", says the Queen after she has settled on the throne. There is next a lengthy wait (in 1978, for instance, it extended to eight minutes) while the charade of Black Rod going off to summon the House of Commons, only to have the door slammed in his face, is played out. Once the leading members of the Commons have arrived, the Lord Chancellor produces the speech (full of the usual bureaucratic clichés and incongruous modern jargon) which the Queen is constitutionally obliged to read out on behalf of her Government. After the ceremony, the crown and the maces have a special coach to themselves on the way back to Buckingham Palace. It is lit up inside so as to enable those lining the route to see the symbols of the Queen's sovereignty.

8. The Queen and the Royal Family

A *family* on the throne", noted Walter Bagehot in his great reference book *The English Constitution*, "is an interesting idea also". This 19th-century sage pointed out that "The women – one half of the human race at least – care fifty times more for a marriage than a ministry . . . a princely marriage is the brilliant edition of a universal fact and, as such, it rivets mankind." Another eminent Victorian, Benjamin Disraeli, Earl of Beaconsfield, also pointed out that the influence of the Crown is not confined merely to political affairs. England is a domestic country. Here the home is revered and the hearth sacred. The nation is represented by a family – the Royal Family; and if that family is educated with a sense of responsibility and a sentiment of public duty, it is difficult to exaggerate the salutary influence they may exercise over a nation.

In recent times the "Royal Family" has come to resemble a sort of family business carrying on the monarchical trade. Indeed the Queen's father used to refer to himself, his Queen (now the Queen Mother) and their daughters, Elizabeth and Margaret, as the "Royal Firm". Today the "Royal Firm" has expanded considerably to constitute an invaluable supporting team to the Queen.

The concept of the "Royal Firm" is certainly shared by Prince Philip who has often referred to the set-up in similar terms. Although now in his mid-sixties, the Prince belies his years as one of the most energetic and hardworking members of the royal family. He has managed to overcome the difficulties of his seemingly impossible position as "consort", carving out a rewarding niche for himself. Never afraid to say what he thinks, he has developed a technique of softening his pithily offensive shafts with a nice line in self-deprecating irony. One of his favourite hobby-horses is Britain's depreciation of what he regards as the vital subjects of engineering, technology and design. Reviewing a collection of Prince Philip's speeches, *Men, Machines and Sacred Cows,* in *The Times*, Professor Nicholas Lash of Cambridge described the Chancellor of his university as the "Homespun Philosopher" – a humanist, an individualist and a rationalist. The Professor likened the Prince's choice of topics ("Helicopters and conservation, fuel technology and propaganda, polo and the mind body problem") to Pope Pius XII's propensity to discourse upon every subject under the sun.

That there is no apparent "generation gap" in the royal family owes most to the Queen Mother who retains a great zest for life in her mid-eighties. She has been a member of the royal family for well over sixty years and her service to the monarchy has been signal – whether bolstering up George VI's self-confidence, providing a natural and happy home for the upbringing of her daughters, supporting Princess Margaret through her emotional troubles or, above all, soldiering on in London through the thick of the Second World War. At the time of the 40th anniversary of the "D-Day" landings in Normandy, the point was made that the Queen Mother was the last surviving war hero. "I shall not go down like the others", she said about her revolver practice at Buckingham Palace.

The Queen Mother still carries out a ceaseless round of royal engagements at home and even abroad on behalf of her elder daughter. When one of the long-serving ladies-in-waiting at Clarence House suggested that she was too old for the job, the Queen Mother replied: "What about me?" There was no more talk of resignation from that quarter. Off duty, the Queen Mother remains essentially a countrywoman with a love of country sports and enjoys a formidable reputation as a fisherwoman (though she has recently hung up her rod). She has pursued her love of gardening at Royal Lodge, Windsor, and at the Castle of Mey in Caithness, which she bought and restored. Her real sympathy for the arts makes a nonsense of the "philistine" charge sometimes laid at the royal family's door. The eclectic collection of pictures at Clarence House includes works by Stubbs, Monet, Sickert, Augustus John, Duncan Grant, Paul Nash, Graham Sutherland, John Bratby and her friend Sir Noel Coward.

George V once observed that if his daughter-in-law was not late sometimes she would be perfect and that would be horrible. "For someone so unaggressive she has a very strong personality", the writer Lord David Cecil has said of his childhood friend, "she *could* be formidable". Sir Woodrow Wyatt, the chairman of the Tote, has pointed out that the Queen Mother "is not all sugar. She can be a little acid when necessary".

It is a sign of the deep affection in which the "Queen Mum" is held ("The great mother figure and nannie to us all", Sir Cecil Beaton noted in his diary) that such gossip as circulates about her only serves to increase her popularity. Whey should not Her Majesty, the feeling runs, overspend her budget, dress like the wedding cake E.M. Forster once claimed to have mistaken her for, enjoy a stiffish tincture or twain, back the odd nag, work her way through some cigarette-burnt eiderdowns, get outside a few chocolate creams, tuck into a lavish tea with her faithful "knitting circle" of courtierly bachelors, and generally enjoy the good things of life?

The key to the Queen Mother's character is surely her great sense of fun. If one can divide the world into Wodehousians (good eggs) and non-Wodehousians (pills, like the politicians who delayed his knighthood on account of some ill-advised but entirely innocent broadcasts in the war), then the Queen Mother firmly belongs in the former category. A Wodehouse fan, she offered to fly out to America to confer the accolade on the ailing old boy. She

Opposite: A determined Prince Philip splashes his horse and four through the water obstacle at the Sandringham Carriage Driving Championships, 1983
Below left: The Queen and Prince Philip at Cowdray Park after his polo team, Windsor Park, had won the Cowdray Gold Cup, 1969

Below right: The Chancellor of Cambridge University receives a soaking
Bottom: Prince Philip shares a joke with George Cole, Pamela Stephenson and the cast of The Pirates of Penzance *after a charity gala performance at the Theatre Royal, Drury Lane, in aid of the World Wildlife Fund, 1982. Sir Peter Scott is to the Prince's left*

herself makes an appearance, at least by implication, in *The Mating Season* (dealing tactfully with an Irish guest at Buckingham Palace who has half-a-dozen helpings of mulligatawny under the impression that there will be no further courses) and her own personality evokes more than a touch of Wodehouse's sparky, effervescent heroines.

P.G. Wodehouse's beloved stepdaughter was married to Peter Cazalet who trained the Queen Mother's racehorses (including the ill-fated *Devon Loch*) until his death when he was succeeded by Fulke Walwyn. National Hunt racing has had no more loyal patron than the Queen Mother who has had several hundred wins as an owner. In 1984 she was rewarded with her two greatest successes so far when *Special Cargo* won both the Grand Military and the Whitbread Gold Cups, the latter in one of the most thrilling steeplechases ever seen at Sandown.

To those who complain that her grandson, the Prince of

Wales (a less successful performer around Sandown) should do a "proper job", the Queen Mother has the answer. "He has a proper job", she says, "he is the Prince of Wales". Indeed from his birth in 1948 Prince Charles has been serving his apprenticeship for sovereignty; he was born to succeed.

Looking back at the educational hoops the Prince was made to jump through it is well to remember that his schooling was planned by a committee. If the Queen Mother had had her way Prince Charles would have gone to Eton. There can be little doubt that this would have suited him much better than his father's *alma mater* of Gordonstoun which, as Prince Edward revealed in an engagingly tactless aside in a television programme eulogizing Kurt Hahn's spartan establishment; Prince Charles did not enjoy. The clinching argument at the time in favour of Prince Charles being packed off to the frozen

127

The Queen presents the Prince of Wales to the people of the Principality gathered underneath the Queen's Gate of Caernarvon Castle where she had invested him

The Queen Mother on her visit to Eton College to open the Museum of Eton Life, 1985. She is seen with the Headmaster, Dr Eric Anderson

north was its distance from the prying eyes of Fleet Street. Certainly his time at Hill House in Knightsbridge (where he became the first prince to attend a day school) and Cheam (Prince Philip's old preparatory school which had removed from Surrey to Headley near Newbury) was subjected to such excessive press coverage that the Queen had to ask Fleet Street editors to lay off. None the less, newspapers have "stringers" everywhere and it was to escape from a group of rubber-necking royalty watchers at Stornoway during his stint at Gordonstoun that Prince Charles took refuge in a bar. He later recalled:

Having never been into a bar before, the first thing I thought of doing was having a drink, of course. It seemed the most sensible thing. And being terrified, not knowing what to do I said the first drink that came into my head, which happened to be cherry brandy, because I'd drunk it before when it was cold, out shooting. And hardly had I taken a sip when the whole world exploded round my ears.

Notwithstanding these alarums and excursions, Prince Charles acquitted himself well at Gordonstoun as if determined to show that he was not the namby pamby some people mistook him for. He won the Silver Award of his father's Award Scheme and undertook vigorous naval training with the cadet force, as well as playing the title role in *Macbeth* and emulating his father as Guardian (head boy).

Prince Charles is welcomed by his housemaster (Robert Whitby)
at the start of his schooling at Gordonstoun. His father and
headmaster (Robert Chew) frame the rather forbidding
photograph

In the cause of "broadening" his education Prince Charles underwent six months at Timbertop, the outpost of Geelong Grammar School in Australia which, he commented, was "tougher than Gordonstoun". A late developer, the Prince's personality began to burgeon at Trinity College, Cambridge, where he gained valuable self-confidence and displayed his "Goonish" humour. The curious thing, however, is that the Goons, to whom Prince Charles is so devoted, had their vogue more than a decade before the Prince was an undergraduate. It was as if the Prince, with his short hair, tweed jacket, brogues and sports car was modelling himself on a generation born nearer 1938 than 1948. His Cambridge contemporaries recall Prince Charles as a character strangely out of step with much of what was going on around him. His values and sense of dedication were certainly not those of the "Swinging Sixties" or the "Nineteen-Sexies". When it was remarked to the Prince's "honorary grandfather" Lord Mountbatten how lucky it was that the heir to the throne was cast in such an old-fashioned mould, the Admiral replied "It's not just luck, it's a bloody miracle". The present writer recalls Lord Mountbatten contrasting his great-nephew with some of the less savoury examples of drug-ridden hedonists to be found among the Prince's aristocratic contemporaries.

The investiture year of 1969 saw the Prince of Wales swim into the centre of the goldfish bowl where the media have placed the modern royal family. The Queen had declared Prince Charles "Prince of Wales" in a recorded message played over the loudspeakers at the Empire Games in Cardiff in 1958, which she was unable to attend through illness, and the new Prince had suffered the embarrassment of hearing this amid the cheers of his Cheam schoolfellows in front of the Headmaster's television set. Now it was time for the Prince to be formally invested in his Principality. To prepare for the investiture Prince Charles was obliged to interrupt his Cambridge studies to learn some Welsh at the University of Aberystwyth, braving some disagreeable "nationalist" behaviour.

Princes of Wales are made, not born. The title does not come automatically, as in the case of the Dukedom of Cornwall. The investiture used to be carried out by the monarch from the throne in Parliament, but in 1911 the then Constable of Caernarvon Castle, David Lloyd George, had other ideas. "With an eye to what would please his constituents", ruefully recalled the Duke of Windsor in his memoirs, " 'L.G.' proposed that the ceremony be transformed into a spectacular pageant". Prince Charles's predecessor as Prince of Wales was duly

fitted up in "a fantastic costume designed for the occasion, consisting of white satin breeches and a mantle and surcoat of purple velvet edged with ermine". Matters were slightly more restrained when the present Prince of Wales was invested at Caernarvon in 1969; though the present Constable, Lord Snowdon, was attired in a natty bottle-green outfit (without a sword, to the dismay of the purists). Lord Snowdon had called in his friend Carl Toms, the stage designer, to create "a kind of theatre in the round so it would read well on television".

A television audience of millions duly watched the Queen invest her eldest son as the 21st Prince of Wales at the beginning of July. The Prince declared that he would become the Queen's "liege man of life and limb" and would "live and die against all manner of folk" before going on to make a speech in English and Welsh (complete with a reference to Harry Secombe). "It is my firm intention", he said in both languages, "to associate myself in word and deed with as much of the life of the Principality as possible."

Until the revival of Welsh traditions in the 19th century, it would not be unfair to say that the "English" Princes of Wales took little interest in their Principality. The present

incumbent is, *pace* the nationalists, the best Prince the Welsh have ever had. He has taken a special interest in Wales through such organizations as the Prince of Wales's Committee and by promoting Welsh industrial opportunities on his travels. As he has said, the motto of the Prince of Wales – adopted by the Black Prince at the Battle of Crecy from the King of Bohemia – is singularly appropriate: "Ich Dien" ("I serve").

Like the Queen, the Prince of Wales believes that an active role in the life of the Commonwealth is one of the most important contributions he can make. He has travelled widely since his University days and there can now be few parts of the Commonwealth that he has not seen. Before settling down to acquainting himself with the workings of government and industry (his current programme) in 1978, the Prince pursued an active career in the Services and spent a year running the successful Silver Jubilee Appeal ("to help young people help others") which raised £16 million.

For someone not naturally tough the Prince displayed admirable courage in earning the sobriquet of "Action Man". He undertook training at RAF Cranwell (winning his wings in 1971) and served in the Royal Navy from 1971 to 1976, ending up as a Commander in charge of a minesweeper, HMS *Bronington*. Reluctant to mount a polo pony as a small boy, he went on to play at international level, to ride under National Hunt rules and to be an enthusiastic follower of hounds.

This thirst for the chase is combined with a genuine feeling for the arts, particularly opera. The Service heartiness is blended with a basic sensitivity; maturity with a residual boyishness, and broad humour with a deep seriousness and a sense of history. In short, the heir to the throne is something of an enigma. For all his "straight" appearance and friends drawn from what Philip Howard has described as "the older Hooray Henrys", the Prince has unconventional views on various subjects. In religion he is strongly opposed to sectarianism and has shown leanings towards mysticism. Like the Queen he is in favour of homeopathy and has spoken out in favour of "alternative medicine". When it was learnt that he had apparently given up shooting game birds, some people made out the Prince was turning into a vegetarian recluse of decidedly eccentric views, but *The Field* reassured its readers that the Prince's heart was still in the right place with the intelligence that he had taken up deerstalking instead.

Ignorant gossips attributed the Prince's alleged abandonment of his gun to the influence of the Princess of Wales, forgetting the fact that the two had first met out shooting at Althorp in 1977. Always a fish out of water in the "hippy" age, the Prince became haunted by a remark he had made that thirty was a good age to marry. Finally in

The investiture of the Prince of Wales at Caernarvon Castle, July 1969. James Callaghan, then Home Secretary, grasps the seal; while spectators adopt some bizarre positions to improve their view of the proceedings

"Action Man". Below: Prince Charles shows the royal family around his ship, the minesweeper Bronington *in 1976. Among those to be seen chatting to the crew are the Queen, Prince Philip, the Queen Mother, Princess Anne, the Duke and Duchess of Gloucester and Princess Alexandra*

Bottom left: A backhand swing from the Prince on the polo ground at Cowdray Park, 1983; and (right) Good Prospect (the Prince of Wales up) canters back after a fall at Sandown Park, accompanied by Devon Mignon (Mr W.A. Bethell), 1981

Below left: In a pose worthy of "Biggles", the Prince stands in front of an old Tiger Moth bi-plane he flew at RAF Benson, 1979; and (bottom) Wales the windsurfer in Australia, 1979

Below: Rising to the occasion among the bare-breasted maidens of Manus, Papua New Guinea, 1984

his 33rd year he chose his bride from a generation younger than his own. Lady Diana Spencer belonged to a breed of level-headed girls who calmly avoided the pitfalls of their 1960s and 1970s predecessors. She was, in effect, the archetype "Sloane Ranger". Although the breed had been identified by *Harpers & Queen*'s style spotter Peter York some years previously, it was not until Lady Diana emerged in 1980 that the "Sloane Ranger" business took off.

Another tag affixed to Lady Diana at the time of her engagement to the Prince of Wales in February 1981 was "the girl next door" for she had been born in a house on the Queen's Sandringham estate at the beginning of July 1961. Park House had first been leased by her maternal grandfather, the 4th Lord Fermoy, an Irish peer who sat in the House of Commons for King's Lynn. He was a

shooting companion of George VI (they were out together on the last day of the King's life) and his Scottish wife Ruth, a musician, became a close friend of Queen Elizabeth (now the Queen Mother). After Lord Fermoy's death, the lease of Park House was taken over by his son-in-law, Viscount Althorp, who had married the Fermoys' younger daughter Frances. Lord Althorp, son and heir of the 7th Earl Spencer, was a former equerry to both George VI and the present Queen and had accompanied the Queen and the Duke of Edinburgh as acting Master of the Household on the epic Commonwealth tour of 1953/4. Indeed Lady Diana was born into a family steeped in royal service; both her grandmothers and four of her great-aunts have served in the household of the Queen Mother, while her Spencer

The proud Earl Spencer prepares to escort his youngest daughter, Lady Diana, down the aisle of St Paul's Cathedral

ancestors alone have included three Lord Chamberlains, as well as a Groom of the Stole. The Queen is a godmother to Diana's brother, Charles, whose chief claim on our attention to date has been his attempt to remove the trousers of a middle-aged disc jockey called Tony Blackburn in a Notting Hill Gate trattoria.

To general surprise (not least to Stanley Gibbons who had already rushed out a commemorative stamp catalogue featuring Westminster Abbey on the cover) the 1981 royal wedding took place at St Paul's Cathedral. Although the Abbey had become the traditional place for royal weddings since the First World War, both the Prince and his bride loved the Cathedral (designed, incidentally, by the husband of her fourth cousin nine times removed, Christopher Wren), with its gloriously resonant acoustics.

Moreover, the Abbey had unfortunate associations through Lady Diana's divorced parents having married there, as well as being the scene of Lord Mountbatten's funeral; whereas St Paul's evoked the joy of the Queen and Prince Philip's Silver Wedding in 1972, the Queen's Silver Jubilee in 1977 and the Queen Mother's 80th birthday celebrations in 1980.

"I remember several occasions that were similar, with large crowds: the Coronation and Jubilee, the various major national occasions", said the Prince of Wales, recalling the wonder of 29 July 1981. "All of them were special in their own way but our wedding was quite extraordinary as far as we were concerned. It made us both, and we have discussed it several times, extraordinarily proud to be British."

Below: The scene in St Paul's Cathedral during the marriage ceremony. Among the figures to stand out in the congregation are, on the bridegroom's side, the Gloucesters and Kents in the front row and the Lascelleses in the second row. The Princess of Wales's former flatmates have the pole position on the bride's side. Opposite: the bride and bridegroom come down the steps of St Paul's after the service

One for the album

Life Guard support

The balcony kiss

Just married . . .

The day was not only "quite extraordinary" for the Prince and the new Princess but for the millions who watched them from all over the world. The Prince said before the wedding that he wanted everybody to leave St Paul's having had "a marvellous musical and emotional experience" and, in the event, it was not just the guests inside the Cathedral who did so. Many an unlikely figure was moved to tears.

Vignettes of the day stay in the mind's eye several years later. Lord Spencer, the bride's father, gamely mounting the steps of St Paul's, his chauffeur at his side. The young Earl of Ulster (son of the Duke and Duchess of Gloucester) waving energetically from his parent's carriage to the packed spectators along the route. The Archbishop of Canterbury in a silver cope that gave him the look of a refugee from *Dr Who*. The bride and bridegroom making a mutual hash of their responses. Kiri te Kanawa, in a somewhat unfortunate hat, singing the Seraphim like a divine bird of paradise. The musical feast was luxuriant: Purcell, Handel, Bach, Holst, Elgar. One recalls the Queen trying to control her laughter when an over-enthusiastic choirmaster knocked off a lampshade; the Queen Mother, in her familiar osprey plumes, dabbing away a tear. Then there was the *coup de théatre* of the kiss on the Buckingham Palace balcony. Finally, the bunch of blue and silver balloons that had been tied to the back of the departure landau seemed to symbolise that, for all the splendour and pageantry, it was ultimately very much a young people's day.

"We still cannot get over what happened that day", said the Prince of Wales. "Neither of us can get over the atmosphere; it was electric, I felt, and so did my wife". Outside his window at Buckingham Palace the noise had been "almost indescribable". Since then he had stood at the same window trying to remember it "so that I can tell my children what it was like".

Under the frightful glare of publicity focused remorselessly upon her, the Prince's bride was billed as "Shy Di" (a diminutive she particularly detests, though her collateral ancestress, who nearly married an 18th-century Prince of Wales, was always known as Lady Di Spencer). Happily for everyone, the Princess turned out to be tougher than she looked. The media having built her up to a celestial plane could not find anything new to say about her (the vocabulary of praise being so much more limited than that of snide remarks), so began the inevitable process of knocking her down. There were stories of bossiness, spoilt behaviour, tantrums, *anorexia nervosa,* insecurity, loneliness and so forth, but the Princess's popularity showed no signs of decline. Her naturalness, youth and exceptional physical attractiveness brought a welcome breeze of fresh air into the royal family.

To her credit the Princess appears to want to do things in her own way and she has no greater supporter along this path than the Queen herself. Just as she felt compelled to try to protect Prince Charles from the attentions of Fleet Street when he was a preparatory schoolboy, the Queen, concerned over the media's obsession with "Princess Di, the National Dish" and its damaging effect on her daughter-in-law, called in the editors in an attempt to make them see reason. Clearly the Queen believes that the Princess, as a unique addition to the royal family, should be allowed to create a new pattern of royal existence, which might well include informal and private excursions in the public eye when off duty. For instance, if the Princess had a sudden craving for wine gums, why shouldn't she feel free to go down to the local village shop to buy some without being confronted by photographers reversing down the pavement? The then editor of the *News of the World*'s observation that a footman could go out and buy the wine gums on the Princess's behalf provoked the Queen's memorable retort that that was one of the most pompous remarks she had ever heard. His fellow editors

took delight in breaching etiquette by quoting this royal rebuke and the wretched man left the editorial chair not long afterwards.

A former nursery school teacher, the Princess of Wales has a special gift with children and has taken on several patronages and presidencies in this connexion, including the Malcolm Sargent Cancer Fund for Children and the Albany, a community centre in South-East London that deals with children at risk. After the birth of her first son, Prince William of Wales, the Princess broke with precedent by taking him along on royal engagements, notably the tour of Australia and New Zealand undertaken by the Prince of Wales and herself in 1983. A boisterous youth, Prince William stole the show at the christening of his brother Prince Henry (known as "Harry", the way the name used to be pronounced in Shakespeare's time) the following year. Both sons were born in St Mary's Hospital, Paddington (the days of home births having largely become a thing of the past) and their arrivals pushed their uncles Princes Andrew and Edward down the line of succession.

*The fashion plate Princess. Opposite: One of the studies by
Snowdon commissioned to mark the stupendous tour of Italy that
the Prince and Princess of Wales made in April 1985*

The Queen's two elder and two younger children are divided by a decade: Prince Charles was born in 1948, Princess Anne in 1950 and then Prince Andrew followed in 1960, Prince Edward in 1964. Prince Andrew, now fourth in line of succession to the throne (after his elder brother and his two nephews Princes William and Henry of Wales), followed Prince Charles to Gordonstoun where he indulged in a variety of outdoor activities, such as gliding with the Air Cadet Corps. His education also included stays in France, Germany and Austria. In 1978 he was awarded his "wings" after a parachute course with the RAF and in the following year he joined the Royal Navy on a twelve-year short service commission, passing through Dartmouth and a series of challenging courses.

Prince Andrew came to the fore as a helicopter pilot in the Falklands Campaign in 1982, the first time a member of the royal family had been in the thick of dangerous action since his grandfather, the future George VI, was a Midshipman (known as "Mr Johnson") on HMS *Collingwood* in the Battle of Jutland in 1915. "I think being shot at is the most character-forming thing of one's life", the Prince said afterwards in a television interview with David Frost. He vividly recalled his experiences:

You tend to become a sort of zombie. All you do is eat, sleep and fly. I had an awful lot of time to myself, sitting in my cabin and now and then ducking the odd missile . . . The worst thing was actually the destruction of everything . . . I saw the *Atlantic Conveyor* hit, and the bits and pieces that rained around . . . there were splashes in the water about a quarter of a mile away. It was an experience I shall never forget. It's still a vivid memory imprinted on my brain. It will be there for a very long time – horrific.

The Queen's expression of joyful relief as Prince Andrew returned in HMS *Invincible* after the victorious campaign in the South Atlantic was the most memorable sight on a glorious day at Portsmouth in September 1982. When the gallant Prince decided to let his hair – and various other things – down during a well-deserved holiday in the West Indies there were more mixed reactions. Some said his boisterous behaviour recalled an earlier age of royal rumbustiousness; an earlier royal sailor, the Duke of Clarence (later William IV), who "swore like a deck hand", had also pleasured himself in the West Indies (where he unfortunately contracted venereal disease). The Buckingham Palace press office chose to make one of their typically gratuitous statements about the Prince being "22 and a grown man who is leading his own life" that earned them a magisterial rebuke from the *Spectator* ("a long way above and beyond the call of duty . . . footling and impertinent"). Others complained of the Prince being distressingly "common" (a word that has never gone out of fashion in royal circles). He was to the Queen rather what Mark Thatcher was to the Prime Minister.

Prince Andrew's problem seemed to be that his girl friends, or would-be girl friends, were all too conscious in the "hype" age of the publicity value to be gained for their careers as "actresses" (or whatever) by a liaison with the Queen's second son. Thanks to the patronage of Lord Pembroke (whose Tudor and Stuart ancestors at Wilton were also patrons of the arts) people were able to form their own opinions of Miss Kathleen ("Koo") Stark's charms in his film *The Awakening of Emily*. When the publicity over the Prince's friendship with "Koo! Starkers!" (as she was inevitably billed) was at its height the BBC Television News sunk to fresh depths by ending its *Nine O'Clock* bulletin with a clip from the noble Earl's soft-porn production. After the camera had panned down the pouting American actress's flesh, the shifty-looking Welsh newsreader leered at the camera: "That's all for now".

The Queen is supposed to have been somewhat over-indulgent to Prince Andrew as a child. As early as the mid-1960s those who had come into contact with the boisterous young prince were predicting that he would become the most charismatic member of the royal family, though his unmannerly relish for his princely status is said

Opposite above: The Queen, Princess Margaret, Prince Charles and Prince Andrew on the royal train; and (below) the Queen's family in the late 1960s

Right: The Queen with Princes Andrew and Edward after Christmas Mattins at St George's Chapel, Windsor, 1968; and (below) Prince Andrew, helicopter pilot

to have caused the Queen and Prince Philip considerable misgivings. Even the most hagiographical studies of the royal family have difficulty in not making Prince Andrew appear an overbearing loudmouth possessing his father's least attractive characteristics, such as a taste for "practical jokes". The look on his face as he "accidentally" sprayed some American photographers with paint on a supposed "goodwill" visit to California did little to inspire any sympathy for this strapping young man. And yet beneath the aggressively extrovert exterior we are asked to believe there lurks a lonely, misunderstood figure. Norman Parkinson, who encouraged Prince Andrew to take up photography, has described his protégé as "the nicest, loneliest man . . . desperately lonely". Loneliness, Prince Andrew himself has pointed out, is a theme of his photography but, though the Prince claims to be "a recluse", he has said "I don't think I am lonely. I try to keep out of people's way and avoid the press."

His younger brother, Prince Edward, as yet less well known than his siblings, has a gentler, more studious image, though friends have said his manner can tend towards the imperious. Like Charles and Andrew, he went to Gordonstoun, where he went gliding with the Air Corps, and he is also destined to receive a similarly tough training to his brothers in the Services after he graduates from Jesus College, Cambridge. In 1986 he is due to join the Royal Marines officer training school at Lympstone in Devon. When he took a short flying course at RAF Cranwell there was speculation that he might be the first member of the royal family to serve full time with the RAF since the late Duke of Kent (killed on active service in the Second World War).

Prince Edward has had several opportunities to travel with the Queen and Prince Philip; his trips have included the 1978 Commonwealth Games in Canada and visits to Germany and Liechtenstein. Again like his brothers, he has done an educational stint in the Commonwealth, acting as a house tutor at a public school in New Zealand. This convinced him that he did not wish to pursue the profession of schoolmastering, though it also resulted in a published spoof on public schools. Prince Edward's examination results (his three "A" levels were gained with modest grades) caused some to question the justification of his place at Cambridge and he has something to prove in his degree course in archaeology and anthropology. There has been speculation that he might take up a professional career later on, but as yet there are no clear pointers as to what this might be.

Prince Edward has managed to shed the misleadingly delicate look he had as an adolescent. He enjoys ski-ing and sailing, has played rugby football for his College 2nd XV and, despite a debilitating bout of glandular fever,

Prince Andrew passes out of Dartmouth in a blaze of sunshine, 1 April 1980

The hero's homecoming: Portsmouth, 1982

"Parks's" photographic protégé, Port Stanley, Falkland Islands

Prince Edward training with the Marines at Lympstone, 1983

Royal ruck, Cambridge, 1984

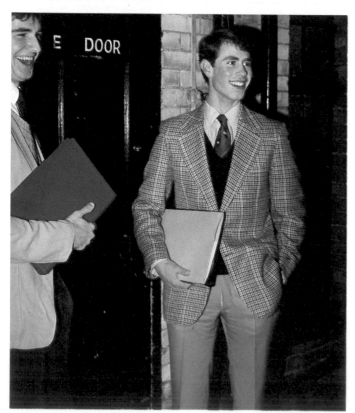

produced the University Rag Week revue in 1984. His girl friends have not received so much attention as Prince Andrew's, tending to be drawn from a less publicity-conscious stratum of society.

While the Queen waits for a suitable moment to confer royal dukedoms on Prince Andrew and Prince Edward (those of York, and, in all probability, Sussex respectively), Princess Anne has never shown any inclination to be granted the title of "Princess Royal" traditionally borne by the eldest daughter of the sovereign. Its last holder was George V's only daughter Princess Mary, Countess of Harewood, who died in 1965 when Princess Anne was in her mid-teens. A no-nonsense young woman, who once said she would like to have been a lorry driver in another life, the Princess has little time for titles. Her husband and fellow-equestrian remains plain Mark Phillips, having declined the peerage the Queen was apparently keen for him to take. Consequently the Phillips children, Peter and Zara, though close to the throne (within the top ten of the order of succession) do not bear so much as a courtesy title in a country where there are still well over 2,000 peerages and baronetcies in existence. The somewhat spurious egalitarianism of this approach to styles and titles is illustrated by the absurd way in which Princess Anne is described in the *Court Circular* as "Mrs Mark Phillips", despite the fact that she is a princess, a duke's daughter and a dame (GCVO).

Princess Anne emerged on the royal scene at about the same time as her elder brother, Prince Charles. Very much her own woman, the Princess has taken on comparatively few patronages and presidencies but those organizations she has accepted have received the benefit of her unstinting time and effort. She has been an outstandingly conscientious President of Save the Children Fund, on whose behalf she has made many overseas visits, often in gruelling conditions which she characteristically took in her stride without any fuss or bother. Although Princess Anne plays a full part in the general round of royal duties (frequently acting, for example, as a Counsellor of State during the Queen and Prince Philip's absences abroad), she has publicly doubted whether her children "will be involved at all". The exuberant Peter Phillips has recently started boarding at a preparatory school in Dorset, Port Regis, a friendly, cheerful establishment housed in an 1890s "Tudorbethan" pile whose old boys include the Phillips' eventing friend, Hugh Thomas.

Since 1977 the Princess and her family have lived at Gatcombe Park, an estate bought for them by the Queen in "Beaufortshire" where the royal family are congregating in such numbers. Here Captain Phillips, an ADC to the Queen (just as his grandfather Brigadier John Tiarks was to the Queen's father, George VI), has farmed some 1,200

Left: Princess Anne, in one of her favourite caps, with her son Peter. Below left: Taking the water at Windsor, 1980. Below (and bottom): Driving one of her beloved lorries. "Any time you get fed up with your present role" Geoff Pygall, the managing director of British Road Services, told the Princess, "you are welcome to a job"

acres since retiring from the Queen's Dragoon Guards. The Princess and the Captain take a hand at harrowing, haymaking and harvesting, as the season demands, but the main activity at Gatcombe revolves around the animals that first brought them together, horses.

Princess Anne took after her mother in being a keen rider as a girl and, under the tutelage of the showjumper Alan Oliver's wife, Ann, achieved phenomenal success in three-day events. In 1971 she won the European Championship at Burghley and was voted the BBC's "Sports Personality of the Year". In 1973, the year of her marriage to fellow equestrian Captain Phillips, Princess Anne took part in the World Championships at Kiev and was a member of the British team in the Olympic Games at Montreal in 1976, where the Queen had the thrill of seeing her daughter compete. Unfortunately Princess Anne has not had the luck or, more to the point, the right horse to repeat her early triumphs in the saddle and with hindsight it could be said she did too well too soon. But

152

Princess Anne, the tireless President of the Save the Children Fund, tours the Boroma refugee camp in Somalia, 1982

she and her husband remain wholeheartedly involved in this increasingly competitive and commercial sport.

The Princess's somewhat prickly personality has not always been appreciated by the press, whom she in turn regards with a certain lack of warmth. "Why don't you just naff off?" was a typical remark addressed to some journalists at Badminton one year. However, during a horrific incident in March 1974 when an unhinged gunman ambushed Princess Anne and Captain Phillips's car in the Mall, it was a gallant pillar of El Vino's in Fleet Street, Brian McConnell, who stopped a bullet or two in coming to the Princess's rescue. Some years later, Mr McConnell's newspaper the *Daily Mirror* christened Princess Anne "PRINCESS SOUR PUSS" after some embarrasing scenes in New Mexico when she said to one journalist who asked her how she was enjoying her visit: "Keep your questions to yourself". Asked how it felt to be an aunt for the first time (the Princess of Wales had just given birth to Prince William), Princess Anne riposted: "That's my business,

thank you". Stories concerning the alleged coolness between the Phillipses and their Gloucestershire neighbours, the Waleses, were magnified when Princess Anne and the Captain did not attend the christening of Prince Henry at Windsor shortly before Christmas 1984. The reason for their absence was said to be a long-standing private engagement. When it was discovered that this engagement was, in fact, a rabbit shoot the gossips had a field day.

Sour puss or not, the Princess's highly individual manner and sense of humour (a nice line in deadpan, sarcastic understatement) have come to be more widely understood and appreciated – especially after a memorable appearance on Terry Wogan's television show. Auberon Waugh has compared her to the original pantomime dame, "a genuine and unmistakable eccentric". He has wittily placed her in the "grand old tradition of English aunts stretching from Wodehouse through Saki and Wilde to Jane Eyre's Aunt Reed and no doubt further back than that".

Princess Margaret backstage at a charity gala. She is at her most relaxed with artists and performers

"Charley's Aunt", as Princess Margaret dreaded being called when her sister Princess Elizabeth gave birth to her first son in 1948, has also experienced a very mixed relationship with the press and the public. "Princess Margaret", wrote *The Times* in 1980 when she celebrated her 50th birthday and her mother's 80th, "has had a relatively unhappy and sometimes difficult life, but her warmth and spontaneity is a reflection of her mother's character and is likely to be of growing importance to the royal family in coming years." Witty, musical, artistic and a talented mimic, Princess Margaret is undoubtedly the most sophisticated member of the royal family. One of her problems has been to combine her taste for the Bohemian life with her equally strong, if contradictory, sense of regality as, in pedantic phraseology, the late King's co-heiress. As the Queen's younger sister, Princess Margaret has always been close to the throne (she was indeed second in line to succession for many years) without ever being likely to occupy it. She often acts as Counsellor of State during the Queen's absences abroad in conjunction with

Prince Charles, Princess Anne or the Queen Mother. Notwithstanding Willie Hamilton's slurs about "this wayward woman" failing to earn her royal keep, Princess Margaret has always undertaken her full share of duties on the Queen's behalf.

Five years after being put in the painful position of having to announce publicly that she was not going to marry her father's protégé, Group-Captain Peter Townsend, because he had been divorced, Princess Margaret married the son of divorced parents, the photographer, Antony Armstrong-Jones (later created Earl of Snowdon) in 1960. As a couple the Snowdons were more closely associated with the arts than any of the other members of the royal family and for a time it looked as though they might bridge the gap between the formality of royalty and the up-and-coming "trendsetters" of the Swinging Sixties. But somehow it never quite worked. However "informal" the Snowdons' approach to life may have appeared, Princess Margaret was still the Queen's sister. After several years of rumours about a rift, the

Snowdons separated officially in 1976 and divorced amicably two years later.

The Queen was "naturally very sad," announced her press secretary Ronald Allison at the time of the separation, adding that "there has been no pressure from the Queen on either Princess Margaret or Lord Snowdon to take any particular course." The Queen has continued to treat Lord Snowdon with exemplary friendliness and consideration. Lord Snowdon has since remarried (his bride Lucy being the daughter of Donald Davies, the maker of "shirt-dresses", and former wife of the film director Michael Lindsay-Hogg). For those who persist in seeing the royal family in terms of the soap opera *Coronation Street*, Princess Margaret has become something of an "Elsie Tanner" figure. Her divorce almost certainly increased the Princess's popularity; in an age where marriage breakdowns have become commonplace it made the royal family seem more human. There was further

concern and sympathy for Princess Margaret when she had to undergo major surgery on one of her lungs in January 1985. As the Princess is a heavy smoker (albeit through her famous prop, a cigarette holder) and suffers from chronic bronchitis, there was no shortage of helpful busybodies to point out that her father had died of lung cancer at about the same age, but happily the medical bulletin stated that the operation on the Princess had not revealed any malignancy.

Both Princess Margaret's children by Lord Snowdon, Viscount Linley and Lady Sarah Armstrong-Jones, were educated at Bedales, the "progressive" co-educational public school in Hampshire. Lord Linley went on to do a crafts course at Parnham, the furniture designer John Makepeace's country house in Dorset, and later set up as a furniture maker in his own right. As "David Linley" he has also dabbled in his father's profession of photography, having sets of pictures published in *Vogue* and *Tatler*, the

Wartime royal group: back row (left to right) the Duke of Gloucester, the Duchess of Gloucester, Princess Margaret, the Princess Royal, the Duchess of Kent (Princess Marina) and the Earl of Harewood. Front Row: Queen Mary, King George VI, Princess Elizabeth and the Queen Mother

latter magazine (edited by his father's old Cambridge friend and *Sunday Times* colour supplement colleague, Mark Boxer) featuring his travels in the Himalayas. Lady Sarah Armstrong-Jones gained a place at Camberwell Art School after Bedales and has also done some odd jobs in the film world, including assisting her father on the set of David Lean's film of *A Passage to India* (where Lord Snowdon was taking the stills) and working for the production company run by Lord Mountbatten's son-in-law, Lord Brabourne. Lady Sarah Armstrong-Jones is best known as a royal bridesmaid, performing that role to Princess Anne in 1973 and the Princess of Wales in 1981. She is also a godmother to Prince Henry of Wales. Although Princess Margaret's spokesman has stated that Lady Sarah "will not undertake public engagements or take on official duties", royalty watchers maintain that as the most senior royal female of her generation after the Princess of Wales, to whom she is known to be close, and

as a particular favourite of the Queen's, the Armstrong-Jones girl may yet join the "Royal Firm".

Princess Margaret continues to live at Kensington Palace, nicknamed the "Aunt Heap" by Edward VIII whose sister-in-law, Princess Alice, Duchess of Gloucester also retains an apartment there for her visits to London from her country house in Northamptonshire, Barnwell. Formerly Lady Alice Montagu-Douglas-Scott, daughter of the 7th Duke of Buccleuch, a territorial magnate descended from the ill-fated Duke of Monmouth (Charles II's son by his first mistress, Lucy Walters), she married Prince Henry, George V's third son in 1935. Prince Henry, the late Duke of Gloucester, was essentially a military man who would have been happiest pursuing the career of an ordinary Army officer; he had to endure many regimental frustrations for the sake of his royal duties. From 1945 to 1947 he was Governor-General of Australia and in the early years of the Queen's reign he and the Duchess

undertook numerous overseas tours together. But in 1966 (the year after he deposited the unfortunate Duchess in a bed of nettles when he crashed his Rolls Royce on the way home from Sir Winston Churchill's state funeral), the Duke's health began to fail and he retired from public life, dying in 1974 after a long illness.

"Uncle Pineapple", as he was known, was a royal duke in the most colourful Hanoverian tradition and became the subject of numerous anecdotes. When someone asked him whether he had read *Wuthering Heights* Prince Henry is supposed to have replied "Yes – jolly funny". When finding himself having to make conversation with a belly-dancer in Cairo during the war all he could think of as an opening gambit was to ask: "Have you ever been to Tidworth?" He would doggedly stick to his "bwief" even if it turned out to be wide of the mark. A critic of Churchill's wartime administration destroyed his own case by suggesting to an incredulous House of Commons that the Duke of Gloucester should be made Commander-in-Chief.

Since the Duke's death his widow, known not as Princess Henry (as she surely should be) but as Princess Alice, has taken on an increased number of Colonelcies of regiments, patronages and presidencies. In 1975 she was appointed the first ever Dame Grand Cross of the Order of the Bath. In her published memoirs, this shy, little-known public figure surprised many people with her wry sense of humour, a quality which must have helped sustain her during a life marred by tragedy.

In 1972 the Duchess, already nursing a dying husband, lost her elder son Prince William, one of the most stylish personalities in the modern royal family, when he was killed in a flying accident while taking part in the Goodyear Air Race near Wolverhampton. As a younger son, the present Duke of Gloucester, born in 1944, should have had an easier life than his elder brother. While Prince William was extrovert and adventurous, Prince Richard is by nature somewhat shyer.

In his early days, particularly at Cambridge, he led a slightly Bohemian existence, studying architecture. He was employed with the Offices Development Group of the Ministry of Public Buildings and Works, before entering practice as a partner in a firm of London architects. He met his Danish bride, Birgitte van Deurs, while at Cambridge and they married in July 1972. They hoped to live in a converted warehouse on the Isle of Dogs, but within a few weeks of his brother's death, Prince Richard (as he was) found himself living at Kensington Palace, his London home today. He was faced with so many royal duties that it proved impossible to continue his architectural practice. Nevertheless, he still takes an active interest in the subject as Vice-Chairman of the Historic Buildings and Monuments Commission (christened "English Heritage" for short by the Chairman, Lord Montagu of Beaulieu) and on behalf of the Victorian Society and other organizations. He has also produced three books of photographs (the first of which, on statues, likens the

159

Below: The wedding group of the Duke and Duchess of Kent (George and Marina) 1934. Princess Elizabeth was a bridesmaid

Opposite: The present Duke and Duchess of Kent

features on Queen Victoria's memorial to those of Harold Wilson). Other interests of the Duke include the rehabilitation of the character of his namesake, that much maligned monarch Richard III (also a former Duke of Gloucester), and a somewhat illiberal campaign against cigarette-smokers. In addition to all this, the bespectacled Duke runs the 2,500 acre estate at Barnwell where he and his family (the three children each divided by three years, are Alexander, the Earl of Ulster; Lady Davina Windsor, and Lady Rose Windsor) spend their weekends.

The Duke of Kent inherited a number of military appointments (and a bearskin) from his late uncle, the Duke of Gloucester, though his own military career in the Scots Dragoon Guards was sadly cut short by the situation in Northern Ireland from where it was thought safer to bring him home. Now he travels extensively in his job as Vice-Chairman of the British Overseas Trade Board and takes an energetic interest in British industry and technology (his other appointments include the chairmanship of the National Electronics Council). In 1961 at York Minster the Duke of Kent married Katharine Worsley, the daughter of a Yorkshire baronet and,

incidentally, a direct descendant of Oliver Cromwell. The Duchess is Controller Commandant of the Women's Royal Army Corps and her various interests include cricket and singing in the Bach choir. A woman of strong religious faith, she pluckily came through a bad bout of depression brought on by a miscarriage in the late 1970s.

The Kents' children are the Earl of St Andrews, Lord Nicholas Windsor and Lady Helen Windsor. A King's Scholar at Eton, George St Andrews, tall, fair-haired and bearded, is reading History at Downing College, Cambridge; Lord Nicholas is a pupil at Westminster School. The glamorous Lady Helen, nicknamed the "Royal Raver" in the press and the first member of the royal family actually to bear the surname of "Windsor" since its adoption in 1917, followed her royal cousins to the sixth-form at Gordonstoun and now works for Christie's in London. The Kents' home used to be Coppins at Iver in Buckinghamshire which the late Duke of Kent, Prince George, inherited from his aunt Princess Victoria. They now divide their time between York House in St James's Palace and Anmer Hall, a late-Georgian country house on the Queen's Sandringham estate in Norfolk.

Prince Michael of Kent, the Duke's younger brother, was born at Coppins in 1942 (President Roosevelt was one of his godfathers, a fact not unconnected with the Prince's birthday being 4 July), only a few weeks before his father was killed. Like his brother, Prince Michael was a serving soldier, becoming a Major in the Royal Hussars. In 1978 he was involved in a religious controversy when it became known that he wished to marry a Roman Catholic, Mrs Troubridge (otherwise Baroness Marie-Christine von Reibnitz), whose previous marriage to a London merchant banker had been dissolved by divorce (although it was to be subsequently annulled in the ecclesiastical courts). Pope Paul XI refused to allow the Baroness and the Prince to marry in a religious service. With hindsight, it was surely a mistake to have gone straight to the top, as it were, for permission rather than seek a solution through the lower echelons of the Catholic hierarchy. Perhaps one can detect the influence of Lord Mountbatten here; certainly he played an avuncular role in the proceedings at the civil ceremony in Vienna. Princess Michael has described their mentor as "our great supporter . . . who could explain a great many things . ."

Having married a Roman Catholic Prince Michael was obliged to surrender his rights to the throne under the Royal Marriages Act of 1772, but the restriction does not apply to his children, who bear the courtesy titles of Lord Frederick Windsor and Laby Gabriella Windsor. Prince Michael now works in the City of London as a director of Standard Telephones and Cables. Although he receives no Civil List allowance from the Government for the engagements he and his wife carry out, Prince Michael has blossomed into a familiar public figure since his marriage. His beard gives him a striking resemblance to his grandfather George V and thus also to that monarch's lookalike cousin Tsar Alexander of Russia. This point will not have been lost on Princess Michael, who takes an enthusiastic interest in history and is reported to be writing a book about princesses.

Lord Mountbatten advised Princess Michael it would take five years for her to be accepted. Certainly when she first arrived on the royal scene Princess Michael was an easy target. Born in Bohemia and brought up, apparently in somewhat reduced circumstances, in Australia, she seemed like a parody of a princess, too regal, too well

161

Princess Michael of Kent

Another evening, another show. . .

The palace glide

The ever-popular Princess Alexandra

Angus Ogilvy

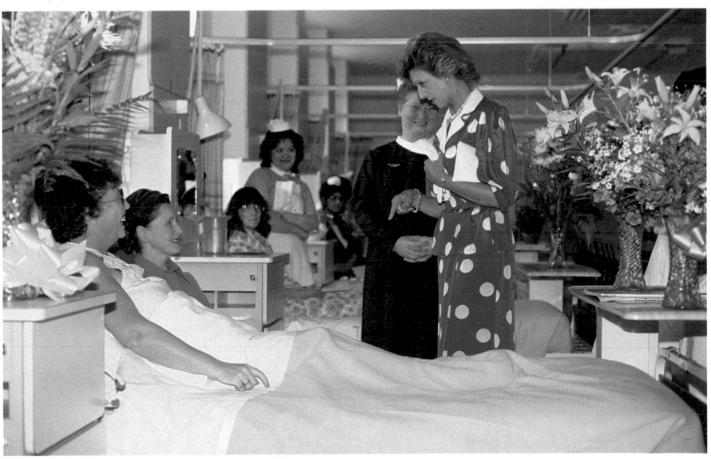

Princess Alexandra visiting the Elizabeth Garrett Anderson Hospital

163

Below: Princess Alexandra on a visit to a factory in Cheshire, 1982

Opposite: Seated on the left of this group for the Christening of Peter Phillips, 1977, is the oldest-ever member of the royal family, Princess Alice, Countess of Athlone, Queen Victoria's last surviving grandchild. Also in the picture (standing left to right): Major and Mrs Peter Phillips, the Queen, Captain Mark Phillips, the Queen Mother and Prince Philip. Princess Anne holds the baby

turned out, too flamboyant, too available, altogether too much. The Queen's alleged pet name for her – "Our Val", short for Valkyrie (an allusion to her strapping Germanic presence) – may have been a myth, but there is no doubt that other members of the family were referring to Princess Michael as "Princess Pushy". Lord Linley was reported as saying that the Christmas present he would give his worst enemy would be dinner with Princess Michael. A well-known peer delighted various grand dinner tables with renditions of a wittily cruel doggerel ode to Her Royal Highness.

The Queen may well have had a hand in putting a stop to all this; in any event, it suddenly became the thing not to knock Princess Michael but to praise her. After all, what was wrong, the buzz went, with a bit of ambition, drive and get-up and go in the 1980s? She had done wonders for Michael and wasn't it useful to have a "royal" on tap prepared to "do the business" for so many charitable and public relations functions? The ugly campaign to visit the sins of her father (sensa-

tionally revealed in April 1985 to have been a member of the SS, though he was, alas, far from the only close connexion of the royal family to have been a Nazi) upon the daughter he hardly knew backfired amid a surge of public sympathy for the contrite Princess.

Whatever digs are made against Princess Michael, one never hears anything but affectionate, warm remarks about her sister-in-law, Princess Alexandra, long one of the most attractive and popular members of the royal family. She was much to the fore in the mid-1960s during a period of transition in the royal family when the older generation were, so to speak, reaching retiring age and the new generation of Prince Charles and Princess Anne were not yet ready to fill their places. Princess Alexandra has continued to undertake a full programme of royal duties; her travels include frequent visits to Hong Kong where she has connexions with the University and the Police Force. In 1963 Princess Alexandra, who inherited a certain look of her beautiful mother Princess Marina of Greece and Den-

mark (Prince Philip's cousin), married Angus Ogilvy, second son of the 12th Earl of Airlie, at Westminster Abbey. The Ogilvys have been close to the royal family for a number of years. Angus Ogilvy's grandmother Mabell Countess of Airlie was the long-serving Lady of the Bedchamber and confidante to Queen Mary, the late Earl was Lord Chamberlain to the Queen Mother and the present Earl succeeded Lord Maclean as Lord Chamberlain to the Queen at the beginning of 1985.

At the time of the marriage Mr Ogilvy (who bears the courtesy title of "Honourable" – a style, it is sometimes said, known only to the postman, though Princess Alexandra, despite being a duke's daughter and a dame is always ridiculously referred to as "the Honourable Mrs Angus Ogilvy" in the *Court Circular*) is said to have declined a title of his own. He decided that he would continue his career in the City of London, but would help Princess Alexandra with her duties on behalf of the Queen whenever possible. Unfortunately his name was linked with "Tiny" Rowland in the Lonrho affair (what Edward

Heath called the "unacceptable face of capitalism") and after the unfavourable report in 1976 Mr Ogilvy announced that he was leaving the City. Today his directorships include the Metropolitan Estate and Property Corporation, the Rank Organization and Sothebys, the art auctioneers. The Ogilvys live at Thatched House Lodge in Richmond Park; their son James went to university at St Andrews and is expected to follow his father into the City; his sister Marina left St Mary's, Wantage, in 1984.

The above names consitute the "royal family" as we generally know it. When the Queen leads her family out of a big ceremony at, say, St Paul's Cathedral or Westminster Abbey, it is they who follow her. At the Queen's Silver Wedding service and Princess Anne's wedding at Westminster Abbey, the late Princess Alice, Countess of Athlone, walked in procession with them out of deference to her position as the only other British "Royal Highness" and the Queen's great-aunt. But there are several others who should really have taken precedence over the late Princess Alice due to their position in line of succession.

Below: The Queen, Prince Edward, Princess Anne, Prince Charles, Prince Andrew and Prince Philip at Windsor in 1965.
Bottom: The wedding group after Princess Anne's marriage to Captain Mark Phillips, 1973

Opposite (above): The Queen Mother on her 80th birthday with her children and grandchildren, 1980.
Opposite (below): Prince William steals the show in front of Snowdon's camera at the Christening of his younger brother, Prince Harry, 1984. The godparents were (standing on the left) Lady Sarah Armstrong-Jones, the artist Bryan Organ and Gerald Ward; and (on the right) Carolyn Bartholomew (née Pride) and Lady Susan Hussey

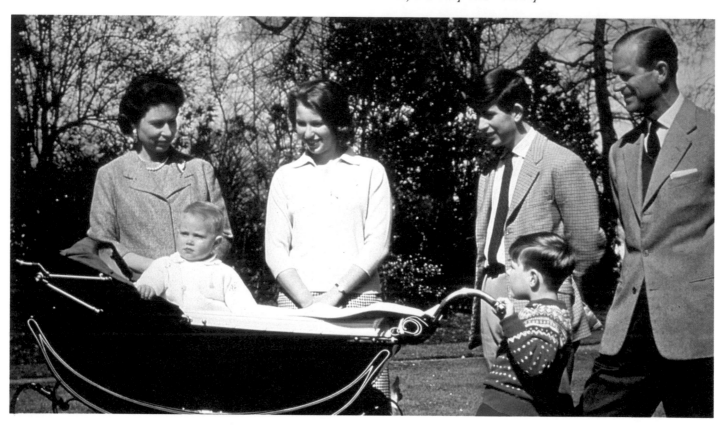

The two sons of the late Princess Royal (George V's daughter) the Earl of Harewood and Gerald Lascelles, are first cousins to the Queen; indeed Lord Harewood was the first of King George V's grandsons to be born and there exists a photograph of him with his mother, the King, and Queen Alexandra, his great-grandmother. Keenly interested in classical music since he was a small boy, he is said to have become an expert musicologist while he was a prisoner of war from 1944 to 1945. Lord Harewood has been an outstanding Managing Director of English National Opera, dividing his time between London and Harewood House, near Leeds, which is one of the most popular showplaces open to the public.

In 1967 Lord Harewood caused a certain amount of controversy by divorcing his wife Marion Stein, the pianist (who later married the Liberal politician Jeremy Thorpe) in order to marry Patricia Tuckwell, by whom he already had a three-year old son. Consequently he did not appear at Court for a number of years. But in 1977 his second wife was given a Silver Jubilee medal and there was a public meeting with the Queen.

When Lord Harewood was born, he was, of course, much closer to the throne than he is now – sixth in line, the equivalent position to a child of Princess Anne today, as opposed to 25th. While the Queen was on her Commonwealth tour from 1953 to 1954, he acted as a Counsellor of State, but now he is so far down the line that he is no longer involved in affairs of State. As a couple, the Harewoods can usually be spotted at major royal ceremonies, sitting about eight rows from the front.

Both the Harewoods and Gerald Lascelles and his second wife (by whom he also had a son out of wedlock) were present at St Paul's Cathedral for the wedding of the Prince and Princess of Wales in 1981. Gerald Lascelles and his first wife lived for some years at Fort Belvedere, Edward VIII's old retreat near Windsor. Mr Lascelles, whose taste in music is jazz rather than classical, is President of the British Racing Driver's Club.

Including the Lascelles children (some of whose musical activities have been more in the mood of "trucking") and grandchildren, there are now 35 descendants of George V, only eleven of whom are princes or princesses. At present the Queen calls on a dozen members of her family to help carry out the business of the "firm". Prince Philip, the Queen Mother, Princes Andrew and Edward, Princesses Anne, Margaret and Alice, Duchess of Gloucester, all have their expenses paid from the public purse through the Civil List. The Dukes of Gloucester and Kent and their Duchesses, and Princess Alexandra also all attend official functions and receive some Civil List help but are chiefly funded by the Queen herself. The Prince and Princess of Wales are supported by the revenues of the Duchy of Cornwall. Prince and Princess Michael of Kent's engagements are of an "unofficial" nature.

The *Court Circular* sometimes uses the phrase "and other members of the Royal Family". This is a specific definition which applies to the members of the "Royal Family" whose names appear in the Court list. Technically it does not include those under age. Several of the names on the list are surprisingly little known to the general public.

The next in line as such is the Duke of Fife. He is a great-grandson of Edward VII through the female line. George V had three sisters, of whom the second, Princess Victoria (best remembered for roaring "Is that you, you old fool" down the telephone to her brother and finding a flunkey at the other end of the line) did not marry, and the youngest, Princess Maud, married King Haakon of Norway. (For obvious reasons their son, King Olav, and his family are not members of the British royal family, though they are in line to the British throne.) The eldest sister was Princess Louise, Duchess of Fife and later Princess Royal, who died in 1931. She had two daughters. The elder, Princess Alexandra, succeeded her father in the Dukedom of Fife and married her first cousin once removed, Prince Arthur of Connaught. Their only son, Alastair (the diminutive 2nd Duke of Connaught), died in Ottawa in 1943. The younger, Princess Maud, who died in 1945, married the 11th Earl of Southesk, and it is their son, James, who is the present Duke of Fife. The Duke is the third holder of the title, which he inherited from his aunt in 1959 at the age of thirty. He and his wife, Caroline Dewar, were divorced in 1966. Eight years later the Duke survived a serious motor accident but seems none the worse for it today.

Then there are the junior descendants of Queen Victoria. The only descendants of her second son, Alfred, Duke of Edinburgh, are through the female line (notably the royal houses of Roumania and Yugoslavia). Those that are not Catholics, or married to Catholics, are in line to the British throne, but are not actually "members of the Royal Family". The third (and favourite) son of Queen Victoria was the Duke of Connaught. The old soldier's younger daughter, Princess Patricia, married Captain Alexander Ramsay, RN, third son of the 13th Earl of Dalhousie. She became known as Lady Patricia Ramsay and he rose to be an Admiral. Both were members of the Royal Family, who continued to attend royal functions in the present Queen's reign while their health permitted. As a former "Royal Highness", Lady Patricia wore full royal robes and coronet at the Coronation in 1953. She was a talented artist, and Colonel-in-Chief of Princess Patricia's Canadian Light Infantry. Both she and the Admiral were touchingly featured in Lord Snowdon's film about old age, *Don't Count the Candles*, sitting together in their garden at

The scene in Westminster Abbey during the Queen's
Coronation, 1953. In the front row of the balcony are (from left
to right): The Duchess of Kent (Princess Marina), the Princess
Royal, the Queen Mother, Princess Margaret, Prince William,
the Duchess of Gloucester (Princess Alice) and Prince Richard.
The Duke of Edinburgh's mother, Princess Andrew of Greece,
can be seen in the nun's habit in the second row; Lord Harewood
is in the peer's ermine robes on the right.

Ribsden Holt, near Windlesham in Surrey. Immensely popular in her youth, "Princess Pat", as she was affectionately known, had faded from the public eye by the time of her death in January 1974 at the age of 87.

Princess Pat's son, Captain Alexander Ramsay of Mar, is very much a member of the royal family. Like the Earl of Harewood, he was a page to George VI at his Coronation in 1937. Later he served in the Grenadier Guards (losing a leg in North Africa) and was an ADC to the Duke of Gloucester for three years, which included the Duke's Governor-Generalship of Australia. His wife is a Scottish peeress in her own right as Lady Saltoun.

Next in the Court list of the royal family come the late Queen Mary's surviving Teck relations (Queen Mary's mother, Princess Mary Adelaide of Great Britain, a granddaughter of George III, married the Prince of Teck). The Marchioness of Cambridge is the widow of Queen Mary's nephew, the former Prince George of Teck, who renounced his German titles in 1917. The Duchess of Beaufort is the late Lord Cambridge's sister. Queen Mary spent the Second World War with her niece at Badminton and when someone recently enquired of the Duchess of Beaufort as to what part of the great house the old Queen had lived in, the Duchess replied: "She lived in all of it."

The present Queen has always been particularly close to the Beauforts (the late Duke, who was her long serving Master of the Horse, died in 1984), staying at Badminton every spring for the celebrated horse trials. When, for one reason or another, there were not many royalties available to attend events such as the State Opening of Parliament, the Duchess of Beaufort would sometimes walk in the royal procession. As a member of the royal family the Duchess was also escorted by a Canon from the Quire of

St George's Chapel after the annual Garter Ceremony. In poor health for some years, the Duchess still lives at Badminton, which she shares with her husband's successor, the former David Somerset and his family.

The remaining two members of the official "royal family" on the Court list are Lady May and Colonel Sir Henry Abel Smith. Lady May, a first cousin of the Duchess of Beaufort and of the late Lord Cambridge, is the daughter of the late Earl of Athlone, Queen Mary's brother (who began life as Prince Alexander of Teck) and of Princess Alice, Countess of Athlone, who was the oldest ever member of the British royal family. Sir Henry was ADC to his future father-in-law when Lord Athlone was Governor-General of South Africa and later he himself became Governor of Queensland, Australia. The Abel Smiths live at Winkfield not far from Windsor Castle.

These, then, are some of the people to bear in mind when one prays in church for "all the royal family". Someone notable by her absence from the Court list is, of course, the widow of the sometime Edward VIII, the Duchess of Windsor. In 1985 the Duchess is still hanging on to a life that has long since lost all meaning, in a pathetic state where even the petty denial of her right to the style "Her Royal Highness" has become an irrelevance. All the old issues were raked up at the time of the Duke's Lying-in-State and funeral in 1972, but in fairness it must be said that during this time, the Queen could not have been kinder to the Duchess of Windsor. She invited her to stay at Buckingham Palace and assured her that she could do exactly as she liked and that no obligations would be put on her. Although many people wondered why no member of the royal family accompanied the Duchess to London Airport on her departure, it was not generally known that when the funeral was over and the committal had taken place, there was not one member of the royal family absent from the porch of Windsor Castle to say goodbye to the Duchess as she stepped into her car.

The following year, the Duchess expressed a wish to see the Duke's grave. The press knew nothing of this visit which took place in July 1973. The Duchess flew from Paris in an aircraft of the Queen's Flight and was met by the Duke of Kent and Lord Mountbatten (the latter, incidentally, was a "member of the royal family", though his daughters are not). She laid flowers at the grave and lunched at Windsor Castle. During lunch a telegram of greeting was brought to her. It came from the Prince of Wales in the Bahamas. Every year the Duchess of Windsor receives a Christmas card from the Queen, and on her eightieth birthday there was a telegram and some roses. When the Duchess dies she will be buried beside her husband at Frogmore in the private burial ground of the royal family.

171

9. The Queen and Her Homes

For the Queen, Buckingham Palace is where she spends the working week. For countless millions the Palace conjures up an imposing, if not particularly inspiring, grey façade of Portland stone looking down the Mall. Although visitors can – at least in theory – sign their names as a gesture of loyal greeting at the Privy Purse Door (on the right of the Mall front) the palace is not open to the public, so it is only the fortunate few who can testify that the inside is much more cheerful and interesting than one might imagine gazing in from outside the railings. Even if now overlooked by the monstrous skyscrapers which were so disgracefully allowed to disfigure London in the 1960s, the 40 acres of Buckingham Palace gardens, with a lake, form a wonderful oasis in the centre of the metropolis. And of the two principal facades, it is the garden front with its golden Bath stone that is by far the more attractive.

Buckingham Palace is largely the creation of that great royal builder George IV who when he ascended the throne in 1820 commissioned John Nash to convert the then Buckingham House into a palace large enough for entertaining. Buckingham House, which had spacious grounds more like a country house park than a town garden, had been bought by George III in 1762. It had been built at the beginning of the 18th century by John Sheffield, Duke of Buckingham, an old friend of Queen Anne who had given him some of St James's Park to enlarge his estate. (The site where Buckingham Palace now stands was covered at the beginning of the 17th century by mulberry trees as part of James I's chequered campaign to boost the raw silk industry.) Although Queen Anne took a dim view of Buckingham building such a fine house looking down the Mall, the Duke was delighted with his creation, taking a special pride in the staircase "with eight and forty steps ten feet broad, each step of one entire Portland stone". The architects were William Talman (the designer of Chatsworth) and Captain William Winde.

George III made various modest improvements and held a celebrated "house-warming", with the grounds being illuminated by 4,000 coloured lamps and a vast picture of the "Farmer" monarch himself, showing this unlikely figure dispensing peace to all the world. George IV managed to extract some £200,000 from Parliament for "a repair and improvement of Buckingham Palace". As things turned out, he spent about three times this in a virtual rebuilding. The "King's House in Pimlico", as it was known, was constructed around a three-sided courtyard, the open side facing the Mall and approached through a triumphal arch – now the "Marble Arch".

Nash's principal front of Bath stone, incorporating the shell of the original Buckingham House, overlooked the gardens which were landscaped by William Aiton. George IV died in 1830 before the "New Palace", as it also had been called, was completed. William IV was not keen to live there, suggesting that it might be used as the Houses of Parliament (following the fire at Westminster of 1834) or as a barracks. The building was eventually finished by Edward Blore (who removed Nash's much-derided dome) and in 1847 this architect provided rooms for Queen Victoria's growing family by enclosing the courtyard with a rather dull range of Caen stone facing the Mall. Nash's nephew, Sir James Pennethorne, added the south wing which contains the State Supper Room and the enormous Ballroom.

Pennethorne's work was finished in 1855, but six years later occurred the death of Prince Albert and the palace was deserted for much of Queen Victoria's long widowhood. In 1873 it was lent to the Shah of Persia for his state visit and there were some bizarre goings-on. Apparently the Shah took his meals on the floor, was reluctant to avail himself of the palace's lavatories and organized a boxing match in the garden. It has even been suggested that he had one of his staff executed with a bowstring and buried in the grounds.

Buckingham Palace cannot be said really to have come into its own until the early years of this century when it was the setting for the brilliant receptions and Court balls held by Edward VII and Queen Alexandra. George V and Queen Mary thought about returning to Kensington Palace, but after they had dropped this idea the last major alterations were made to the palace in 1913 by Sir Aston Webb. He refaced Blore's shabby east front with a facade of Portland stone looking out on to the newly-erected Victoria Memorial.

Inside Buckingham Palace, the principal rooms on the first floor include the 60-foot long Throne Room, with a ceiling and decoration that followed the designs of Nash. Some of the interior features came from Carlton House, George IV's sumptuous building capriciously pulled down in 1827. The Music Room, with its bold reliefs of putti in the spandrels of the domed ceiling, and the Blue Drawing Room are further examples of Nash's surviving designs. The Music Room is where royal christenings take place; whereas the Blue Drawing Room was used for balls until Pennethorne added the largest of all the State apartments, the Ballroom, in the 1850s. Here investitures are held, as well as the occasional state banquet and ball. The throne canopy was designed by Sir Edwin Lutyens out of the Imperial Shimiana used at the Delhi Durbar of 1911.

The highly impressive Picture Gallery is 155 feet long with an arched glass ceiling and occupies the whole of the central area of the first floor on the west side of the palace. It houses some of the finest pictures in the royal art

The stage and 'front of house' at Buckingham Palace:
The Centre Room and the Balcony (opposite); and (below)
Jubilee crowds seen from the Queen Victoria Memorial in
The Mall

collections including works by Rembrandt, Hals, Cuyp, Van Dyck and Poussin. Early in her reign Queen Victoria salvaged many of these paintings (collected by George IV) from store, where they had been placed after the destruction of Carlton House, and hung them four deep in the Picture Gallery. The hanging arrangements were no less of a muddle in Queen Mary's time, though today the old masters are sensitively arranged against a newly painted peach-coloured background.

The Chinese Dining Room, in the north-east angle of the east front facing the Mall, is the most exotic room in Buckingham Palace. It is a colourful confection of Blore's and Cubitt's made up from parts of the Music and Banqueting Rooms at Brighton Pavilion from which Queen Victoria and Prince Albert decamped in 1847. The old Queen enjoyed lunching in the room, though in modern times it has tended to be used more for meetings. This extraordinary corner room has just recently been comprehensively restored, recapturing all its vivid – not to say overwhelming – effect.

The first floor of the east front is known at the palace as the "principal floor". Along it are such rooms as the Yellow Drawing Room (with a fantastic Chinese chimneypiece) and the Blue Sitting Room. Also decorated in the Chinese taste is the Centre Room from which, on special occasions, the Queen and the royal family emerge on to the balcony overlooking the forecourt. It is a surprisingly small room; somehow one had always imagined a larger "backstage" area.

The semi-state apartments on the ground floor of Buckingham Palace include the 1855 Room (commemorating the occupation of Napoleon III and the Empress Eugénie); the Bow Room (through which the garden-party guests make their way to the lawn); the 1844 Room (named because of its occupation by Emperor Nicholas of Russia); and the Belgian Suite where Edward VII used to live. Prince Andrew was born in the Orleans Bedroom here in 1960. The Garden Entrance on the north front of the palace is the one used by the Queen and her family. After the notorious invasion of the Queen's bedroom the layout of the palace became all too familiar.

In July 1982 the Queen woke up one morning to find an unkempt, bare-footed young man drawing her bedroom curtains about half-an-hour before that chore was usually performed by her maid. The intruder, who was dripping blood from a cut thumb, then proceeded to sit on the

The Glass Coach containing Princess Anne and her father,
Prince Philip, sets off from Buckingham Palace for her marriage
to Captain Mark Phillips at Westminster Abbey, 1973

Queen's bed and pour out his troubles to the bemused but magnificently calm monarch. A few weeks earlier the strange man, Fagan by name, had broken into the palace and was alleged to have made off with half a bottle of wine; this time he had set off an alarm when he climbed through an unlocked window into the Stamp Room, only for the alarm to be promptly switched off with a curse as to the system's idiosyncracies by the bored police sergeant on duty in the control room. Having failed to gain access to Her Majesty through the locked door of the Stamp Room, Fagan climbed back out of the window and shinned up a drainpipe, to the open window of the Master of the Household's room which had been opened by a maid to let in some air. Once inside, Fagan purposefully made his way – past servants who took him for a workman – around the

Palace to the Queen's bedroom on the first, or principal, floor above the entrance on the north front. He had a notion to slash his wrists in front of his Sovereign and smashed a glass ashtray, cutting his thumb in the process, before entering the Queen's bedroom. There was no one on duty outside the room, the policeman not having been replaced earlier that morning. The corgis were taking a constitutional with a footman in the gardens.

The lamentable lack of security was now compounded by incompetence of a degree that would have been farcical if it were not so appalling. While keeping Fagan talking, the Queen pressed the night alarm bell. No response. Then the corridor bell. No response. The Queen next picked up the telephone and told the Palace telephonist in a matter of fact voice that she wanted a police officer. Six minutes later

the Queen spoke to the switchboard again to enquire why nothing had happened. Finally, on the pretext of foraging for some cigarettes for Fagan, the Queen managed to make her exit to the corridor where she encountered a maid from Middlesbrough, Elizabeth Andrew. "Bloody 'ell, Ma'am, wot's 'e doin in 'ere?" quoth this worthy – a remark the Queen was later to enjoy mimicking. The Queen herself was apparently soon employing a similar expletive when a posse of policemen finally hove into view pausing to adjust their dress the while. By this time, which must have seemed like an eternity, the Queen, Miss Andrew, the returned footman and the corgis were holding an increasingly agitated Fagan at bay in the pantry. At Fagan's subsequent trial for stealing the half bottle of wine (he was, in fact, acquitted on this charge and the asinine law of

trespass did not enable him to be prosecuted for his invasion of the Queen's bedroom), the accused told the jury: "It might be that I've done the Queen a favour. I've proved that her security system was no good."

The way the Queen had coped with her unwelcome caller emulated her mother's handling of a deserter in the Second World War. Having gained access to Queen Elizabeth's bedroom the man, who had lost all his family in an air raid, grabbed her ankles. "Tell me about it . . .", said Queen Elizabeth in her most soothing tones. In September 1940 Buckingham Palace itself had been hit, the Chapel being gutted by a salvo of bombs. In 1959 the Queen decided to create an art gallery on part of the bombed site so that the public could see masterpieces from the royal collection. Three years later a spectacular

Opposite: Interior views of Buckingham Palace. The family photographs in the Queen's Audience Room (above) indicate that this is a semi-private room unlike the more elaborate White Drawing Room (below) where members of the royal family assemble before State functions

Below: Christening group for the baptism of Zara Phillips in the Music Room at Buckingham Palace, 1981

exhibition opened "The Queen's Gallery", as it was called, and ever since there has been a rotating series of shows.

Also open to the public is the Royal Mews at Buckingham Palace which displays the collection of coaches, including Sir William Chambers's Rococo State Coach first used for the opening of Parliament in 1762. This is now the coach for Coronations; the Irish State Coach is used for the State Opening of Parliament and the Glass State Coach for royal weddings. Numerous other coaches, landaus, barouches, broughams, phaetons and sociables can be inspected, together with the Windsor greys themselves, state saddlery and other horsy tackle.

Every morning at half past eleven the guard is changed at Buckingham Palace. When the Queen is in residence, her standard flying, there is a guard of four sentries, otherwise only two. For herself and the "Royal Firm" "Buck House" is "the shop" (as her father used to call it). On the ground floor of the north wing are the offices of some of the principal members of the Royal Household. Above, on the first floor, are the suites of the Queen and Prince Philip – in effect "flats" within the Palace. The Queen's suite of rooms includes her own bow-windowed study, sitting room, Audience Room for visitors, bedroom, bathroom, dressing room and dining room; Prince Philip has an office, a library, a bedroom, bathroom and dressing room. On the floor above are bedrooms and bathrooms for members of the royal family.

If Buckingham Palace is the office, Windsor is very much home. The extent to which the royal family identifies with Windsor is illustrated by the fact that since 1917 they have taken their surname from the place. For the Queen, Windsor has become the regular weekend retreat (notwithstanding the frightful aeroplane noise); she seldom stays away, apart from her annual sojourn at Badminton for the horse trials in April. She also spends Christmas and Easter here (generally staying down for about a month around the latter holiday) as well as Ascot week in June.

Like Buckingham Palace, the Windsor Castle we see today is largely the creation of George IV. From 1824 his architect Sir Jeffrey Wyatville gave the castle a fairy-tale "medieval" air, pulling the disparate elements together to give the impression of a composite building. However absurd, and even downright ugly, Wyatville's Gothic touches may appear close up, from a distance Windsor looks like everything a castle should be.

Windsor Castle was founded by William the Conqueror as one of a chain of fortresses designed to control the Thames Valley and the environs of London. At first it was a construction of earthwork and timber erected overlooking an old Saxon palace, but the strategic position of the fortress, on the hill overhanging the river soon offset the greater comfort of the palace in the valley.

The familiar Round Tower, on top of the mound which the Conqueror had piled up, dates from the reign of the first Plantagenet monarch, Henry II, who began replacing the wooden defences of the castle with stone brought from Bagshot. In the 14th century the fortress was transformed into a magnificent castle by Edward III, carrying out an ambitious building programme with the help of William of Wykeham. Edward was not amused, however, when Wykeham had 'Hoc fecit Wykeham' carved on a wall of a tower.

The decaying old chapel was replaced by Edward IV with what he wanted to be "another and altogether more glorious building". It is said that he wanted St George's to outshine the glories of his predecessor Henry VI's chapel across the river at Eton. Work began in 1472 and the final result was a most noble Perpendicular Gothic edifice, with Henry VII being responsible for the nave and Henry VIII setting the choir roof. As it is the chapel of the Order of the Garter, the banners of the knights are hung above their stalls; the Queen's stall is marked by the Royal Standard.

Henry VIII rebuilt the entrance to the Lower Ward of the castle (the gatehouse is still named after him) and added the original wooden North Terrace overlooking what is now the Home Park. His daughter Elizabeth rebuilt the North Terrace in stone and made a pretty garden below, but the castle was too cold for her taste. For her indoor walks she built a long gallery (later adapted in the present Library) and she is said to have asked Shakespeare to write *The Merry Wives of Windsor*, reputedly first performed in the castle.

181

After the Civil War, the diarist John Evelyn recorded that the castle was "exceedingly ragged and ruinous". All this was to change with some splendour under the stylish Charles II. The King had spent much of his youth in France, forming plans to rival Versailles at Windsor, and the years of exile had increased his leanings towards the Baroque. He reconstructed the Sovereign Apartments to the design of Hugh May and if the exterior was austerely classical in style, with only an enormous Garter Star for decoration, the interior was a riot of lavish magnificence. There was an abundance of exuberant wood carvings by Philipps and the great Grinling Gibbons. Twenty vast painted ceilings were executed by Antonio Verrio, though sadly only three of these survived the redecoration by Wyatville for George IV.

Then Charles II set about constructing a grand avenue stretching away from the south front of the castle right up to the top of Snow Hill three miles away in the Great Park. This was the beginning of the Long Walk where, later, Queen Anne made a road for her chaise in which she would enjoy bowling along at a good lick, often in pursuit of a stag. The avenue which runs for another three miles through the park from Queen Anne's Gate to the Prince Consort's Gate at Windsor is still known as "Queen Anne's Ride".

The third Hanoverian monarch, "Farmer George", decided to remodel the castle. James Wyatt began work in the Gothic style at Windsor and his nephew Jeffry Wyatville carried on in earnest for George IV. His name was originally Wyatt but he had asked George IV if he could adopt this somewhat affected nomenclature to avoid confusion with the other architects in the family. "Veal or mutton, call yourself what you like," the King is said to have replied.

Sir Jeffrey Wyatville gave the Upper and Middle Wards of Windsor Castle a Gothic appearance by the romantic additions of curious windows, corbels and crenellations. In his sixteen years of work up until 1840, Wyatville also redesigned much of the interior, doubling the length of St George's Hall and building the 550 foot long Grand Corridor joining the east front to the south front. George IV was the first king to use the east front for his private apartments – a tradition actually begun by Queen Charlotte and continuing to this day – leaving the north front as the state apartments.

The best known of the state apartments is the Waterloo Chamber which the King planned towards the end of his reign to commemorate Wellington's mighty victory. It displays a stupendous series of portraits of the monarchs, soldiers and statesmen who contributed to the downfall of Napoleon; some 30 of them are by Sir Thomas Lawrence. The dining table seats 150 and every year the Queen holds

a Waterloo Banquet here on the anniversary of the battle.

George IV's other achievement at Windsor was the completion of the Long Walk. He commissioned an imposing statue of his father, George III, in the improbable garb of a Roman emperor, astride a gigantic copper horse, which was placed as an eye-catcher at the far end of the Long Walk. In June 1977 the Queen lit the "Royal Beacon" bonfire here to mark the beginning of her Silver Jubilee festivities.

Although Windsor acquired its central place in the life of the British monarchy in the Victorian era, Queen Victoria herself was not especially fond of the castle. "Windsor always appears very melancholy to me," she wrote at the beginning of her reign, "and there are so many sad associations with it". Her beloved Albert dying there did not improve matters.

Albert was buried in the Royal Mausoleum at Frogmore in Windsor Park and, in time, the Queen's own effigy was added to that of her husband. Queen Charlotte's house at Frogmore has not been lived in since the Second World

The Queen with Prince Philip in the Grand Corridor at Windsor

War, but this pretty place remains a peaceful sanctuary for the Queen and the royal family. On two or three days every year, generally in May, the public are allowed in to see the Royal Mausoleum and this specially secret garden.

Other royal buildings in the Windsor Park include the Queen's childhood home, Royal Lodge, which the Queen Mother still uses for weekends. In 1932 the small replica of a thatched Welsh cottage (*Y Bwthyn Bach*) was installed in the garden here – a present from the people of Wales to Princesses Elizabeth and Margaret.

The little Welsh cottage is a rural complement to Queen Mary's Dolls House in the castle itself which the eminent architect Sir Edwin Lutyens designed to the scale of one-twelfth. It is a wonderfully elaborate spoof, with the work of noted artists and writers of the day well represented in miniature, and is one of the most popular attractions for the public. The state apartments are open regularly, affording a glimpse of the rich variety of paintings, furniture, armoury, china and other treasures

that form part of the fabulous royal heritage that was celebrated in the eponymous television series presented by Huw Wheldon in the late 1970s.

This sumptuous series of programmes caused the normally level-headed American writer Louis Auchincloss to exclaim: "Watching the handsome and charming members of the royal family in the television series *Royal Heritage*, as they show off the treasures of their palaces, one wonders if they are finer, even rarer, than the beautiful objects which they expose gracefully to our view . . . such perfect clothes, such soft modulated voices, such stately progress". One of the most charming sequences features the Queen showing her first grandchild, Peter Phillips, round *Y Bwthyn Bach*.

The *Royal Heritage* films also touched on the work of Sir Hugh Casson, the President of the Royal Academy, who has acted as architectural adviser to the Queen concerning the renovation and – to use the word that so tickled Her Majesty when enunciated by the orotund American Ambassador Walter Annenberg in the *Royal Heritage* film –

185

Below: Driving a four-in-hand at Smith's Lawn: Prince Philip and the Queen with their granddaughter, Zara Phillips

Opposite above: The Queen's Audience Chamber, Windsor Castle. Below: The Lower Ward of the Castle, with St George's Chapel on the left and, on the right, the Round Tower flying the Royal Standard

"refurbishment" of the royal residences. Sir Hugh's firm has carried out internal redecoration and installed new bedroom suites at both Windsor and Sandringham during the Queen's reign.

In the mid-1960s the Queen switched the royal celebrations of Christmas from Sandringham to Windsor. The "Royal Firm" assembles at the castle on Christmas Eve, the immediate family staying in the Queen's Tower, the Queen Mother in the Lancaster Tower, the Gloucesters in the York Tower, the Kents in the Edward III Tower. Presents are opened at tea-time on Christmas Eve in the Red Drawing Room and then arranged in piles on a long table where they are meant to stay for general inspection. When Sir Osbert Sitwell removed his present to the privacy of his own room, he was ticked off. "Members of the family", he said, "were fond of coming down in any spare moment to gloat over the presents, other people's as well as their own". On Christmas morning there is early communion and then matins in St George's Chapel. Then comes celebratory champagne in the Green Drawing Room and lunch at one o'clock, served with the minimum of state (one chef to carve the turkey), in readiness for the Queen's Christmas broadcast at three.

For the New Year the royal caravan moves on to Sandringham. In the 1960s the aggressively forward-looking Prince Philip wanted to pull down the old pile and to build an almost equally large new one "in the style of our time". The architect David Roberts of Cambridge was commissioned to design the ambitious structure, but the Queen put the kibosh on this drastic scheme. Doubtless she had in mind how much her beloved father had cared for Sandringham. "I have always been so happy here", George VI once wrote to his mother, Queen Mary, "and I love the place". When the Queen gave birth to Prince Charles, George VI wrote excitedly that now there was the prospect of five generations at Sandringham.

It had originally been Prince Albert's idea that his wayward son Albert Edward, Prince of Wales (later Edward VII) should have a country house, where he could put down rural roots away from the fleshpots, on his coming of age in 1862. Various possibilities were mooted – including the Cholmondeleys' splendid Palladian palace in Norfolk, Houghton Hall – but the wily Lord Palmerston managed to steer the Prince Consort in the direction of the unprepossessing Sandringham Hall in the same county, with which the statesman's stepson, Charles Spencer

Cowper, was only too happy to part. Prince Albert died at the end of 1861 before the deal could go through and Albert Edward himself did not come to inspect the place until February 1862. Its initial attractions to the young Prince were the shooting and the distance from his mother at Windsor.

After toying with various improvements to the existing house, Albert Edward decided to pull the building down (save for the conservatory which became a billiard room) and start again. Prince Albert's architect A.J. Humbert, who had worked at Osborne and Frogmore, was given the go-ahead to construct a sort of "Jacobethan" structure in red brick with yellowish Ketton stone dressings. "THIS HOUSE WAS BUILT BY ALBERT EDWARD AND ALEXANDRA HIS WIFE IN THE YEAR OF OUR LORD 1870" was proudly inscribed above the door.

Colonel R.W. Edis, a rather superior architect to Humbert (which was not saying a great deal), added a ballroom and was later called in again to remodel the house after a bad fire just before Albert Edward's 50th birthday celebrations. As far as the appearance of the house was concerned, the fire was something of a blessing in disguise. Even so, no one could claim that Sandringham is a work of much architectural merit – it has been compared, unfavourably, to an hotel in Harrogate.

The point is, though, that Sandringham was, in Albert Edward's words, "the house I like best". George V also loved "dear old Sandringham" better than anywhere else in the world. His eldest son, Edward VIII, took a less sympathetic view, describing Sandringham as a "voracious white elephant" and apparently vowing to "fix those bloody clocks" on the night of his father's death in 1936. Shooting has always dominated life here and the clocks used to be kept half-an-hour fast in order to fit in an extra half-hour's shooting on the dark winter days.

The Queen and the royal family often use the more homely six-bedroomed Wood Farm (where her little-known epileptic uncle, Prince John, lived out his thirteen years) on the estate when they come to stay. Apart from Sir Hugh Casson's "improvements", the "big house", which is open to the public in the summer months, remains much as it was in Queen Alexandra's day. There

Below: The Saloon at Sandringham. The clocks used to be set half-an-hour fast so as to squeeze in the maximum amount of shooting

Bottom: The cosy six-bedroomed farmhouse at Wolferton, Wood Farm, where the Queen's epileptic uncle Prince John used to live and in which the royal family stay from time to time as a break from the "big house"

are notable collections of Fabergé's work, Worcester porcelain, Edwardian knicknacks, sporting pictures and cases of game. The gardens are Sandringham's best feature with two lakes and more than 200 different varieties of rhododendron, as well as daffodils, camellias, azaleas and primulas.

One of the lakes, York Cottage Lake, takes its name from the "most undesirable residence" where Prince George, Duke of York, and Princess May of Teck (later George V and Queen Mary) brought up their family. Sir Harold Nicolson, George V's official biographer, described York Cottage as:

A glum little villa . . . The rooms inside, with their fumed oak surrounds, their white overmantels framing oval mirrors, their Doulton tiles and stained glass fanlights, are indistinguishable from those of any Surbiton or Upper Norwood home.

For all the sneers about Sandringham, it still expresses the role of monarch as simple country squire better than anywhere else among the Queen's homes. In Norfolk the Queen lives the life of a local landowner, driving herself around the estate, popping into shops, attending the Women's Institute. Once when she was in a teashop, clad in her customary headscarf and "Husky", the Queen was buttonholed by what can only have been a stranger to those parts. "Excuse me", the woman said, "but you do look awfully like the Queen". The Queen replied, with a smile: "How very reassuring".

At Holyroodhouse, however, her official residence in Edinburgh, the Queen is very much on duty during her annual stint in the Scottish capital. A garden party and other state occasions take place here, enhanced by the presence of the Queen's Body Guard, the Royal Company of Archers, in their historic green uniforms. State visits have been paid to Scotland in recent years by the Kings of Norway and Sweden when the special character of the palace was seen at its best. For all its somewhat forbidding appearance, Holyroodhouse is one of the most fascinating of royal palaces; with a combination of intimacy and grandeur that is particularly Scottish.

Below the cliffs of that brooding, extinct volcano, Arthur's Seat, David I, King of Scots, established a house of Augustinian canons, presenting the community with a reliquary containing a fragment of the True Cross; in consequence the abbey was dedicated to the Holy Cross or Holy Rood. Like other religious houses, Holyrood was used by the Kings of Scotland, though their Edinburgh stronghold remained the castle. Of the medieval abbey all that now remains are the ruined nave of the church and the foundations of its transepts and quire. The guest house, west of the main monastic building, was altered and enlarged by James IV (1488–1513), who was determined to make Edinburgh the undisputed capital of Scotland and to give it a suitably magnificent royal palace. James V carried on the building work at Holyroodhouse and the Great Tower (of 1529–32) survives from this period.

Mary Queen of Scots's son James VI came to live at Holyroodhouse in 1578 at the age of twelve and spent more time here than any other monarch; but after travelling south to become King James I of England he only returned once, in 1617, when some repairs and improvements were carried out to the palace. Holyroodhouse ceased to have regular occupation for nearly 200 years. Nevertheless, major building plans were put in hand after the Restoration of Charles II. In works lasting from 1671 to 1680, the great 16th-century tower was remodelled and the rest of the palace was rebuilt. Sir William Bruce and Robert Mylne produced a new quadrangle in an austere style, though the plain walls were relieved in places by typically Scottish turrets. Inside, however, were rich furnishings and tapestries; the Gallery was adorned with 111 portraits, many of them fanciful, of Scottish kings painted by an enterprising Dutch artist called Jacob de Witt. In spite of these elaborate preparations Charles II never turned up.

At long last, interest in the palace was revived by George IV's popular visit to Scotland in 1822. Inspired by Sir Walter Scott, the ample George donned a kilt, wearing flesh-coloured tights to preserve his modesty. The success of this adventure can be seen as a prologue to Queen

Right: The porte-cochère *and main entrance to the new castle at Balmoral, which was ready for occupation in 1855. Below: the entrance front at Birkhall, the Queen Mother's Balmoral retreat, with its sturdy rustic porch*

Victoria's attachment to Scotland and to Holyroodhouse remaining intact as a royal palace. As early as the 1850s the Queen ordered that the royal apartments should be open to the public. She was fond of driving round Arthur's Seat, where the impression of being far away from it all in the Highlands (although still on the edge of a city) is just as striking today as it was then. The route has become known as "The Queen's Drive". Queen Victoria started the custom, continued by the present Queen, of occupying Holyroodhouse for a brief period every year.

The Queen's other residence in Scotland, Balmoral Castle in Aberdeenshire, remains a special private holiday home for herself and her family, a world apart. Here, in the words of Balmoral's historian Ronald Clark, the Queen can still "take a deep breath on her own property and – with the exception of an unending stream of dispatch boxes – live with her family the life of a Scottish landowner". Stalking, walking, fishing, barbecuing, picnicking, sketching – interspersed with visits to Crathie Church and the Highland games at Braemar and Ballater nearby – are the order of the day. The Prince of Wales's best-selling book for children (originally written for Prince Edward), *The Old Man of Loch-na-Gar,* was inspired by Balmoral.

Up until the mid-19th century previous royal residences had all been Crown property but when Queen Victoria and Prince Albert bought Balmoral from the Duff family in 1852 it was a private sale; the purchase price came out of a bequest from an idiosyncratic old miser, John Camden Neild, who died that year leaving his considerable fortune to the Queen. For Albert, with his passion for architectural projects, this buckshee cash was like an answer to a prayer. Together with his architect William Smith, Prince Albert chose a site only 100 yards from the old house for a new castle to be built in the now highly popular Scotch Baronial style. Albert and Smith's idea was to create a piece of scenic architecture so that the new castle and the new gardens should be in keeping with the range of foothills rising to the summit of Loch-na-Gar. The landscaping was deputed to James Giles.

The new castle was ready for occupation by September 1855, the old being demolished. Multi-turreted with castellated gables, a *porte-cochère* and a 100-foot tower, the new castle was built of grey Invergelder granite, had 180 windows and 67 fireplaces as well as a central heating system, four bathrooms and fourteen water-closets. "The new house looks beautiful", wrote Queen Victoria in her journal, ". . . charming; the rooms delightful; the furniture, papers, everything perfection".

At the end of each summer, Victoria and Albert returned to their beloved Balmoral. Every year, as the Queen wrote in her journal:

My heart becomes more fixed in this dear Paradise and so much more so now that *all* has become my dear *Albert's* own creation, own work, own building, own laying-out . . . and his great taste and the impress of his dear hand, have been stamped everywhere.

Inside the castle the main effect of this impress was in the ubiquitous overwhelming tartan and the motif of the thistle. One of the Queen's granddaughters described the décor as "more patriotic than artistic and had a way of flickering before your eyes and confusing your brain".

The castle is essentially Victorian, and George V, who was more of a "Victorian" than his father, Edward VII, had a greater affection for it. He and his son George VI used to come for at least two months in the autumn, a practice followed by the Queen. Lord Home has described the Queen's sojourns as "the big rest".

The Queen's hereditary love of the Highlands has, of course, been amplified by the Scots blood of the Queen Mother who has made Birkhall into a charming retreat on the Balmoral estate, adding a bow-fronted wing to the old Scottish "ha-house" in the 1950s. The Queen Mother's friend and courtier Ruth Lady Fermoy, who hails from Aberdeenshire, is chiefly responsible for the high proportion of Scots blood in her granddaughter the Princess of Wales (though the press would have one believe she finds life at Balmoral boring) – and hence her sons. The Prince and Princess of Wales, alias the Duke and Duchess of Rothesay, make their Scottish home in another house on the Balmoral estate, Delnadamph Lodge.

10. The Queen and Her Court

During the preparations for the Queen's Coronation in 1953 there was much delving in documents to establish orders of precedence and so forth. With the help of Henry VIII's 1539 "Acte for the placing of the Lordes in the Parliamt" it was established that the following . were "Great Officers of the Realm": the Lord Chancellor; the Lord President of the Council; the Lord Privy Seal; the Lord Great Chamberlain; the Lord High Constable; the Earl Marshal; the Lord Steward of the Household; the Lord Chamberlain; and the Master of the Horse. Of these, the Lord Chancellor, the Lord Privy Seal and the Lord President are now politicians rather than courtiers.

The Lord Great Chamberlain's duties are largely ceremonial. He should not be confused with the Lord Chamberlain, who is very much a full-time courtier. Although at one stage the Lord Great Chamberlains of old had responsibility for all the royal palaces, the office's modern duties extend only to the administration of the Queen's apartments at the Palace of Westminster – that is to say the robing room, the staircase, anteroom and royal gallery. At the State Opening of Parliament the Lord Great Chamberlain walks backwards in front of the Queen in the royal procession. He is also to the fore at other ceremonial occasions at Westminster; for example, when President Reagan addressed the Houses of Parliament in the Royal Gallery during his 1983 visit, the Lord Great Chamberlain conducted him in and out.

The hereditary office of Lord Great Chamberlain was first granted to Alberic de Vere by Henry II in 1133. In default of male heirs, the post was able to pass through the female line. At one stage there were five sisters who all had equally valid rights as co-heiresses to appoint their husbands as deputies for the job. Since they could not agree, some confusion ensued. The matter was thrashed out once and for all in the Committee of Privileges of the House of Lords at the beginning of this century. The upshot was that the family of Cholmondeley was entitled to the office in alternate reigns and that the Earl of Ancaster and the Marquess of Lincolnshire should alternate in those reigns when the office was not in the keeping of the Marquess of Cholmondeley.

In the reign of George VI the acting Lord Great Chamberlain was the Earl of Ancaster. The late Earl was married to the only daughter of the 2nd Viscount Astor and of his outspoken American wife Nancy, the first female to sit in the House of Commons. The Ancasters' only son, was lost at sea in the Mediterranean in 1963; his sister Jane, who has inherited the ancient Barony of Willoughby de Eresby, was one of the Queen's Train Bearers at the Coronation.

At the beginning of the Queen's reign Lord Ancaster was succeeded as Lord Great Chamberlain by the late Marquess of Cholmondeley, husband of the beautiful heiress Sybil Sassoon, who has restored the family's Palladian palace in Norfolk, Houghton. Their son, the present Marquess and Lord Great Chamberlain, lives at Cholmondeley Castle in Cheshire where the family has been seated since the 12th century. Lord Cholmondeley won the Military Cross at the Battle of Alamein in the Second World War and has run the family estate since retiring from the Army. Rather in the traditions of P.G. Wodehouse's the Earl of Emsworth, the Lord Great Chamberlain is a dedicated breeder of rare farm animals, notably a pig that is a cross between a black Berkshire boar and a chestnut Tamworth sow. His son, the Earl of Rocksavage, is a former page of honour to the Queen; one of his daughters is a concert pianist, another married the son of John Huston, the film director.

As the Marquessate of Lincolnshire is now extinct, the office of Lord Great Chamberlain in the next reign will be filled by the late Marquess's nearest male relation. At the present this is Lord Carrington, the Tory statesman who resigned as Foreign Secretary after the Argentine army landed on the Falkland Islands in 1982 and later became Secretary-General of NATO.

The office of Lord High Constable, traditionally held in the past by the commander-in-chief of the army, is now only revived on special ceremonial occasions. Thus at the Queen's Coronation, Field-Marshal Lord Alanbrooke, one of the extraordinary number of Ulstermen to become Chief of the Imperial General Staff in recent times, rode near the Queen's coach in his temporary capacity as Lord High Constable.

The Earl Marshal, originally the Lord High Constable's deputy, is, in effect, the master of ceremonies for "state" – as opposed to "court", or family – occasions. In the Queen's reign the principal state occasions, apart from the regular Openings of Parliament, have been the Coronation, the Investiture of the Prince of Wales and the funeral of Sir Winston Churchill. The Earl Marshal is also head of the College of Arms, a late 17th-century building near St Paul's Cathedral housing the Kings, Heralds and Pursuivants of Arms of England who assist him in the marshalling of State ceremonial, as well as registering pedigrees and armorial bearings.

The Kings of Arms (the three senior heralds) are authorized by the Queen to grant coats of arms to "eminent men", subject to the Earl Marshal's approval. The heralds, incidentally, define a gentleman as a man entitled to bear arms; in other words, a grant of arms is given to a man on the assumption that he is a gentleman already and does not in itself make him one. Even today, the Kings of Arms like to satisfy themselves that the 150 or

so people to whom arms are granted each year are
gentlemen. The question of how they manage to do so
gives rise to a certain amount of cynical speculation – there
are stories of heralds taking candidates for grants out to
luncheon, in order to observe how they eat their peas.

The office of Earl Marshal is hereditary in the Howard
family. First conferred on Thomas of Brotherton in 1385,
it was later held by the Mowbrays before Richard III
created John Howard Duke of Norfolk and Earl Marshal in
1483. The present Duke of Norfolk, Miles Fitzalan-
Howard, has played a leading part in Catholic affairs since
succeeding his cousin in 1975 (it is one of the nice ironies of
British life that the job of organizing the Anglican ritual of
the Coronation of the "Defender of the Faith" should vest
in a Catholic dynasty). Being Duke of Norfolk and Earl
Marshal is, so to speak, his third career; the other two
being the Army, in which he rose to the rank of Major-
General, and merchant banking. His son and heir is a
motor-racing driver (known on the tracks as "Eddie
Arundel"); one of his daughters, the actress Marsha
Fitzalan, is married to a fellow thespian Patrick Ryecart;
another to David Frost, the television tycoon.

By contrast, the Earl Marshal's predecessor, Bernard,
the 16th Duke, inherited the dukedom at the age of eight
and thus devoted the whole of his adult life to being Duke
of Norfolk and everything that it entailed. His masterly
management of the ceremonial for the great State
occasions, which displayed a sharper awareness of the
modern world (particularly as to the importance of the
television coverage) than his forbidding external
appearance might have suggested, helped make him a
national figure more like the dukes of former times than
those of the present.

The office of Lord Steward of the Household, which
chiefly involves the formal arrangements for State
Banquets and other ceremonial occasions, is not
hereditary. Since 1973 it has been held by the Duke of
Northumberland, owner of Alnwick Castle in
Northumberland, the medieval stronghold of the Percys
(his ancestors in the female line) and Syon House,
overlooking the Thames opposite Kew Gardens. Would-
be debunkers of the antiquity of the peerage find the
Duke's male-line descent from the Yorkshire Smithsons an
unfailing source of ammunition. After Sir Hugh Smithson
had married the eventual heiress of the extinct Percys,
changed his name to Percy and inherited his father-in-law's
Earldom of Northumberland, he solicited the Order of the
Garter from George II. The King gave it to him, but
remarked that he was "the first Smithson to have it". The
present Hughie Northumberland also has the Garter and
can claim more ducal connexions than any other peer at the
present time, when it is less usual for dukes to marry the

199

Below: The Queen is presented with a whale's tooth by a Fijian chief on Britannia's *arrival in Suva during the Silver Jubilee tour of the Commonwealth. Behind the Queen are some of her back-up team led by Sir Martin Charteris, the then Private Secretary (the bald-headed figure to the left of the Queen's hat)*

Opposite: The Princess of Wales presents her hand to be kissed by the Crown Equerry, Sir John Miller, at Waterloo Station on route for her honeymoon at Broadlands. Sir "Johnny" Johnston, the Comptroller of the Lord Chamberlain's Office in the left foreground, received a kiss on the cheek from the Princess

daughters of dukes than it was formerly. He is himself married to a duke's daughter, both his sisters married dukes; his mother was the daughter of a duke and so was his paternal grandmother.

In the past many of the Court appointments were political, that is to say the personnel changed according to the party in power. For example, Queen Anne's reign saw the jockeying for position at Court between the fiercely Whiggish Sarah Duchess of Marlborough and her detested Tory cousin Abigail Hill (Lady Masham). At the beginning of Queen Victoria's reign there was the "Bedchamber Crisis" when the Queen refused to have her Whig ladies of the bedchamber replaced by Tories after the defeat of Lord Melbourne by Sir Robert Peel. Until the advent of Ramsay MacDonald and the first Labour Government in 1924, a new Lord Chamberlain, the senior officer in the Royal Household, was appointed not upon the accession of a new monarch but rather upon the formation of a new political administration. As poor old MacDonald did not feel he could come up with anyone who would be palatable both to the King and his Socialist

comrades, George V and the Prime Minister came to the conclusion that it would be best to make the Lord Chamberlain a non-political appointment. So it has remained.

The Lord Chamberlain looks after the organization of State Visits by foreign Heads of State, Court ceremonies (such as royal weddings and funerals, but not State funerals) and garden parties. His wide range of responsibilities range from the maintenance of the royal palaces and residences to matters of precedence (in which his department is sometimes in conflict with the College of Arms over, for instance, such thorny questions as the definite article in front of courtesy titles), from the flying of flags to the care of the Queen's Swans. The Lord Chamberlain sees to all appointments to the Household including the Queen's ecclesiastical and medical functionaries, the Marshal of the Diplomatic Corps, the Gentlemen Ushers, the Gentlemen at Arms, the Queen's Bodyguard, the Master of the Queen's Music, the Poet Laureate and the Queen's Bargemaster. The Central Chancery of the Orders of Knighthood and the various

experts who look after the royal collections also come under the authority of the Lord Chamberlain. The Puritan legacy of the responsibility for stage censorship was relinquished in the late 1960s, ushering in the exposure of *Hair* (and little else). This thankfully abandoned chore had yielded some richly absurd exchanges between the Court and the theatre. For instance, when the script of the early 1960s satirical revue *Beyond the Fringe* was submitted for the Lord Chamberlain's approval, the gentleman responsible for the licensing of plays in the Lord Chamberlain's Department at St James's Palace pointed out that a stage direction reading *"Enter two outrageous old queens"* would be acceptable if altered to *"Enter two aesthetic young men"*.

The Lord Chamberlain's Office, which has its own Comptroller ranking with the heads of the other four departments of the Household (those of Private Secretary to the Queen, the Keeper of the Privy Purse, the Master of the Household and the Crown Equerry), also issues Royal Warrants to tradesmen basking under royal patronage. At the end of each year a list of names of individuals and firms

holding "warrants of appointment" is published in the official organ, the *London Gazette*. The thousand or so tradesmen can then display the royal arms above their premises and on their merchandise with the legend "By Appointment".

The present Lord Chamberlain is the Earl of Airlie, who took over from his fellow Scot Lord Maclean at the beginning of 1985. The owlish perfectionist "Chips" Maclean had a busy programme of special ceremonial events on top of his normal Household chores in his fourteen years at St James's Palace. The funeral of the Duke of Windsor in the spring of 1972 gave him something of a baptism of fire. Eagle-eyed royalty watchers noted how, in accordance with Court etiquette, Lord Maclean did not bow to the Duchess of Windsor as he bade her farewell at Heathrow afterwards.

Happier occasions in the Maclean era were the Queen's silver wedding celebrations that autumn and Princess Anne's wedding the following year. During the rehearsal for the latter, Lord Maclean took the part of the Queen amid general hilarity. His wife, a member of the Mann

brewing and sporting dynasty, completed a remarkable double by standing in for the Queen at the rehearsal for the Silver Jubilee service at St Paul's Cathedral in 1977. The 1981 wedding of the Prince and Princess of Wales saw the climax of yet more beavering away in the background by the Lord Chamberlain and his staff. He and the Comptroller of the Lord Chamberlain's Office, Sir "Johnny" Johnston, were rewarded for their trouble by a kiss each from the Princess of Wales at Waterloo Station before she boarded the honeymoon special for Broadlands.

Lord Airlie is perhaps best known as the elder brother of Princess Alexandra's husband, Angus Ogilvy. The Ogilvy family has a romantic Jacobite past, remaining staunchly loyal to the Stuarts during the 18th century and only having the attainted Earldom of Airlie restored to them in 1826, but this has not prevented more recent members of the family from being faithful courtiers of the House of Windsor. Lord Airlie's father, the 12th Earl, was a Lord-in-Waiting to George V and Lord Chamberlain to the Queen Mother, and the 12th Earl's mother, Mabell Countess of Airlie, was a Lady of the Bedchamber to Queen Mary and also wrote some engaging memoirs of her life at Court, *Thatched with Gold*. Formerly a merchant banker in the City of London, Lord Airlie is married to Virginia Ryan, who comes from an American family prominent at Newport, Rhode Island, and is a Lady of the Bedchamber to the Queen. Their son, Lord Ogilvy, a former page of honour to the Queen, is married to a daughter of Viscount Rothermere, owner of the *Daily Mail*, and his wife, the ebullient hostess "Bubbles".

After the Lord Chamberlain in the roll of "great officers" at Court comes the Master of the Horse, whose traditional duties include being responsible for the Queen's safety whenever she is mounted on a horse or in a carriage. At the Queen's Birthday Parade, he can be seen riding in the group immediately behind the sovereign. Since 1978 the Master of the Horse has been the Earl of Westmorland, previously a long-serving Lord-in-Waiting and a former Captain in the Royal Horse Guards (the "Blues"). He and his wife Barbara are particularly close friends of the Queen, sharing her passionate love of the Turf. Westmorland's heir, Lord Burghersh, was once a "greeter" at Wedgie's nightclub in the King's Road but has now taken up a more respectable career in the City.

The Westmorlands live only a few miles away from Badminton, the seat of the previous Master of the Horse, the late Duke of Beaufort, aptly described by Randolph Churchill as "the greatest horseman in the kingdom". The doyen of the equestrian world and a legendary figure in the hunting field, the Duke served a record 42-year stint as Master of the Horse to Edward VIII, George VI and the present Queen until a hunting accident caused his retirement. The nickname of "Master", by which the Duke was known to this family and friends, did not, however, originate from this, or from the fact that he was Master of the Beaufort Hunt – as is often erroneously stated – but goes back to when he was eight and his father, the 9th Duke, gave him his own pack of harriers. The great sportsman, an endearingly simple and straightforward figure, brought an historic touch of Plantagenet to the Queen's Court for he was a direct descendant in the male line (albeit broken by illegitimacy in early Tudor times) of John of Gaunt. As a farewell present to her loyal and devoted "Master", the Queen, who used to stay at Badminton every year for the Horse Trials he started in 1949, commissioned a special portrait by Terence Cuneo. The picture shows Master mounted in the courtyard at Buckingham Palace with the unprecedented appearance of the Queen and Prince Philip in, so to speak, supporting roles looking on. It used to decorate the Duke's study at Badminton, together with an autographed picture of Basil Brush, the pursuit of whose fur-and-blood kinsfolk was Master's unremitting vocation.

The Master of the Horse has overall responsibility for the royal stables but the Royal Mews and Garages are run on a day-to-day basis by the Crown Equerry, Sir John Miller, who has been in the saddle since leaving the Welsh Guards in 1961. Similarly the practicalities of the domestic arrangements of the Court are handled not by the Lord Steward, as his title might suggest, but by the Master of the Household. From 1973 until 1985, this post was held by Vice-Admiral Sir Peter Ashmore, a former Chief of Allied Staff at the NATO Naval HQ. Unfortunately Sir Peter was thus at the helm during the invasion of the Queen's bedroom in 1982 and, as his responsibilities

Right: Derby Day, 1980. (Left to right: Lord Porchester, the Queen's racing manager, the Queen Mother, the Crown Equerry, Sir John Miller and the Queen.) Opposite: The late Lord Rupert Nevill, Prince Philip's adviser. Centre: The Marchioness of Abergavenny, Lady of the Bedchamber. Top right: The Duchess of Grafton, Mistress of the Robes.
Below: Security for the Queen's visit to Jordan, 1984. Sir Philip Moore and Michael Shea, the press secretary, bring up the rear

include the Palace police, he had to endure some heavy fire across the bows in the wake of the appalling security lapses. To make matters worse there was the contemporaneous blaze of publicity about the Queen's personal bodyguard Michael Trestrail. Seeing the policeman's name in the newspapers at the time of the enquiry into the Fagan intrusion (with which Trestrail had no connexion), an unscrupulous homosexual acquaintance of his had attempted to blackmail the Queen's bodyguard, leading to the wretched man's resignation. Amid the distasteful hysteria that erupted after this revelation the gossips would have had one believe there was hardly a heterosexual employed in the Household. The "glamour" of Court life, it was claimed, held a "gay" allure.

The senior lady in the Queen's Household is the Mistress of the Robes, who accompanies the Queen on important occasions and arranges the rota for the other ladies-in-waiting. Since 1967 this part-time job has been held by the Duchess of Grafton, wife of one of the old wartime "Body Guard" attendant on Princess Elizabeth at Windsor. The Duke of Grafton, descended from Charles II's bastard son by his mistress Barbara Villiers and sometimes known as the "Duke of Conservation" on account of his multifarious activities on behalf of the heritage, married Fortune Smith, from a family long associated with the National Provincial Bank, shortly after the war. They live at Euston Hall in Suffolk, originally built for the Duke's ancestor, the 1st Earl of Arlington (the first "A" in Charles II's "Cabal") whose London house once occupied the site of the present Buckingham Palace. The Graftons rank among the Queen's closest friends. The Duchess is the *doyenne* of the Queen's Court, having first become a Lady of the Bedchamber in 1953.

The present Ladies of the Bedchamber are the Marchioness of Abergavenny and the Countess of Airlie. The Abergavennys must also rank among the Queen's intimate friends. Lord Abergavenny was formerly the Queen's representative at Ascot and his son the Earl of Lewes was a page of honour to the Queen before he died of leukaemia at the age of seventeen. Tragedy has stalked the historic medieval dynasty of Nevill in modern times for the Abergavenny's third daughter also died as a child and the present Marquess's brother, Lord Rupert Nevill, died well before his time in 1982. The Duchess of Grafton described his loss as "an appalling blow". As Norman St John-Stevas wrote in a valedictory tribute to Lord Rupert:

On important matters of state his discretion, as befitted a counsellor of the monarch, was rock-like. He was near the centre of that magic circle, both as servant and friend, but you would never have guessed that from his conversation. Prince Philip, whom he served so faithfully and well (as Treasurer and then Private Secretary), paid him a rare and right last tribute when he read the lesson from the Book of Wisdom of Solomon at his obsequies.

Below (left): William ("Bill") Heseltine, the Western Australian who has been deputy private secretary to the Queen since 1977. Right: The Marquess of Abergavenny, head of a courtierly family
Bottom: The wedding group of Robert Fellowes, now the Queen's assistant private secretary, and Lady Jane Spencer. The senior bridesmaid (on the right of the back row) was the future Princess of Wales

Opposite: Behind the Queen and the Prime Minister of Jamaica, come the courtly camp followers. Brian McGrath, Prince Philip's private secretary, and Sir Philip Moore are on the top steps; below them are Surgeon-Captain Norman Blackrock (medical officer), Squadron-Leader Adam Wise (equerry in waiting to the Queen), Michael Shea (press secretary) Robert Fellowes (assistant private secretary), Lady Susan Hussey and Lady Abel Smith (ladies in waiting), Air Vice Marshal John Severne (Captain of the Queen's Flight) is on the tarmac

For the Queen Lord Rupert's death was doubtless the most severe of the many misfortunes (the others including the Fagan intrusion, the Trestrail resignation and the devastation of her Household Cavalry in Hyde Park) that befell her in the black month of July 1982.

Next in the pecking order after the Ladies of the Bedchamber (who are usually Countesses or upwards) come the Women of the Bedchamber. The current quartet are: Mary Morrison, Lady Susan Hussey, Lady Abel Smith and Mrs John Dugdale. "Mossy" Morrison is the unmarried daughter of the Tory elder statesman Lord Margadale, a great-grandson of the 19th-century Scots haberdashery tycoon James Morrison and the owner of large estates in Wiltshire and on Islay. Lady Susan Hussey, youngest daughter of the Earl Waldegrave and sister of the young Tory politician William Waldegrave (widely tipped to be a future Prime Minister), is married to "Duke" Hussey, the former managing director of Times Newspapers. Their son James was a page of honour to the Queen and Lady Susan is a godmother to Prince Henry of Wales. Lady Abel Smith, a Cadogan by birth, is the sister-in-law of the most junior member of the "royal family" on the Court list of precedence, Colonel Sir Henry Abel Smith. Mrs Dugdale, daughter of politician Oliver Stanley, is the wife of the Lord-Lieutenant of Shropshire.

All these aristocratic names might seem to bear out the erstwhile Lord Altrincham's rather prissy strictures made nearly thirty years ago. "The present composition of the Court", he wrote, "emphasises the social lopsideness to which the Monarchy is still prone". He continued:

The Queen's entourage – those who serve her from day to day, who accompany her when she travels and sit with her when she eats – are almost without exception people of the "tweedy" sort. Such people may be shrewd, broad-minded and thoroughly suitable for positions at Court, but the same is true of many who are not "tweedy"; and the fact that the Queen's personal staff represents almost exclusively a single social type creates an unfortunate impression. Worse still, courtiers are nearly always citizens of one Commonwealth country – the United Kingdom. In other words, the Court has lamentably failed to move with the times; while the Monarchy has become "popular" and multi-racial, the Court has remained a tight little enclave of British "ladies and gentlemen". This cannot be right.

Lord Altrincham (later John Grigg) went on to call for a truly classless and Commonwealth Court".

At what could be called the sharp end – as opposed to the ceremonial fiddle-faddle – Altrincham's point has, however, clearly had some effect. Sir Philip Moore, the holder of by far the most important job at Court – Private Secretary – is cast in a different mould from his predecessors. A career civil servant and diplomatist, Sir Philip is said to have favoured a fundamental change in the whole Palace set-up, wanting to make it all tick over more

along the lines of a Government department than an "anachronistic" Court. In this aim he has not, perhaps, been able to count on the wholehearted support of his "chief", the Queen, who tends to like things to go along as they did in her dear father's day. However, under the progressive influence of Prince Philip, an Australian civil servant who first came to prominence as private secretary to Sir Robert Menzies has been steadily groomed as "Number Two" to Sir Philip Moore (who, incidentally, will be 65 in 1986). When he became assistant press secretary to the Queen in 1960, Bill Heseltine was reported to be the first grammar-school educated person to work at "executive" level in the Palace. As press secretary from 1967 to 1972, Heseltine is credited with initiating the "walkabout", playing a key role in setting up the *Royal Family* film and generally polishing up the media "image". His successors in that job have not enjoyed his run of luck; one unfortunate felt obliged to resign after denying (doubtless in good faith as the press office is often the last to know about such matters) that there was any question of Princess Anne and Mark Phillips becoming engaged only a few months before they duly did so. Too often in the post-Heseltine era the press office has felt obliged in its desire to be helpful to the media to say something, however inane and impertinent. There have been times when the attitude of the Queen's much-maligned first press secretary Commander Colville (an exemplar of the silent service whose main qualification for his job seemed to be a singular distaste for journalists) would have been infinitely preferable. The present incumbent is Michael Shea, an able Scot on secondment from the Foreign Office whose interests include sailing and writing thrillers.

Heseltine (now Sir William), no apparent relation to his possible future counterpart at Number Ten Downing Street, moved up to become assistant private secretary and then deputy private secretary. The present assistant private secretary, Robert Fellowes, comes from the traditional "tweedy" background; his father Sir William Fellowes, a scion of an East Anglian squirearchical dynasty, was agent at Sandringham for 28 years. Robert Fellowes is married to the Princess of Wales's middle sister, Lady Jane Spencer.

Under the Private Secretary come the royal archives, the secretariat and the press office. The Privy Purse Department looks after the royal accounts (including the Duchy of Lancaster). In addition to the Queen's Household, the Duke of Edinburgh, the Queen Mother, the Prince and Princess of Wales, Princess Anne, Princess Margaret, Princess Alice, the Duke and Duchess of Gloucester, the Duke and Duchess of Kent, Prince and Princess Michael and Princess Alexandra all have "Households" of their own even if in some cases this only runs to a private secretary and a lady-in-waiting. In the

The "wedding of the year" 1975: a key event for students of the "outer circle" of royalty — the Queen's cousin, the Earl of Lichfield marries Lady Leonora Grosvenor, daughter of the Duke of Westminster Lord Lichfield's mother, Princess Georg of Denmark, was a Bowes-Lyon. The royal turn-out included the Queen, the Queen Mother, Princess Beatrix (later Queen of the Netherlands), King Constantine and Queen Anne-Marie, Prince Michael of Kent, Princess Benedikte of Denmark and Lord Mountbatten

spring of 1985 there was a surprising departure from the Court when Edward Adeane, private secretary and treasurer to the Prince and Princess of Wales, left his post amid groundless press speculation that he and the Princess had not seen eye to eye. An able lawyer, the bachelor Adeane had been expected to follow in the footsteps of his father, Lord Adeane (Private Secretary to the Queen from 1953 to 1972) and great-grandfather, Lord Stamfordham (Private Secretary to Queen Victoria and George V). He may, of course, yet do so – notwithstanding tittle-tattle about the "Fall of the House of Adeane".

The Queen, unlike say Charles II, George IV or Edward VII, is not a sociable monarch. She has never shown any inclination to go on royal progresses staying at grand country houses. In this she takes after her father who rather prided himself on not being "smart" (a distinctly uncomplimentary term in certain circles as Evelyn Waugh observes in *Vile Bodies*) or fashionable. Once when some young man produced a swizzle stick in the royal presence to stir his drink, George VI, after mildly remonstrating with him over this social solecism, added that it was, of course, "all right with *us*" – but it would never do in "Society". The Queen's closest friends tend to be drawn largely from those who help share her burden at Court. Even the apparent exceptions, such as the Martens of Crichel in Dorset, tend to have Court connexions; George Marten, a naval commander, was an equerry to George VI. The other basis for the Queen's friendships is, of course, a mutual interest in sport, or more specifically the Turf.

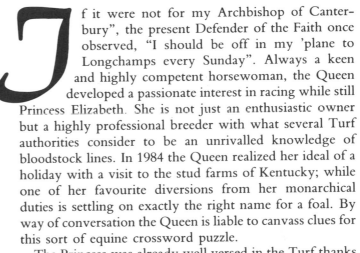

*I*f it were not for my Archbishop of Canterbury", the present Defender of the Faith once observed, "I should be off in my 'plane to Longchamps every Sunday". Always a keen and highly competent horsewoman, the Queen developed a passionate interest in racing while still Princess Elizabeth. She is not just an enthusiastic owner but a highly professional breeder with what several Turf authorities consider to be an unrivalled knowledge of bloodstock lines. In 1984 the Queen realized her ideal of a holiday with a visit to the stud farms of Kentucky; while one of her favourite diversions from her monarchical duties is settling on exactly the right name for a foal. By way of conversation the Queen is liable to canvass clues for this sort of equine crossword puzzle.

The Princess was already well versed in the Turf thanks to her racing mentor Captain Charles Moore (the Irishman who was her father's racing manager) when the expansive Aga Khan gave her a filly as a wedding present in 1947. *Astrakhan*, as she called her, won at the now defunct Hurst Park, on the flat in 1949 and in that year Lord Mildmay of Flete, the celebrated amateur rider, persuaded Queen Elizabeth (now the Queen Mother) and the Princess to buy *Monaveen*, a strapping Irish steeplechaser. Trained by "Lordy" Mildmay's great friend Peter Cazalet, *Monaveen* won several races over the sticks before a disappointing run in the Grand National. In 1950 *Monaveen* broke his leg at the Hurst Park water jump and had to be put down. Bitterly upset, Princess Elizabeth never recovered her enthusiasm for National Hunt racing and dedicated herself to the flat. Her mother, however, stuck with the "winter game", buying Anthony Mildmay's horse *Manicou* after the peer was mysteriously drowned off the Devon coast and then another Irish 'chaser, *Devon Loch* which even more inexplicably spreadeagled on the run–in to the finish of the 1956 Grand National with the race at his mercy.

Together with the crown, the Queen inherited the royal studs and several racehorses in training with Captain Cecil Boyd-Rochfort (a scion of an Irish Ascendancy family and stepfather of the future champion trainer, Henry Cecil) and Noel Murless at Newmarket. The Queen's first major success as an owner came through *Aureole* which won the Derby Trial at Lingfield and was strongly fancied to win the blue riband of racing itself in the summer of the Coronation. A story is told of how, not long before the Queen was due to set out for Westminster Abbey for the ceremony, a lady-in-waiting asked if all was well. "Oh yes", replied the Queen, her mind on the Derby to be run a few days later, "the Captain has just rung up to say that *Aureole* went really well". But *Aureole* finished second to *Pinza* (Sir Gordon Richards up, finally winning his first Derby) and did not fulfil his promise as a three-year-old.

211

Below: The Queen showing that special sympathy for the equine species

Opposite: The Queen leads in Carozza (the young L. Piggott up) after winning the Oaks at Epsom, 1957. Noel Murless, the royal trainer, takes a close hold

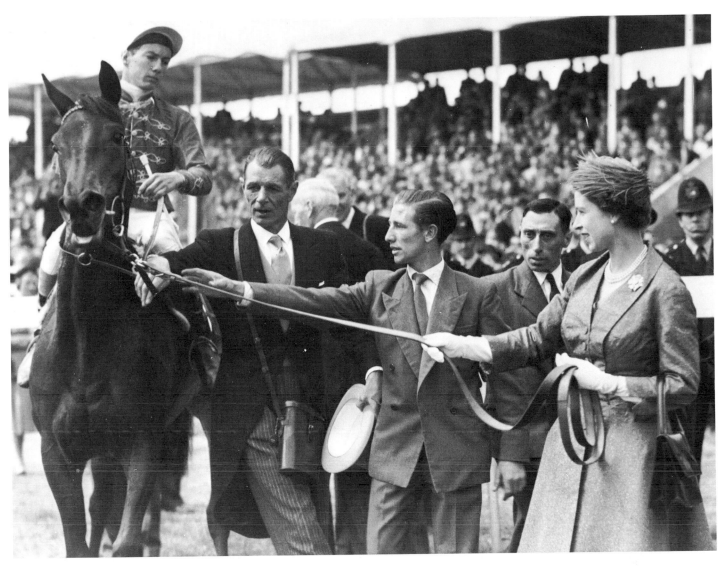

Something was wrong and the Queen took a hand in solving the problem. First she recommended a neurologist *(sic)* to examine the horse and then a change of jockey. In 1954 *Aureole* carried all before him, winning the King George VI and Queen Elizabeth stakes at Ascot to the Queen's undisguised delight and helping to make her leading owner for the season. The great horse retired triumphantly to stud at Wolferton where he became an oustanding sire.

The Queen was leading owner again in 1957 with 30 wins (23 trained by Boyd-Rochfort and seven by Murless), the most notable being the Oaks with *Carrozza*, cleverly ridden by Lester Piggott. She also had two other outstanding fillies racing that year, *Almeria* and *Mulberry Harbour* which both won good races. In 1958 her home-bred colt *Pall Mall* won the Two Thousand Guineas but in this year of constant colds the Queen was unable to be at Newmarket to cheer the 40 to 1 outsider home.

The 1960s were not so successful for the Queen on the Turf. It was a time of transition: Captains Moore and Boyd-Rochfort (the latter knighted in 1968) retired; the National Stud from which the Queen had previously leased young stock switched to a centre for stallions; and Lord Porchester became the Queen's new racing manager, a post he holds to this day. Son and heir of the rakish sportsman and *bon vivant* Earl of Carnarvon, and grandson

of the ill-fated Earl who helped discover the tomb of Tutankhamun, Henry Porchester and his wife Jean Wallop from Big Horn, Wyoming, are among the Queen's special friends. With Lord Porchester's imaginative help the Queen adopted a different breeding policy that owed something to the method she had observed on fact-finding missions to France. A new royal stud was set up near Highclere, the Carnarvon seat outside Newbury, and the Queen's horses were sent to the local yards of Major Dick Hern and Ian Balding.

In the early 1970s the Queen won some useful races across the Channel in France, but it was not until 1974 that she topped the owners' table in Britain again. Her star performer was *Highclere* (sired by Lord Porchester's *Queen's Hussar* out of a granddaughter of *Hypericum*, George VI's filly which the Queen saw win the One Thousand Guineas in 1946). Ridden by Joe Mercer, *Highclere* emulated her ancestress's feat in winning the One Thousand Guineas, albeit by a narrow margin, and excelled herself by giving the Queen her first French "Classic" in winning the Prix de Diane at Chantilly. There was a possibly prophetic vignette in the winners' enclosure at the York spring meeting that year when the Queen welcomed the victorious *Escatorial*. As Piggott jumped off the filly's back landing at the Queen's feet, a jubilant racegoer shouted: "Arise, Sir Lester!"

Below: The Queen with her trainer Sir Cecil Boyd-Rochfort at Epsom in 1958; and (bottom) also with Ian Balding (left) and Lord Porchester (right)

Opposite above left: The Queen at Ascot, escorted by her representative on the course, the moustachioed Lieutenant-Colonel Piers Bengough, 1984. Above right: The Queen at Newmarket in the same season. Below: The royal procession down the course at Ascot

The Queen is a regular spectator of the polo at Smith's Lawn in Windsor Great Park – favourite haunt of the Windsorian royalty watchers where the Queen and her family can be studied in their most natural habitat. The language to be heard on the field often recalls Windsor's Saxon past. Before taking up four-in-hand driving as his main equestrian pursuit, Prince Philip (whose own interest in horse-racing is lukewarm, to say the least) was a top-class performer at polo, entertaining the crowd as much with his nautical oaths as with his aggressive play. Prince Charles played for Cambridge and captained Young England at polo, but was less successful in his race-riding exploits under National Hunt rules.

The Queen shot as a girl but, perhaps bearing in mind Queen Victoria's dictum that "To look on is harmless but it is not ladylike to kill animals and go out shooting", she has, again, not pursued the sport. However, she still goes out with the guns at Sandringham from time to time. Urban-minded critics enjoy pointing up the supposed paradox of the conservationist Prince Philip, so active in the World Wildlife Fund, blasting away at game birds. In any event, the sport has apparently lost its flavour for the Prince of Wales.

A little-known sporting interest of the Queen's is in gun dogs. *The Field* reported in the late autumn of 1984:

The Queen's presence as one of the judges in the Kennel Club's two-day All-Aged Retriever Trial at Sandringham came as an unavoidable surprise, not least to competitors. It scarcely needs saying that security requirements dictated this. First disclosure of Her Majesty's participation came on the card for the meeting. This was not, as some thought, her first judging appointment. She had previously acted in a retriever stake at Balmoral.

Competitors and judges in gundog events have long known of Her Majesty's interest and knowledge, gained from working her labradors at Royal Family shoots. Some of the great field trial dogs of the past have ended their careers as her personal shooting companions, including the Championship winner of 1975, FT Ch Lugwardine Jade, and her own FT Ch Sandringham Sydney.

Some also know of her regret at having to decide that, as Sovereign, the full rigour of the game in handling her dogs in public was not for her. Her pleasure at being able to take an active part in one of the field trial season's major occasions was greater as a result.

She has long enjoyed private gundog trials organized for neighbours, friends from further afield, and estate workers during the mid-winter holidays at Sandringham. These have done more than prove her competence against professional and well-practised amateur rivals; they gave her an insight into the receiving end of the judging process, in which she was already keenly interested.

Throughout her reign she has entered her labradors in field trials. Most of them have been handled by W. Meldrum, now one of the senior professionals. Her knowledge of situations and problems, and of reasons for success and failure, is acute. Her presence as a spectator when the demands of royal time permitted, little publicized, by her own wish, has made her anything but an absentee owner.

So when she invited the Kennel Club to hold its major retriever trial at Sandringham the suggestion that she should be one of the judges came naturally, and was graciously accepted.

Appropriately enough the Queen's Silver Jubilee year of 1977 saw more triumphs on the Turf, with the Queen topping the British winning breeders' list. On the eve of the Silver Jubilee celebrations *Dunfermline*, ridden by the courageous Scot Willie Carson, won the Oaks by three-quarters of a length, despite a rough passage down the notoriously difficult Epsom course, went on to win the St Leger (surviving a Stewards' enquiry), but could only finish fourth in the coveted Prix de l'Arc de Triomphe. In 1979 *Highclere's* first foal, *Milford*, sired by the mighty *Mill Reef*, was widely backed to win the 200th running of the Derby but ran disappointingly and the 1980s have yet to produce a really exceptional racehorse in the Queen's colours.

The Queen's other sporting interests have inevitably had to take second place to the Turf. She hunted as a girl with the Pytchley when her parents rented a hunting box unsuitably close to the Civil War battlefield of Naseby (where the Cavaliers were decisively beaten by the Parliamentarians), but did not continue the sport. The Queen has been a patron of three-day eventing at Badminton and elsewhere, encouraging her daughter Princess Anne, the greatest equestrian in the family. As a girl Princess Anne was sent by the Queen to the redoubtable riding instructress Sybil Smith, at Holyport near Bray who had taught her and her sister, Princess Margaret, the rudiments of horsemanship.

Below: Among those registering varying degrees of disturbance on an old farm cart beside an obstacle at Badminton in the early 1960s are (back row, left to right): the Duke and Duchess of Beaufort, the Princess Royal, Lord Snowdon (partly obscured, with camera), Princess Margaret, Prince Charles (partly obscured), the Queen Mother and the particularly horrified Queen. In the front row, Princess Anne casts a cooler eye on the proceedings

Below: A happy moment for the Queen spectating at Windsor Horse Trials; and (bottom) with one of her black labradors at Sandringham

Below left: A graphic exposition of equestrianism from Prince Philip; and (right) a courtly gesture from Prince Charles clearly delights the Queen at Windsor
Bottom: The Queen's enthusiasm for sport is unaffected by the "going"

Opposite: A contrast in seats. The Queen rides out at Windsor with President Reagan, veteran of many a "western"

The quite exceptional photographs by Colin Jones accompanying *The Field's* report showed the Queen in her element – attired in headscarf and waterproof jacket, smiling broadly, relaxed and patently happy in the country setting she likes best.

At Balmoral, the Queen enjoys stalking. She killed her first stag at the age of sixteen and in 1958 shot an "eleven pointer", regarded as one of the best heads in Scotland that season. During her tour of India in 1961 the Queen took part in an elephant drive as a guest of the Maharajah of Jaipur. Fishing, however, is another country sport that the Queen is happy to leave to her mother and elder son.

The Queen is not a good sailor, only going out once with Prince Philip at Cowes in the early years of their marriage, nor is she a particularly enthusiastic swimmer. Winter sports have also passed her by, as have ball games, though she enjoys driving her own cars.

The Queen and the royal family are often accused of being "philistine" but in this narrow-minded age some people forget that it is perfectly possible to indulge in outdoor activities and yet still be genuinely interested in the arts. The Queen has a fondness for the music of Handel whose advancement owed much to her Hanoverian ancestors. Prince Philip, often portrayed as a boor, paints and collects pictures, by Sidney Nolan among others. The Queen Mother is a connoisseur of the arts. The Prince of Wales is an archaeologist, frustrated actor, cellist, and sometime contributor to *Punch* and *Books and Bookmen*; the Princess, a dancer *manqué*, shares his love of opera and ballet. Even the much criticised Prince Andrew has produced some sensitive photographs and was an enthusiastic potter and actor at school.

Princess Margaret takes a particularly lively interest in the arts; whether collecting china and modern pictures, singing, playing the piano, going to the theatre or ballet. Together with the Queen she used to take part in amateur theatricals as a girl. Princess Alice, Duchess of Gloucester paints in water-colours and likes cinematography; her architect son, the present Duke, has published books of his photographs and is knowledgeable about art. The Duke of Kent is another royal photographer and music-lover; the Duchess is an accomplished pianist and sings with the Bach Choir. Princess Michael of Kent, who runs her own design company, is a keen student of historic buildings. Princess Alexandra, like her mother Princess Marina, is also a cultured lady who enjoys a wide variety of music and plays the piano. The up-and-coming generation of royalty, as represented by Lord Linley, Lady Sarah Armstrong-Jones, Lord St Andrews, Lady Helen Windsor, James and Marina Ogilvy, are also proving to be a bunch of lively individualists.

Much as she may like the pictures of Edward Seago, Sir Peter Scott and others, there is no doubt as to what present the Queen would most like for her sixtieth birthday in 1986. To own the home-bred winner of the only English "Classic" to have eluded her, the Derby.

221

12. The Queen at Sixty

In an opinion poll conducted by *Woman* magazine early in 1985, 52 per cent of this cosy weekly's readers expressed their belief that the Queen should abdicate at some stage rather than retain the crown for life, 16 per cent stipulating that she should go in 1986 when she becomes a "senior citizen" at the age of sixty. Always ready with a quote, the Buckingham Palace spokeman commented: "There is absolutely no question of the Queen abdicating; it is quite contrary to the tradition of the country". Certainly from a historical viewpoint talk of the possibility of the Queen abdicating seems wide of the mark.

The monarchy, after all, is not a job; it is an hereditary office. The Queen's overriding sense of duty would militate against any idea of stepping down. As the Prince of Wales himself has said, the longer the Queen is on the throne the better sovercign she becomes. The advantages to the country of having a monarch who can take a long view of things cannot be emphasized too strongly. Already in her 30-odd years as Queen, Elizabeth II has acquired considerable political experience that will stand her in good stead if faced with the constitutional crisis of a "hung" Parliament (more than ever likely since the advent of the Social Democratic/Liberal Alliance) which only she has the power to untangle.

The emergence of the Princess of Wales on the scene is suggested as the key to the *Woman* opinion poll. When the magazine conducted a similar poll in 1978 two-thirds of those questioned were against the Queen's abdication. But despite a majority wishing her to make retirement plans the Queen remains the most popular member of the royal family, polling a 40 per cent vote.

In the 1970s apathy seemed to pose the greatest threat to the Queen and the survival of the monarchy. Before the celebration of the Queen's Silver Jubilee got under way there were fears expressed as to it being an embarrassing flop. "We are scarcely into 1977 yet", wrote somebody on the London *Evening Standard*, "but already everybody is looking pretty shell-shocked in the ceaseless barrage of Jubilee propaganda, nostalgia and exploitation . . ." Then suddenly, in the spring a tremendous tide of benevolence welled up. It was directed specifically at the Queen as a very personal thank-you and message of love from the great mass of her passionately loyal and devoted subjects. The silent majority had found its voice. For certain media-brainwashed pseudo-sophisticates the warmth of feeling expressed by the "provincials" for horsy old "Brenda" came as a complete revelation. It also clearly caused some touching surprise to the Queen. Rather in the manner of her grandfather George V during his Silver Jubilee 42 years earlier, the Queen's reaction might well have been to observe that she had not realized they liked her for herself.

"We have come here because we love you", cried one well-wisher in the crowd that packed the "walkabout" route between St Paul's Cathedral and the Guildhall on Tuesday 7 June 1977. "I feel it and it means so much to me", replied the Queen.

Another exchange overheard on this most successful of all "walkabouts" (something which the shy Queen had finally come to terms with) began with a child asking: "Do you have a mechanical arm to keep waving all the time, the way that you do?"

"I haven't reached that stage yet", said the Queen.

In her speech at the Guildhall, the Queen observed in her vastly improved, lighter, deeper tone of voice: "If this is not exactly a period of rest for us, it is certainly one of refreshment and of happiness and satisfaction".

The crowds which gathered outside Buckingham Palace a couple of days later after the fireworks display had not been matched in size or euphoria since VE night. "We want the Queen" was the endlessly repeated refrain. The message communicated itself. After the Silver Jubilee the Queen's shyness in public was less marked; she smiled more, relaxed, risked a few more jokes.

In the years since there have been further causes to smile – the Queen Mother's 80th birthday celebrations, the Prince and Princess of Wales's wedding – but other feelings have inevitably clouded the Queen's serenity. The disgust at learning that Sir Anthony Blunt, her adviser on pictures and drawings, and a friend and cousin of her mother's, had been a Stalinist spy. The shock and horror of the murder of Lord Mountbatten, Doreen Lady Brabourne, Nicholas Knatchbull and an Irish boy at Mullaghmore. The revulsion on learning of a film about the sex life of Jesus Christ. The distaste for cheque-book journalism benefiting the relations of mass-murderers. The impatience and annoyance with intrusive or indeed utterly fabricated "reporting". The shooting incident at the Birthday Parade. The Fagan intrusion. The Trestrail resignation caused by homosexual blackmail. And, above all individual incidents, the constant exposure to danger. It would be small wonder if this concatenation of traumas has – as some observers claim – deeply affected and aged the Queen. No sooner had the smile become a feature of her face on public view than it was wiped off again.

The Queen has also found herself under attack from the Right over her attachment to the Commonwealth. Writing in the *Spectator* Peregrine Worsthorne asked:

Over whom, or what, does the Queen reign? Where do her loyalties lie? When the Australians depose her, as they certainly will before long, how are the British meant to take this humiliation to their Queen? Will they accept the sophistry that it won't be the British Queen who is insulted; only the Australian Queen and although the two are the same, they must never be confused, or put up for long with the shaming pretence of neutrality under which the Queen as head of the Commonwealth, must not be pro-British, or criticise black Commonwealth dictatorships which torture her former officers, since that would be to take sides, which an impartial head should never do. It takes all sorts to make a Commonwealth and the Queen must love them all equally.

In a masterly analysis the essayist argued that in this matter alone the Queen's instinctive judgment about public opinion ("which hitherto has been absolutely right") is letting her down: "She may take pride in the Commonwealth, but her people for the most part, don't, and regard her love for this hybrid offspring of the empire with deepening distaste". Worsthorne's warning is that the unpopularity of the Queen's infatuation with the Commonwealth is dangerously under-estimated in high places. It could well soon shake the monarchy in Britain and the Queen would surely be well advised to play down her commitment to the Commonwealth. Perhaps, to avoid further controversy, separate messages could be recorded for transmission in different countries.

It is also high time that the Queen and the royal family became more involved in European affairs. Britain is now very much part of Europe and our own royal family's background could hardly be more European. This is something that the xenophobic British like to ignore; but it is surely long overdue to revive the links with the continent which were so strong in 1914. Less talk of the price of butter and more inspiring education on the wider issues of European unity might eventually lead to the dream of a Federal Europe becoming a reality. If it does, who might be a suitable head? A rota system of European monarchs – similar to the Malaysian practice – could perhaps be employed. Doubtless it would be regarded as too chauvinistic to suggest that the Queen herself could be given the job outright. One theory then goes that if she did this, she could make way for the Prince of Wales on the British throne.

When the present writer put forward a suggestion along these lines a few years ago it was denounced as "balderdash" coming from "the back of his ostrich neck" by a then obscure Labour backbench Welsh MP. He had thinning red hair and a somewhat garrulous manner; it was the now somewhat better known Mr Neil Kinnock.

The jubilation of Jubilee Day, 1977.
Below: The Queen and Duke of Edinburgh in The Mall,
returning to Buckingham Palace
Opposite (above): On the steps of St Paul's Cathedral, having
alighted from the State Coach, and (below) acknowledging the
crowds from the 1902 State Landau

When he becomes king, Prince Charles could find no better exemplar than the recently restored King of Spain. Juan Carlos manages to be both regal and informal. To avoid pomposity on the one hand and bogusness on the other is one of the problems of modern monarchy. "Perhaps the most remarkable aspect of our Queen's reign", wrote Lord Mountbatten, "is how she and her husband and children have succeeded in moving with the times without detracting from the dignity of their duties or sacrificing the royal ceremonial which other countries envy."

The monarch has to symbolize the nation and the Queen somehow succeeds in representing Britain's modern aspirations, as well as its heritage. To link the past with the present and future is a tricky but vital part of the monarch's function. In an unstable atmosphere the monarchy provides continuity and a very necessary reminder that the history of Britain did not begin this morning. The older an institution is, the better it adapts to change; and the monarchy is changing all the time.

There are, however, problems in packaging the monarchy as an idealized, "instant" middle-class family unit suitable for democratic mass-consumption. This anti-historical approach has resulted in worrying side effects. People seem to have forgotten that the monarchy is actually hereditary. However unpalatable this may be in an egalitarian age, it must be faced. If one supports the monarchy one is also supporting the hereditary principle. To defend the hereditary principle – and it is perfectly defensible in theory and in practice – is to risk being considered of unsound mind; to attack the monarchy can still provoke violent reactions. This conflict spells danger. The more people think of the royal family as being "just like us", the less they will be inclined to bow the knee. The younger members of the royal family are now expected to chat away in press interviews like a footballer or a pop star. Happily a certain divinity still hedges the Queen herself and one hopes the day will not dawn when she is asked "how she feels" about something or other. The mystique of monarchy needs to be preserved.

Willie Hamilton and company might ask what about the "*Mustique* of the Monarchy?" This eccentric MP has probably done more for the British monarchy, in his perverse way, than anyone else over the last few years. At least he has provoked reactions, made people think about and vigorously defend the system. To survive it needs rational as well as just emotional support. Criticism of the monarchy is certainly healthier than the apathy of its notional worshippers. Where Hamilton and others of his kidney go wrong is in insulting individuals, who cannot answer back, rather than concentrating on the institution. The personal invective, though, is nothing compared to

Below: The Hamilton handshake: The Queen meets her most vociferous critic at Glenrothes New Town, 1982 — a few days after the birth of another William (the elder son of the Prince and Princess of Wales)

Bottom: The Queen and Sir John Kerr, the Governor-General of Australia who dismissed Gough Whitlam's Labour government

the lambasting Queen Victoria used to receive a hundred years ago.

Modern republicans are a fairly unimaginative crew. Philosophical arguments about the monarchy, or even constructive suggestions as to what they would like to see put in its place, are seldom forthcoming. Instead all their energies are devoted to endless discussion of the royal finances. The vulgar and boring subject of money is brought up again and again. Naturally the monarchy is not cheap, but neither is it extravagant. Surely no one wants a skimped monarchy; either one has a splendid show or one has nothing. In every respect the British monarchy gives magnificent value for the running expenses it receives from the State. Nevertheless a radical Chancellor of the Exchequer could save everybody a great deal of bother if he arranged for the Queen to receive back a direct share of her own revenues in order to cover her and the royal

family's expenses, thereby scrapping the Civil List. There is an admirable precedent for such a simple course: the Prince and Princess of Wales do not cost the public any money at all as they live off the revenues of the Duchy of Cornwall. If it works for that Duchy why not for the Duchy of Lancaster?

Just as putting forward the pat historical arguments against the principle of the Queen's abdication will not necessarily obviate its being put into practice should an even greater majority of *Woman* readers (doubtless a significant barometer) come out in favour of such an unwelcome course, so being aware of the dangers of the Prince of Wales entering what is known in Court circles as "an Edward VII situation" is no guarantee against that eventuality. Nobody wants a repetition of the circumstances whereby the heir to the throne is not given enough to do. We all know that the Prince of Wales has

A 1950s portrait in the stately tradition by James Gunn

Michael Noakes's more informal study of the 1970s

Opposite: Royal celebrations. Above: the Thanksgiving Service for the Queen's Silver Jubilee at St Paul's; and (below) the Queen Mother and the Queen listen to a rendition of "Happy Birthday" outside Clarence House on the former's 80th birthday Right: The Prince of Wales and Lady Diana Spencer at Clarence House on the evening following the announcement of their engagement. With the Queen Mother was Ruth Lady Fermoy, Lady Diana's maternal grandmother

plenty to keep himself busy. His "industry programme" has been co-ordinated by the National Economic Development Council, he visits the City and Government departments, he fulfils the usual round of royal engagements at home and abroad. As Philip Howard has pointed out, he also "does a great deal of work on his trusts, charities and estates. But that is the sort of work that retired major-generals were invented to perform." The question still nags: What about a proper job? And the Queen Mother's spirited answer about him having a proper job – "He is the Prince of Wales" – begins to sound a little hollow especially in the light of recent idle gossip that he has been exhibiting signs of listlessness, boredom and withdrawal.

Like the Queen, the Prince of Wales is a firm believer in the Commonwealth. Suggestions have been made from time to time that he should, like Hilaire Belloc's Lord Lundy, "go out and govern New South Wales". However, the Australian Governor-Generalship no longer seems a realistic proposition for the Prince. While Malcolm Fraser's coalition government seemed to favour the idea, the Australian Labour Party remained unconvinced that the job could be kept out of the political fray after the Kerr-Whitlam brouhaha of 1975. It is also a mistake to over-emphasize the esteem in which the Australians hold the Prince of Wales. Although it was a popular decision to send him to school there and his subsequent visits, especially with his gorgeous "Sheila" of a Princess, have been successful, it is facile to assume that he is a blue-eyed boy Down Under. The Australian mind does not work quite like that. As for Canada there is nothing doing since the new Constitution of 1982.

One of the most important reasons why any chance of the Queen abdicating seems remote is that she wants to give the Prince and Princess of Wales a period of relatively carefree, and "normal", family life denied herself and Prince Philip by her father's tragically early death. It is indeed almost impossible to imagine the Queen ever retiring but as time goes by it is to be hoped that the Prince will be brought increasingly into state affairs through, for example, the Privy Council. Perhaps, in years to come, some new constitutional wheeze – rather along the lines of a Regency – could be worked out whereby the Queen became a sort of "Chairperson" and the Prince of Wales's position was made analogous to a "Managing Director".

Looking to the future, a move by the Prince and Princess of Wales from Highgrove, a distinctly unsatisfactory residence for the heir to the throne, should be on the cards. The Prince's deplorable muddle (reminiscent of Denis Compton's calling between the wickets – "no, yes, wait, no, yes . . . sorry") over whether to take up poor old Lord Stanhope's most generous bequest of a first-class seat at

Chevening has since, one suspects, been compounded by a fear of bad public relations in failing to buy a decent place elsewhere within reach of good hunting country. Belton, the glorious late-Stuart seat of the Brownlows, was mentioned as a possible candidate for the Waleses a few years ago but it ended up having to be financially rescued by the National Heritage Memorial Fund and then handed over to the National Trust.

Since the triumphant tour of Wales after their wedding the Prince and Princess of Wales have been somewhat notable by their absence from the Principality and it would be a popular gesture were they to settle in a Welsh home. Debating with some disaffected teenagers on a BBC Radio One *Talkabout* programme, whether or not the Prince and Princess were a good thing for Wales, the present writer had to concede to his interlocutors that they had a point when they asked why the Waleses did not live in Wales.

Genealogically the Princess of Wales's ancestry provides a healthy new mix for the Blood Royal with Irish, Scotch, American and even a dash of something more exotic – her illegitimate great-great-great-great-grandmother was an Armenian living in Bombay – added to the mainstream English aristocratic lines. Thanks to all this, Prince William of Wales will eventually become the most 'British' sovereign since James I with some 58.8 per cent British blood (and 4.69 per cent American).

The Princess of Wales's style of motherhood will surely set the standards for the present generation. She is, of course, singularly well qualified for her new role and her former colleagues at the Young England Kindergarten are

233

Below: A farewell wave from the Queen and Prince Philip in Canada September 1984

Opposite: "Queen's weather" (or "rain without end"): the cloudbursts that seem to have accompanied Her Majesty's footsteps have never dampened the Queen's enthusiasm for the task in hand

in no doubt that she will make an excellent mother. Princes William and Harry are understood to be destined for a play school run on similar "Montessori" lines. The precedents of the Prince of Wales's fairly tough education are not necessarily going to be followed. Indeed, Hill House (the Knightsbridge day school) and Prince Philip's *almae matres* Cheam and Gordonstoun might well be given a wide berth. After a prep school not far from home, Eton should be the obvious choice for the young Princes and, in due course, the obligatory stint in the Commonwealth and in the services. Like the monarchy, Eton is a good example of the maxim that the older the institution the better it adapts to change; those establishments where boys wear shorts and shin up mountains now seem oddly dated. Moreover, the Princess of Wales's father and brothers are Etonians. Co-education does not seem in order somehow, despite the Armstrong-Jones children going to Bedales. It is noticeable that, apart from the great schools (Eton,

Harrow, Winchester), private education is increasingly geared to local patrons; thus schools close to the family home are sure to be carefully considered.

Security is a key factor in royal education and, apart from anything else, opting for boarding schools makes it less likely that we shall witness the disagreeable sight of an armed motorcade escorting the young Princes to and from school, as happens in Spain. It should be borne in mind that one of the factors in favour of Gordonstoun was its distance from Fleet Street.

The intrusiveness of the press is one of the biggest headaches for the Queen and the royal family and it is not a problem that is going to disappear. The hounding of the Princess of Wales in 1981 became so intolerable that the Queen stepped in on her behalf to try to reason with the newspaper editors. The Queen apparently made it clear that she did not want to force the Princess to change her nature so as to conform to royal tradition. It was especially interesting that the Queen herself did not seem to be going along with the traditional view that personal restrictions have to go hand in hand with royal duties. This can be regarded as a significant pointer to a new style of life for the next generation of royalty. It remains to be seen, though, whether the media can resist the temptation of treating the royal family as a tacky soap opera. The Queen opening the new set of *Coronation Street* was a sight overloaded with symbolism.

The Queen's sympathy for the Princess of Wales's predicament and her encouraging support for the Princess's independent attitude surprised some of the Fleet Street editors. Behind it lies not merely the humanity of a kindly mother-in-law, but the shrewd common-sense of a constitutional sovereign. The Queen has learnt from her husband, Prince Philip, that to survive the monarchy has to change. It is therefore as well for the future King Charles III, Queen Diana and indeed King William V to start putting their own acts together in readiness for the 21st century show. The Queen wants it to run and run, but she is wise enough to allow plenty of scope for cast changes. How long the leading lady stays in the starring part, the only name above the title, should be decided not by a *Woman* opinion poll but by the Queen herself.

The Queen in her sixtieth year, is a grandmother with hair greying at the temples, often bespectacled and sometimes showing the strain of recent traumas. Her appearance is perhaps becoming a little more Hanoverian with the passing of the years. But she is still very far from old and remains a vital figure not to be underestimated. She has been Queen for more than half her life and there is no reason to suppose she will not reign over us for many years to come. All over the globe her peoples will be wishing the Queen many happy returns on 21 April 1986.

234

Chronology of the Queen's Reign

1952

February King George VI dies at Sandringham aged 56 – Queen and Duke of Edinburgh fly home from Kenya – Queen holds Accession Council – Queen Elizabeth II proclaimed – Lying-in-State of late King in Westminster Hall – Queen receives High Commissioners, Commonwealth representatives and foreign royals – Funeral of late King in St George's Chapel – Queen holds 1st investiture – Queen approves wording of prayers for Royal Family

March Duke flies in Comet jet aircraft – Duke of Kent confirmed at Buckingham Palace

April Queen becomes Colonel-in-Chief of all Guards regiments – Declaration that Queen's family will be known as House and Family of Windsor – Queen invests Duke as KT

May Queen takes up residence at Buckingham Palace – Duke and Duchess of Gloucester visit Northern Ireland – Queen Mother and Princess Margaret make tour of Europe in Comet jet aircraft

June Court Mourning ends – Queen holds 1st Trooping the Colour – Queen holds Coronation Council – Queen's Coronation proclaimed – Queen holds 1st presentation party at Buckingham Palace – Queen undertakes engagements in Edinburgh

June Duke promoted Commander RN – Wedding of Gerald Lascelles to Miss Angela Dowding – Duke and Duchess of Gloucester visit Channel Islands

August Queen Mother buys Barrogill Castle, Caithness

September Duchess of Kent visits Malaya and Hong Kong

October Queen opens Claerwen Dam

November Queen opens 1st Parliament of reign – Queen lays foundation of new Hall of Inner Temple – Duke of Windsor visits Queen Mary – Queen approves new coinage

December Duke of Edinbugh makes 1st solo flight – Queen makes 1st Christmas broadcast

1953

January Duke promoted to top rank of all Services – Princess Royal visits West Indies

February Queen visits flooded areas of Britain

March Queen Mary ill – Marshal Tito of Yugoslavia lunches with Queen – Queen Mary dies at Marlborough House – Lying-in-State of Queen Mary in Westminster Hall – Funeral of Queen Mary in St George's Chapel

April Queen appoints Winston Churchill KG – Duke of Gloucester represents Queen at enthronement of King Feisal of Iraq

May Duke of Edinburgh receives pilot's wings – Queen Mother and Princess Margaret move to Clarence House

June Coronation of Queen at Westminster Abbey – Queen reviews fleet at Spithead – Queen makes Coronation visit to Edinburgh – Duke installed KT – Queen Mother and Princess Margaret visit Southern Rhodesia

July Queen and Duke visit Northern Ireland and Wales – Queen reviews RAF – Queen and Duke witness Royal River Pageant on Thames

October Queen unveils Runnymede air memorial – Queen opens new Trinity House – Queen invests Lt-Col James Carne with VC – Queen Mother receives Freedom of City of London

November New Regency Act receives Royal Assent (Duke of Edinburgh can act as Regent) – Counsellors of State appointed – Queen and Duke receive addresses of god-speed before Commonwealth Tour – Queen and Duke sail in *Canopus* for Bermuda and Jamaica – they leave in *Gothic* via Panama Canal

December *Gothic* arrives in Fiji – Queen and Duke received by Queen Salote in Tonga – they sail for New Zealand – Queen broadcasts Christmas message from Government House, Auckland – Queen and Duke visit survivors of Tangiwai rail accident

1954

January Queen and Duke make tour of New Zealand – Queen opens New Zealand Parliament – Queen holds 1st Privy Council meeting outside Britain – they sail for Australia in *Gothic*

February Queen and Duke tour Australia – Queen opens Federal Parliament in Canberra – Queen unveils memorial to US help in war – they visit Sydney, Melbourne and fly to Tasmania – Princess Alice and Lord Athlone celebrate golden wedding

March Queen and Duke visit Victoria, Great Barrier Reef, Adelaide and Perth (no hand-shaking due to poliomyelitis epidemic) – Queen Mother attends rededication of Temple Church

April Queen and Duke leave Australia – Queen broadcasts her thanks – they visit Ceylon, Uganda (where Queen inaugurates Owen Falls Dam)

May They fly to Libya and are united with their children – they return to London via Malta, Gibraltar and English Channel – Sir Winston Churchill comes on board at Isle of Wight – Royal Family greet Queen at Westminster – Loyal address from House of Commons – Queen lunches at Mansion House

June Jubilee Review of 2,000 officers of RNVR – Sir Winston Churchill installed KG – King Gustaf VI Adolf of Sweden pays State Visit to London

July Queen reviews 10,000 UK Police in Hyde Park – Duke visits Canada – Queen launches *Southern Cross* at Belfast – Duchess of Kent and Princess Alexandra return from tour of Canada and USA

October Emperor Haile Selassie of Ethiopia pays State Visit to London – Queen appoints Anthony Eden KG – Queen Mother leaves for USA and Canada – Queen and Duke tour Lancashire and Yorkshire

December Duke made honorary Freeman of Cardiff

1955

January Princess Margaret leaves for Caribbean tour

February Queen entertains Shahanshah of Iran to lunch

March Duke attends opening of Maltese Parliament – Queen presents Duke of Gloucester with Field-Marshal's baton

April Queen and Duke dine with Sir Winston Churchill at No. 10 on eve of his retirement as Prime Minister – Sir Anthony Eden becomes Prime Minister – Queen Mother makes 1st helicopter trip

May Queen and Duke attend service in Gloucester for 800th Anniversary of Royal Charter – Queen receives 1st German Ambassador since the war

June Trooping the Colour cancelled due to railway strike – Duke of Cornwall and Princess Anne make 1st flight – Queen Victoria Eugénie of Spain visits Queen at Windsor – Queen launches liner at Glasgow – Queen pays State Visit to Norway

July Queen receives Nehru at Windsor – Queen sees *Jardiniere* win at postponed Ascot meeting – Duke of Kent has motor accident – Duke of Edinburgh visits Scilly Isles

August Duke of Kent commissioned in Royal Scots Greys – Queen and Duke visit Wales – Queen inaugurates Usk reservoir for Swansea – Queen and Duke visit Isle of Man

October Queen invests Albert Schweitzer with OM – Queen attends rededication of Lambeth Palace – Queen unveils National Memorial Statue of King George VI in Carlton Gardens – President Cravero Lopes of Portugal pays State Visit to London – Princess Margaret announces she will not marry Group-Captain Peter Townsend

November Queen and Duke visit Midlands – Queen Mother installed as Chancellor of London University

December Princess Margaret launches *Carinthia* – Queen opens buildings at London Airport

1956
January–February Queen and Duke make three-week tour of Nigeria

March Queen Mother opens Franco-Scottish exhibition in Paris – Queen lays foundation stone at Coventry Cathedral

April Queen and Duke receive Bulganin and Khrushchev at Windsor Castle

May Queen and Duke visit West Country

June Queen and Duke visit Teesside – Queen pays State Visit to Sweden – Princess Margaret and Duke and Duchess of Gloucester join Queen for Equestrian Olympics – Queen sees *Alexander* win Royal Hunt Cup at Ascot – Queen reviews 300 VC holders in Hyde Park – Queen and Duke entertain Commonwealth Prime Ministers for dinner

July Queen and Duke tour Berwickshire and East Lothian – King Feisal of Iraq pays State Visit to London – Queen and Duke visit Lee-on-Solent

September Royal Family at wedding of Lord Carnegie in Perth – Princess Margaret begins East African tour

October Queen at 21st birthday party of Duke of Kent – Duke of Edinburgh leaves for four-month Commonwealth tour – Queen opens world's 1st large-scale nuclear power station at Calder Hall, Cumberland – Duke opens Olympic Games in Melbourne – Queen and Duke of Gloucester install new GCBs at Westminster Abbey – Queen and Royal Family at Army Council dinner

December Princess Marie Louise dies in London aged 84 – Guneral of Princess at St George's Chapel – Queen broadcasts to Commonwealth – Duke also speaks from *Britannia* in South Pacific – Memorial tablet to King George VI dedicated in Sandringham Church

1957
January Sir Anthony Eden resigns as Prime Minister – Queen sends for Harold Macmillan to form a government – Earl of Athlone dies at Kensington Palace aged 82

February Duke joins Queen at Lisbon for Commonwealth tour – Queen pays State Visit to Portugal – Duke of Edinburgh granted style and dignity of a Prince of the UK

March Duchess of Kent opens 1st Parliament in Ghana

April Duke gives lecture on his tour to 2,000 schoolchildren in Festival Hall – Queen pays State Visit to France – Queen distributes Royal Maundy at St Albans Abbey (1st time outside London since Charles II)

May Duke makes 1st flight in glider – Queen pays State Visit to Denmark

June Queen opens *Cutty Sark* to the public – Queen Mother unveils Dunkirk memorial

July Queen Mother visits Rhodesia and Nyasaland – Queen attends Wimbledon for 1st time – Queen and Duke visit Channel Islands

August Duke of Gloucester represents Queen at Independence celebrations in Malaya

September Queen unveils memorial bust to King George VI at Crathie Church

October Duke of Gloucester represents Queen at funeral of King Haakon of Norway – Queen and Duke visit Canada – Queen addresses UN General Assembly in New York

November Princess Royal visits Nigeria – announcement that presentation parties would cease after 1958 – Queen Mother opens new Lloyd's building

December Queen's bounty for triplets and quadruplets ceases – Princess Margaret visits Lewisham train disaster victims – Queen's Christmas broadcast televised for 1st time

1958
January–March Queen Mother makes world tour, visiting Australia and New Zealand

March Queen pays State Visit to the Netherlands

April Royal Family attend RAF 40th Anniversary dinner – Queen and Duke give dinner party for Chancellor Adenauer at Windsor – Princess Margaret inaugurates legislature of new West Indies Federation on behalf of Queen

May Queen and Duke at gala of *My Fair Lady* – Royal Family at dedication of new high altar at St Paul's Cathedral – President Gronchi of Italy pays State Visit to London

June Princess Royal ordered to rest for two months – Queen opens extended airport of Gatwick – Duke of Gloucester promoted Marshal of RAF – Queen reviews 8,000 Territorials on their golden jubilee – Queen and Duke tour North of England and Scotland – Queen descends coalmine for 1st time

July Princess Margaret represents Queen at British Columbia centenary celebrations – Portland Island renamed Princess Margaret Island – Duke of Edinburgh opens Empire Games – Queen unwell – Queen's recorded message announces creation of Prince Charles as Prince of Wales

The royal matriarch, wearing her Canadian orders, photographed by Karsh of Ottawa

The Prince of Wales in his uniform as Colonel-in-Chief of the Gurkha Regiment

Princess Anne at a charity clay-pigeon shooting event at Chester organised by Jackie Stewart, 1984

Prince Andrew: one of "The Team"

Prince Edward: 21 in 1985

August Queen and Royal Family make cruise of Western Isles – new Prince of Wales lands on Welsh soil

September Princess Margaret visits World Exhibition in Brussels

October President Heuss of West Germany pays State Visit to London – Opening on Parliament televised for 1st time – Duke flies to Canada in BOAC Comet IV jet airliner for ESU conference

November Duke and Duchess of Gloucester make East African tour – Queen and Royal Family present at dedication of American War Memorial Chapel at St Paul's Cathedral

December Queen inaugurates British trunk-dialling system at Bristol Telephone Exchange

1959

January Duke of Edinburgh makes world tour until April

February Queen Mother visits East Africa – Duchess of Kent and Princess Alexandra begin Latin American tour – Queen makes Marlborough House available for Commonwealth conferences – Princess Arthur of Connaught dies in London aged 67

March Queen attends memorial service for Princess Arthur at Chapel Royal, St James's Palace

April Queen Mother and Princess Margaret visit Rome and Paris – Princess Margaret atends WVS 21st anniversary party

May Shahanshah of Iran pays State Visit to London – Duke of Gloucester represents Queen at self-government celebrations in Nigeria – King Olav of Norway visits Windsor and is appointed KG

June Queen and Duke at cententary garden party of Royal Botanical Gardens at Kew – Princess Margaret visits Portugal – Duke lays keel of 1st British atomic submarine *Dreadnought* – Queen opens new St Lawrence Seaway in Canada

July Duchess of Kent opens 1st section of new road Route 11 in City of London

August Announcement that Queen is expecting a baby – Princess Alexandra visits Queensland for centenary and visits Thailand, Cambodia, India, France and Turkey

October Sentries outside Buckingham Palace moved into forecourt – Queen becomes Colonel-in-Chief of Royal Sierra Leone Military Forces – new Ministers take oaths after general election

November Princess Alexandra launches 40,000 ton *Oriana* – Royal Family attend RNR centenary service at St Paul's Cathedral – Duke pilots himself to Ghana to visit development schemes

December Duke of Kent takes seat in House of Lords – Duke of Edinburgh pilots hovercraft across the Solent

1960

January Princess Anne is bridesmaid at wedding of Lady Pamela Mountbatten to David Hicks – Princess Royal sails for three-month Caribbean tour

February Queen declares that future generations of family wil be called Mountbatten-Windsor – Queen gives birth to Prince Andrew at Buckingham Palace (1st time a reigning Sovereign has had a baby since 1857) – Countess Mountbatten of Burma dies in North Borneo – Marquess of Carisbrooke (last grandson of Queen Victoria) dies at Kensington Palace aged 73 – Lady Mountbatten buried at sea – Engagement of Princess Margaret to Antony Armstrong-Jones announced

April General de Gaulle pays State Visit to London – President of Pakistan spends weekend with Queen at Windsor

May Queen gives dinner for Commonwealth Prime Ministers at Windsor – Marriage of Princess Margaret to Antony Armstrong-Jones at Westminster Abbey – Queen Mother opens Kariba Dam in Rhodesia

June Duke visits Canada and USA

July President Frondizi of Argentina pays State Visit to London – King Bhumibol of Thailand pays State Visit to London

August Queen and Duke visit National Eisteddfod

October Princess Alexandra represents Queen at Independence celebrations in Nigeria – Queen and Duke attend service for 400th anniversary of Reformation in Scotland in Edinburgh – King Mahendra of Nepal pays State Visit to London – Queen and Duke make private visit to Denmark

November Queen lays foundation stone of St Catherine's College Oxford – Duke and Duchess of Gloucester celebrate silver wedding

December Duke of Kent appointed to staff of CIGS – Princess Margaret represents Queen at wedding of King Baudouin of the Belgians – Queen appoints Duke of Kent and Princess Alexandra GCVOs.

1961

January Antony Armstrong-Jones takes unpaid job at Council of Industrial Design – Queen nominates Dr Ramsey as Archbishop of Canterbury – Queen visits Cyprus and India

February Queen visits Pakistan

March Queen pays State Visits to Iran and Nepal and visits Turkey – Engagement of Duke of Kent to Miss Katharine Worsley announced

April Queen Mother visits Tunisia – Duke of Kent represents Queen at Independence celebrations of Sierra Leone

May Queen pays State Visit to Italy – Queen and Duke received by Pope John – Duke and Duchess of Gloucester join Queen on *Britannia* – Gloucesters sail for Greece and Turkey – Queen attends consecration of Guildford Cathedral – Duchess of Kent to be known as Princess Marina, Duchess of Kent after son's wedding – Announcement that Princess Margaret is expecting a baby

June Queen and Duke entertain President Kennedy at Buckingham Palace – Marriage of Duke of Kent to Miss Katharine Worsley at York Minster

July Queen opens Baden-Powell House

August Queen and Duke visit Northern Ireland

September Funeral of Queen's uncle, Sir David Bowes-Lyon – Queen opens Commonwealth Parliamentary Conference at Westminster Hall

October Antony Armstrong-Jones created Earl of Snowdon – Queen attends banquet to commemorate 600 years of JPs – President Senghor of Senegal lunches with Queen – Princess Alexandra makes Far Eastern tour

November Princess Margaret gives birth to Viscount Linley at Clarence House – Queen and Duke make West African tour

December Duke represents Queen at Independence celebrations in Tanzania – Queen inaugurates submarine telephone cable between Britain and Canada – Announcement that Duchess of Kent is expecting a baby

1962

February Duke of Edinburgh sets out on 36,000 mile tour of South America returning April – Princess Royal makes six week visit to Mediterranean and Near East

March Duke and Duchess of Gloucester return from tour of Kenya – Queen entertains Mrs Kennedy to lunch – Queen inaugurates Queen Elizabeth II Reservoir at Walton-on-Thames

April Queen Mother tours Northern Ireland – President Soekarno of Indonesia cancels State Visit to London – Queen Mother opens Tamar Bridge

May Queen, Duke, Princess Marina and Princess Alexandra attend silver wedding celebrations of Queen Juliana of the Netherlands – Duke visits Montreal – Queen attends consecration of Coventry Cathedral – Queen attends service at St Paul's Cathedral for 300th anniversary of Book of Common Prayer

June Queen Mother visits New York – Queen and Royal Family attend hallowing service of new Private Chapel at Buckingham Palace – Duchess of Kent gives birth to Earl of St Andrews at Coppins

July Princess Margaret installed as Chancellor of Keele University – President Tubman of Liberia pays State Visit to London

August Princess Margaret represents Queen at Independence celebrations in Jamaica – Queen entertains Eisenhowers at Buckingham Palace – Princess Royal represents Queen at Independence celebrations in Trinidad

September Queen and Duke give dinner party for Commonwealth Prime Ministers

October Duke of Kent represents Queen at Independence celebrations in Uganda – King Olav of Norway pays State Visit to Edinburgh

November Queen opens new Commonwealth Institute – Duke opens Commonwealth Games in Perth – Engagement of Princess of Alexandra to Angus Ogilvy announced

December Duchess joins Duke of Kent in Hong Kong where he is stationed

1963

January Queen and Duke visit Canada

February Queen and Duke visit Fiji, New Zealand and Australia

March Snowdons move to new home at Kensington Palace – Queen appoints Robert Menzies KT – Gloucesters visit Jordan and Cyprus

April Marriage of Princess Alexandra to Angus Ogilvy at Westminster Abbey

May Queen Mother visits Channel Islands – Queen opens New Zealand House – King Baudouin of the Belgians pays State Visit to London

June Princess Margaret and Lord Snowdon visit Northern Ireland – President Radhakrishnan of India pays Commonwealth Visit to London

July Queen installs Sir Robert Menzies as KT in Edinburgh – Queen Mother visits Isle of Man – King Paul of the Hellenes pays State Visit to London – Announcement that Princess Alexandra is expecting a baby

August Queen and Duke visit Wales – State Visit of President Ayub Khan of Pakistan postponed

September Announcement that Queen is expecting a baby

October Queen visits Mr Macmillan in hospital after his resignation as Prime Minister – Queen receives Lord Home who forms a government

November Duke opens West London Air Terminal – Queen and Duke entertain President Asgeirsson of Iceland to lunch at Buckingham Palace – Princess Royal visits Cyprus – Duke of Edinburgh represents Queen at funeral of President Kennedy in Washington – Queen and Royal Family attend dedication of rebuilt Guards Chapel

December Queen and Royal Family attend memorial services for President Kennedy – Queen opens Pacific section of Commonwealth telephone cable between Australia, New Zealand, Fiji and Canada in recorded message – Duke represents Queen at Independence celebrations in Zanzibar

1964

February Queen Mother cancels tour of Canada, New Zealand and Australia due to operation – Princess Alexandra gives birth to James Ogilvy at Thatched House Lodge on Leap Year's Day

March Queen gives birth to Prince Edward at Buckingham Palace – Duke and Princess Marina attend funeral of King Paul of the Hellenes

April Duke attends 40th anniversary celebrations of Shakespeare's birth at Stratford – Duchess of Kent gives birth to Lady Helen Windsor at Coppins

May Princess Margaret gives birth to Lady Sarah Armstrong-Jones at Kensington Palace – Duke visits Northern Ireland – President Abbood of Sudan pays State Visit to London

June Queen attends Beating of Retreat of RM massed bands for tercentenary

July Duke represents Queen at Independence celebrations in Malawi – Snowdons at premiere of Beatles film *A Hard Day's Night*

Below: Norman Parkinson's 80th birthday study of the Queen Mother with her two daughters, 1980

Opposite (above left and right): The monarch on manoeuvres; (below) the Queen with Prince Philip after the service at St Paul's to celebrate the Queen Mother's 80th birthday, July 1980

September Queen inaugurates Forth Road Bridge – Duke, Prince of Wales and Princess Anne attend wedding of King Constantine of the Hellenes – Duke represents Queen at Independence celebrations of Malta – Princess Marina visits Australia and Malaysia – Princess Margaret opens British Week in Copenhagen

October Sir Alec Douglas-Home resigns after general election – Queen asks Harold Wilson to form a government – Queen and Duke visit Canada – Princess Royal represents Queen at Independence celebrations in Zambia

November Princess Alexandra installed as Chancellor of University of Lancaster

December Duke visits Germany, France and Belgium – Duke visits Morocco as guest of King Hussan – Duke, Prince of Wales and Princess Anne holiday in Liechtenstein

1965

January Queen and Royal Family attend State Funeral of Sir Winston Churchill – Duke and Duchess of Gloucester's motor accident on A1

February Queen pays State Visit to Ethiopia and Sudan – Duke makes 21,000 mile world tour – Duke of Kent represents Queen at Independence celebrations in Gambia

March Princess Margaret and Lord Snowdon visit Uganda – Princess Royal represents Queen at funeral of Queen Louise of Sweden – Queen visits Duke of Windsor in hospital in London – Duke and Duchess of Gloucester make four-week tour of Australia – Princess Royal dies at Harewood aged 67

April Funeral of Princess Royal at Harewood – Prince of Wales confirmed at Windsor

May Queen inaugurates Kennedy memorial at Runnymede – Princess Margaret opens British Week in Amsterdam – Queen pays State Visit to West Germany

June Queen receives address for 700th Anniversary of Simon de Montfort's Parliament in Westminster Hall – Queen Mother visits Toronto – Queen attends Salvation Army centenary in Albert Hall

July President Frei of Chile pays State Visit to London – Queen and Duke visit Isle of Wight

August Queen reviews Home Fleet in Firth of Clyde

September Princess Alexandra visits Japan and Hong Kong – Queen and Duke attend 25th anniversary Service of Battle of Britain in Westminster Abbey

October Queen writes to Ian Smith about Rhodesian problem

November Princess Margaret and Lord Snowdon visit USA – Princess Marina represents Queen at funeral of Queen Elizabeth of the Belgians

December Queen and Royal Family spend Christmas at Windsor for 1st time – Queen and Royal Family attend 900th Anniversary Service of Westminster Abbey

1966

January Duke and Duchess of Gloucester visit Singapore and Malaysia – Prince of Wales leaves for Geelong Grammar School, Australia

February Queen and Duke undertake a month's Caribbean tour

March Princess Margaret and Lord Snowdon visit British Week in Hong Kong – Princess Margaret represents Queen at wedding of Princess Beatrix of the Netherlands – Queen Mother tours Australia, Fiji and New Zealand – Princess Marina installed as 1st Chancellor of University of Kent at Canterbury

April Princess Anne confirmed by Archbishop of Canterbury – Princess Anne breaks nose

May Duke visits Oslo for British Trade Fair – Duchess of Kent installed as Chancellor of Leeds University – Queen pays State Visit to Belgium – President Jonas of Austia pays State Visit to London – Queen signs proclamation of emergency due to seamen's strike – Duke of Kent represents Queen at Independence celebrations in Guyana

July Queen's car dented by concrete slab in Belfast – King Husain of Jordan pays State Visit to London – Prince of Wales leaves Timbertop – Princess Alexandra gives birth to Marina Ogilvy at Thatched House Lodge – Lord Snowdon opens aviary at London Zoo

August Duke opens Empire Games in Jamaica

September Queen opens Severn Bridge – Queen Mother launches Polaris submarine *Resolution* – Duke visits Argentina – Princess Marina represents Queen at ceremonies for founding of Republic of Botswana

October Queen opens St George's House, Windsor – Queen and Duke visit Aberfan after disaster

November Queen opens Imperial War Museum extension – Prince of Wales comes-of-age at 18 – President Ayub Khan of Pakistan pays Commonwealth Visit to London

December Queen Mother has operation

1967

January Queen Mother to rest for a few months

February Queen and Duke entertain Kosygin in London – Princess Alexandra visits Burma, Hong Kong, Australia and Canada – Duke makes world tour

March Queen opens Queen Elizabeth Hall on South Bank – Snowdons holiday in Bahamas

May Queen Mother tours Cornwall, North Devon and Northern France – King Faisal of Saudi Arabia pays State Visit to London – Queen attends 50th anniversary service of OBE at St Paul's Cathedral – Princess Margaret and Lord Snowdon visit Northern Ireland – Queen visits Normandy privately

June Duke and Duchess of Windsor present when Queen unveils plaque to Queen Mary at Marlborough House – Duke of Kent rides in Queen's Birthday Parade for 1st time

July Queen knights Francis Chichester at Greenwich – Queen and Duke visit EXPO 67 in Canada – Queen Mother tours Canada – Queen opens new sports centre at Gordonstoun

August Queen and Royal Family visit Scilly Isles

September Queen launches *Queen Elizabeth 2* at Clydebank –
Lord Snowdon opens British Week in Brussels

October Queen opens new Tyne Tunnel for vehicles – Queen
Mother installed as Chancellor of Dundee University – Prince of
Wales goes up to Trinity College Cambridge – Prince of Wales
and Princess Anne attend Opening of Parliament for 1st time

November President Cevdet Sunay of Turkey pays State Visit
to London – Princess Marina attends memorial service for Sir
Malcolm Sargent – Queen and Duke visit Malta – Queen Mother
lays foundation stone of new Stock Exchange

December Queen inaugurates Sir Isaac Newton telescope at
Herstmonceux – Prince of Wales represents Queen at memorial
service for Harold Holt in Melbourne

1968
February Queen Mother attends wedding of Princess Benedicte
of Denmark

March Queen Mother opens new library of Royal Academy of
Music – Queen opens Salvation Army's Booth House

April Queen and Royal Family attend RAF 50th anniversary
banquet – Queen entertains King Frederik of Denmark during
Danish Week

May Duke makes world tour – Queen attends ceremony
granting Brigade of Guards Freedom of Royal Borough of New
Windsor

June Queen attends TUC centenary banquet at Guildhall – Duke
of Kent becomes honorary Chief of Blackfoot tribe at Calgary –
Duke of Edinburgh receives OM – Prince of Wales installed KG

July Queen knights Alec Rose – Queen receives President of
Pakistan at Buckingham Palace – Queen opens Matisse Gallery

August Queen opens new oil refinery at Milford Haven –
Princess Marina, Duchess of Kent dies at Kensington Palace

September Prince Andrew goes to Heatherdown – Princess
Alexandra opens British Week in Stockholm – Miss Peebles,
royal governess, dies

October Queen opens extension to Royal Courts of Justice –
Duke attends Olympic Games in Mexico City – memorial service
for Princess Marina in Westminster Abbey

November Prince of Wales takes part in Cambridge revue –
Queen pays State Visits to Brazil and Chile and visits Senegal –
Princess Margaret opens Scottish Design Centre, Glasgow –
Queen Mother sees sextuplets in Birmingham – Duke faces
demonstrators at Salford University – Queen attends RA
bicentenary dinner – Queen strikes 1st decimal coin at new Royal
Mint at Llantrisant

1969
February Quen opens National Postal Museum – Queen
entertains President Nixon to lunch

March Prince of Wales makes 1st broadcast – Princess Anne
undertakes 1st solo engagement at St David's Day Parade –
Queen opens Victoria Underground Line – Queen attends
dedication of King George VI Memorial Chapel at Windsor –
Lord Mountbatten represents Queen at General Eisenhower's
funeral

April Duke of Kent represents Queen at funeral of Queen
Victoria Eugénie of Spain – Prince of Wales arrives at University
College of Wales, Aberystwyth for course – President Saragat of
Italy pays State Visit to Windsor

May Princess Anne launches *Esso Northumbria* – Queen pays State
Visit to Austria – Queen reviews ships of twelve NATO
countries at Spithead – Queen addresses General Assemblies in
Scotland

June Prince of Wales presents new colours to Royal Regiment of
Wales at Cardiff Castle – Richard Cawston's *Royal Family* film
shown on television

July Investiture of Prince Charles as Prince of Wales at
Caernarvon Castle – Prince of Wales makes four-day tour of
Wales – President Kekkonen of Finland pays State Visit to
London – Queen reviews ships of Western Fleet at Torbay

August Princess Alexandra visits Singapore – Queen and Royal
Family sail to Norway on private visit – Duke and Duchess of
Kent visit Australia

September Princess Margaret and Lord Snowdon open British
Week in Japan

October Queen receives *Apollo 11* astronauts at Buckingham
Palace – Duke visits Canada and USA

November Prince of Wales celebrates 21st birthday – Prince of
Wales visits Malta

December Princess Andrew of Greece dies at Buckingham
Palace aged 84 – Funeral of Princess Andrew at St George's
Chapel

1970
February Duke and Prince of Wales visit Strasbourg for
European Conservation conference – Duchess of Kent visits
Singapore – Prince of Wales takes seat in House of Lords –
Annigoni's new portrait of Queen unveiled at National Portrait
Gallery

March Queen, Duke, Prince of Wales and Princess Anne visit
Fiji, Tonga, New Zealand and Australia – Duke of Gloucester is
70

April Prince of Wales visits EXPO 70 in Japan – Viscount Linley
guarded at school against kidnap attempt

May Prince William of Gloucester represents Queen at
Independence celebrations in Tonga – Gloucesters move to
Kensington Palace

June Princess Margaret and Lord Snowdon visit Yugoslavia –
Harold Wilson resigns after general election – Queen asks
Edward Heath to form a government – Queen gives party for
70th birthdays of four members of Royal Family – Queen attends
Westminster Hall ceremony for 25th Anniversary of signing of
UN Charter

July Queen, Duke, Prince of Wales and Princess Anne visit
Canada – Prince of Wales and Princess Anne stay at the White
House – Queen attends Commonwealth Games in Edinburgh –
Duchess of Kent gives birth to Lord Nicholas Windsor at King's
College Hospital

August Queen Mother is 70

September Duke visits Helsinki Trade Fair

The Queen in Portugal, March 1985. Below: A display by the Portuguese School of Equestrian Art. Bottom: Students at Evora University honouring the Queen. Opposite (above): Unveiling a statue of her great-grandfather, the European traveller, Edward VII; and (below) at the Palace of Belen, the Portuguese President's official residence in Lisbon

October Queen attends lunch given by Edward Heath for President Nixon at Chequers – Prince of Wales represents Queen at Independence celebrations in Fiji

November Princess Alexandra opens British Industrial Exhibition in Argentina – Queen attends inauguration of General Synod of Church of England at Westminster Abbey – Prince of Wales represents Queen at memorial service for General de Gaulle in Paris

1971

January Prince Michael in bobsleigh accident – Duke and Princess Alexandra tour Pacific Islands

February Prince of Wales and Princess Anne visit Kenya – Prince of Wales drives tank at Osnabruck

March Prince of Wales receives Freedom of City of London – Queen Mother attends Royal Film Performance of *Love Story* – Prince William of Gloucester buys Piper Cherokee aircraft

April Princess Margaret opens British Design exhibition in Paris – Queen restores Emperor Hirohito of Japan to Order of Garter – Princess Alexandra visits New Zealand

May Queen visits British Columbia – Queen asks for revision of Civil List

June Princess Anne visits Norway – Queen launches guided missile destroyer – Duke of Edinburgh is 50 – Queen declares 2nd Mersey Tunnel open – Queen and Duke visit York despite shooting threat

July Princess Anne has emergency operation – Prince of Wales parachutes into Channel

August Princess Anne celebrates 21st birthday on *Britannia* – Duke, Prince of Wales and Princess Anne welcome Chay Blyth home from solo round-world voyage – Prince of Wales receives pilot's wings

September Princess Anne wins European Championships at Burghley – Prince of Wales becomes Sub-Lieutenant at RNC Dartmouth

October Duke and Duchess of Windsor receive Emperor Hirohito in Paris – Emperor Hirohito pays State Visit to London – Duke and Princess Anne attend Persepolis celebrations – Queen pays State Visit to Turkey – Princess Anne visits Hong Kong – Prince of Wales joins HMS *Norfolk*

November President Tito lunches with Queen – Princess Anne voted BBC Sports Personality of the Year

December King Mohamed Zahir Shah of Afghanistan pays State Visit to London – House of Commons votes for Civil List increase from £475,000 to £980,000 p.a.

1972

January Duke pilots *Concorde* – Duke represents Queen at funeral of King Frederik IX of Denmark – Queen pays State Visit to Thailand and tours SE Asia and Indian Ocean – Engagement of Prince Richard of Gloucester to Birgitte van Deurs announced

March Princess Margaret atends tercentary celebrations of British Virgin Islands – Queen opens Tutankhamen exhibition

April Queen Juliana of the Netherlands pays State Visit

May Princess Margaret, Lord Snowdon, Prince William of Gloucester and Duke of Kent make *Concorde* flight – Queen pays State Visit to France and calls on Duke and Duchess of Windsor – Princess Anne visits Channel Islands – Duke of Windsor dies in Paris aged 77

June Lying-in-State and funeral of Duke of Windsor at St George's Chapel – Grand Duke Jean of Luxembourg pays State Visit to London – Princess Anne visits Monaco

July Princess Anne attends wedding of Prince Alexander of Yugoslavia in Seville – Marriage of Prince Richard of Gloucester to Birgitte van Deurs at St Andrew's Church, Barnwell

August Prince William of Gloucester killed in flying accident near Wolverhampton aged 30 – Queen cancels visit to Munich Olympics but Duke and Princess Anne attend

September Funeral of Prince William at St George's Chapel

October Admiral Sir Alexander Ramsay dies aged 91 – Queen pays State Visit to Yugoslavia – President Heinemann of West Germany pays State Visit to London

November Queen opens exhibition for 50th Anniversary of BBC – Queen and Duke celebrate silver wedding with thanksgiving service at Westminster Abbey and lunch at Guildhall

1973

January Queen attends gala for Britain's entry into Common Market – Prince of Wales serves in West Indies in HMS *Minerva*

February Princess Anne visits Ethiopia and Sudan – Duke of Kent starts work at Ministry of Defence – Princess Alice, Countess of Athlone is 90

March Queen opens community centre at Aberfan – Queen opens new London Bridge

April President de Echeverria of Mexico pays State Visit

May Engagement of Princess Anne to Lieutenant Mark Phillips announced

June Princess Anne visits Germany – Duke visits Portugal – General Gowon of Nigeria pays State Visit to London – Queen and Duke visit Canada

July Prince of Wales represents Queen at Independence celebrations in the Bahamas – Queen and Duke visit Canada for meeting of Commonwealth Heads of Government

August Queen and Duke attend service at Bath Abbey to mark millennium of Edgar's coronation

September Princess Anne competes in Kiev and falls from *Goodwill* – Prince Andrew goes to Gordonstoun – Queen opens Commonwealth Parliamentary Conference at Westminster – Duke and Duchess of Kent visit Japan and Burma – Prince and Princess Richard of Gloucester visit Mexico – Duke represents Queen at funeral of King Gustaf VI Adolf of Sweden

October Queen opens Sydney Opera House

November Queen attends unveiling of statue of Sir Winston Churchill in Parliament Square – Marriage of Princess Anne to Captain Mark Phillips at Westminster Abbey

December Princess Anne and Captain Phillips tour Latin America – President Mobutu of Zaire pays State Visit to London

1974

January Prince Richard of Gloucester appointed GCVO – Prince of Wales joins firgate *Jupiter* in Singapore – Lady Patricia Ramsay dies aged 87 – Princess Margaret visits Cyprus – Duke opens Commonwealth Games in Christchurch – Queen leaves for Australasian tour

February Prince Richard attends ceremony in London to mark Independence of Grenada – Queen flies home for general election

March Edward Heath resigns and Harold Wilson forms a government – Queen pays State Visit to Indonesia – Princess Anne escapes kidnap attempt in Mall

April Lord Snowdon makes maiden speech in House of Lords – Queen Margrethe of Denmark pays State Visit to London

May Princess Margaret visits USA and Canada – Queen Mother visits Churchill Centenary exhibition – Prince of Wales accepts Chevening House

June Duke of Gloucester dies at Barnwell aged 74 – Prince of Wales makes maiden speech in House of Lords – Funeral of Duke of Gloucester at St George's Chapel – Queen Mother visits Canada

July The Yang-di-Pertuan Agong of Malaysia pays State Visit to London – Queen attends game fair at Stratfield Saye

August Princess Anne appointed GCVO

September Prince of Wales represents Queen at funeral of Norman Kirk in New Zealand – Prince of Wales takes helicopter course at Yeovilton

October Prince of Wales visits Fiji and Australia – Duchess of Gloucester gives birth to Earl of Ulster at St Mary's Hospital Paddington – Princess Anne and Captain Phillips visit Toronto Royal Fair

November Duke visits IRA bomb victims in Birmingham

December Queen attends première of *Murder on the Orient Express*.

1975

January Prince of Wales undergoes commando assault course in Devon – Princess Alexandra launches International Women's Year – Prince of Wales attends enthronement of Dr Coggan as Archbishop of Canterbury

February Prince of Wales and Princess Alexandra attend funeral of Duke of Norfolk – Queen abandons scheme to modernize Sandringham – Queen sees bomb squad at work at Scotland Yard – Queen pays State Visit to Mexico – Prince of Wales represents Queen at coronation of King Birendra of Nepal – House of Commons vote for Civil List increase

March Queen attends wedding of Earl of Lichfield – Queen Mother visits Iran

April Prince of Wales grows beard in Canada – Queen and Royal Family attend Quincentenary service in St George's Chapel – Queen invests Princess Alice, Duchess of Gloucester as GCB – Queen attends Commonwealth Prime Ministers' Conference in Jamaica

May Earl of St Andrews awarded scholarship to Eton – Queen pays State Visit to Japan – Prince of Wales installed as Grand Master of Order of Bath at Westminster Abbey

June Prince of Wales takes part in Birthday Parade for 1st time – Queen visits new Covent Garden Market

July King Carl XVI Gustaf of Sweden pays State Visit to Edinburgh – King of Nigeria attends Garden Party at Buckingham Palace

August Queen Mother is 75

September Prince of Wales visits Caterham IRA bomb victims – Prince of Wales represents Queen at Independence celebrations in Papua New Guinea

October Princess Alice, Duchess of Gloucester opens new Battersea Dogs Home

November President Nyere of Tanzania pays State Visit to London – Duke represents Queen at Accession celebrations of King Juan Carlos of Spain in Madrid

1976

January Duke of Kent flies on *Concorde's* inaugural flight to Bahrain – Duke of Kent becomes Vice-Chairman of British Overseas Trade Board

February Prince of Wales takes command of HMS *Bronington* – Queen Mother has 300th National Hunt winner – Queen and Duke visit Fleet Street – Princess Anne receives freedom of City of London

March Princess Margaret and Lord Snowdon separate – Harold Wilson resigns and James Callaghan becomes Prime Minister – Prince Andrew and Viscount Linley confirmed at Windsor – Queen opens *1776* exhibition at Greenwich – Duke of Edinburgh at funeral of Lord Montgomery

April Queen celebrates 50th birthday at Windsor – Princess Margaret visits Morocco and Tunisia

May President Geisel of Brazil pays State Visit to London – Queen pays State Visit to Finland

June President Giscard d'Estaing of France pays State Visit to London – Duchess of Windsor is 80 – Sir Harold Wilson installed KG – Duke of Gloucester represents Queen at wedding of King Carl XVI Gustaf of Sweden – Queen buys Gatcombe Park for Princess Anne and Captain Phillips

July Prince Andrew makes solo glider flight – Queen pays State Visit to USA – Queen opens 21st Olympic Games in Montreal – Princess Anne competes in Olympic Games

September Princess Margaret opens Commonwealth Speakers' Conference – Prince of Wales announces resignation from RN

October Princess Alexandra attends Vatican ceremony for canonization of John Ogilvy – Tercentenary celebrations of Royal Company of Archers – Queen Mother visits Paris

November Queen Mother opens exhibition in Windsor to mark 50 years of Queen's life – Queen pays State Visit to Luxembourg

1977

January Prince Andrew begins two terms at Lakefield College School, Ontario

February Queen and the Royal Family attend Morning Service at St George's Chapel, Windsor to mark start of Silver Jubilee year – Queen and Duke visit Western Samoa, Tonga, Fiji, New Zealand, Australia and Papua New Guinea

March Queen and Duke attend Centenary Test Match at Melbourne – Queen returns from Australia – Duke of Edinburgh in Saudi Arabia

April Prince of Wales launches Silver Jubilee Appeal

May Queen launches HMS *Invincible* at Barow-in-Furness – Queen receives addresses from both Houses of Parliament on Silver Jubilee – Prince of Wales invested KT – Silver Jubilee Gala at Covent Garden

June Silver Jubilee week – Countrywide chain of bonfires – Thanksgiving Service in St Paul's Cathedral and Guildhall lunch – Buckingham Palace dinner for Commonwealth Heads of Government – River pageant and fireworks display – Duke of Edinburgh installed as Chancellor of Cambridge University – The Queen and Duke tour Lancashire, Greater Manchester, Merseyside and Wales – Silver Jubilee Review of the Fleet at Spithead

July Centenary Wimbledon Championships (Queen presents trophy to Virginia Wade) – Silver Jubilee Review of the Army in Germany – The Queen and Duke tour Yorkshire, Humberside, Cleveland, Durham, Tyne and Wear, Northumberland, West Midlands, Derbyshire and Nottinghamshire

August Queen and Duke tour Devon, Avon and Northern Ireland

October The Queen and Duke visit Canada, the Bahamas, British Virgin Islands, Antigua and Barbados – Queen opens new sessions of Parliament in Ottawa and Nassau – Prince of Wales fundraising in Australia

November Queen and Duke return from Caribbean on *Concorde* in 3 hours 42 minutes – Princess Anne gives birth to son (Peter Phillips) at St Mary's Hospital, Paddington and moves to Gatcombe Park, Gloucestershire

December Queen entertains French President at Windsor – Queen opens Piccadilly Line extension to Heathrow

1978

January The Queen entertains King and Queen of Spain at Sandringham

February Prince Andrew's 18th birthday

March Prince of Wales visits Brazil and Venezuela – Queen entertains President Tito at Buckingham Palace

April Confirmation of Prince Edward, Lady Sarah Armstrong-Jones, Lady Helen Windsor and James Ogilvy

May Prince of Wales announces that Silver Jubilee Appeal raised £16 million – Divorce of Princess Margaret and Lord Snowdon – Prince of Wales represents the Queen at State fungeral of Sir Robert Menzies in Melbourne – Queen's State Visit to Federal Republic of Germany – Queen grants permission for Prince Michael of Kent to marry Baroness Marie-Christine von Reibnitz (formerly Mrs Tom Troubridge)

June State Visit of President Ceausescu of Rumania – Pope refuses permission for Prince Michael and the divorced Baroness to marry in a Catholic church – Queen and Duke tour Channel Islands

July Queen and Duke tour Borders Region of Scotland – Diamond Jubilee of English Speaking Union – Queen and Royal Family visit Canada

August Queen opens XIth Commonwealth Games in Edmonton, Alberta – Prince of Wales represents the Queen at State funeral of President Kenyatta in Nairobi

September The Queen Mother appointed Lord Warden of the Cinque Ports in succession to Sir Robert Menzies (first lady to hold post) – Princess Margaret taken ill on way to independence celebratins at Tuvalu

November The Queen Mother visits Army in Germany – State Visit of President Eanes of Portugal

December Queen entertains King Husain of Jordan at Buckingham Palace

1979

February Queen and Duke go on three-week visit to the Middle East, tourng Kuwait, Bahrain, Saudi Arabia, the United Arab Emirates and Oman – Princess Alexandra and Angus Ogilvy attend independence celebrations of St Lucia

March The Duke of Edinburgh attends Olympic meeting in Moscow – James Callaghan asks Queen to dissolve Parliament – The Prince of Wales visits Hong Kong, Singapore, Australia and Canada

April Princess Michael of Kent has a son (Lord Frederick Windsor) – Prince of Wales opens Jubilee Underground Line

May Queen asks Margaret Thatcher to form a new administration after General Election – Queen opens new galleries at Tate – 'The Great Children's Party' in Hyde Park

June The Duke of Kent opens British Energy Exhibition in Peking (first member of the Royal Family to visit China) – Queen and Duke attend 100th birthday concert of Sir Robert Mayer – 200th Derby atEpsom

July Princess Anne visits Gilbert Islands (independence celebrations), Thailand, New Zealand and Australia – Queen and Duke visit Isle of Man (millennium of Tynwald) – Queen, Duke and Prince Andrew go on 17-day visit to Tanzania, Malawi, Botswana and Zambia

August Lord Mountbatten assassinated by the IRA

September Funeral of Lord Mountbatten at Westminster Abbey

October Queen opens new Lyric Theatre, Hammersmith

November State Visit of President Soeharto of Indonesia

December Queen entertains President Tolbert of Liberia

1980

February Queen entertains Malcolm Fraser (Australian premier) at Sandringham

March The Duchess of Gloucester has a daughter (Lady Rose Windsor) – Enthronement of Most Reverend Robert Runcie as Archbishop of Canterbury – Prince of Wales visits Canada

April Prince Andrew passes out of Dartmouth – Prince of Wales represents the Queen at accession ceremony of Queen Beatrix of the Netherlands

May The Duke of Edinburgh represents the Queen at State funeral of President Tito of Yugoslavia – Queen and Duke visit Australia – opening of new High Court building in Canberra

June Queen entertains President Rahman of Bangladesh at Windsor

July Garden Party at Holyroodhouse in honour of the Queen Mother's 80th birthday – Prince of Wales gives up tenancy of Chevening House, Kent – Buckingham Palace press office deny so-called "official" report that the Prince of Wales will marry Princess Marie-Astrid of Luxembourg – Special Thanksgiving Service at St Paul's Cathedral in honour of Queen Mother's 80th birthday (Queen Mother takes precedence over the Queen at the latter's express wish) – Queen opens new grandstand at Goodwood

August Special Royal Ballet performance at Covent Garden to celebrate the Queen Mother's 80th birthday – Prince of Wales purchases Highgrove House

September The Duke of Edinburgh visits Canada, USA and Venezuela

October The Queen's State Visit to Italy, the Vatican, Tunisia, Algeria and Morocco

November Queen entertains the President of the European Parliament (Mme Veil) at Buckingham Palace – State Visit of King Birendra of Nepal – Prince of Wales visits India and Nepal

1981
January Funeral of Princess Alice, Countess of Athlone at St George's Chapel

February 25th anniversary dinner at the Mansion House for the Duke of Edinburgh's Award Scheme – engagement of the Prince of Wales to Lady Diana Spencer

March State Visit of President Shehu Shagari of Nigeria – Duke of Edinburgh visits Egypt, Hong Kong and Australia – Queen gives official approval in Privy Council to marriage of Prince of Wales

April Princess Michael of Kent has a daughter (Lady Gabriella Windsor)

May Queen's State Visit to Norway – Prince of Wales opens Mountbatten Exhibition at Broadlands – Princess Anne has a daughter (Zara Phillips)

June State Visit of King Khalid of Saudi Arabia – The Queen opens National Westminster tower in City of London – Dance at Windsor to celebrate Prince Andrew's 21st birthday

July Queen opens Humber Bridge – Buckingham Palace Garden Party to mark International Year of Disabled People – Wedding of Prince of Wales to Lady Diana Spencer in St Paul's Cathedral

August Queen entertains President Sadat of Egypt at Buckingham Palace – Prince and Princess of Wales entertain Sadats on Britannia at Port Said

September Queen and Duke visit Australia for the Commonwealth Heads of Government meeting

October Queen and Duke tour Australia, New Zealand and Sri Lanka – Prince of Wales represents Queen at funeral of President Sadat in Cairo – Princess Anne installed as Chancellor of London University – Prince and Princess of Wales tour the Principality – Princess Margaret represents the Queen at independence celebrations of Antigua and Barbados

November Queen opens Tyne & Wear Metro System – Princess Anne visits Nepal on behalf of Save the Children Fund

December Prince Andrew attends 100th University rugby match – Queen entertains the President of Zaire at Buckingham Palace

1982
February 30th anniversary of the Queen's accession

March Queen opens Barbican Centre – State Visit of the Sultan of Oman – Queen entertains Mrs Gandhi at Buckingham Palace

April Queen proclaims new Canadian Constitution in Ottawa – Queen entertains the President of Cameroon at Windsor – Argentina invades the Falkland Islands

May Queen entertains the President of the Maldives at Buckingham Palace – Queen re-opens restored Temperate House at Kew – Queen and Duke visit Winchester Collete for its 6th centenary – Queen entertains the Prime Minister of Zimbabwe at Buckingham Palace – Queen opens Kielder water project

June Queen entertains President Reagan at Windsor – The Queen Mother welcomes home survivors of HMS Coventry, Antelope and Ardent from the Falklands – Princess of Wales has a son (Prince William of Wales)

July Service in St Paul's for Diamond Jubilee of BBC – Queen entertains the Prime Minister of Singapore at Buckingham Palace – Falkland Islands service in St Paul's Cathedral

August Christening of Prince William at Buckingham Palace

September Prince Edward takes up post as junior house tutor at Wanganui Collegiate, New Zealand – Queen, Duke and Princess Anne welcome Prince Andrew back from Falklands on HMS Invincible at Spithead – Duke of Edinburgh opens XIIth Commonwealth Games in Brisbane

October Queen visits Australia, Papua New Guinea, Solomon Islands, Nauru, Kiribati, Tuvalu and Fiji – Prince of Wales sees Mary Rose raised from the seabed at Portsmouth – Princess Anne tours Africa on behalf of SCF

November Princess Anne visits Beirut on behalf of SCF – State Visit of Queen of the Netherlands – Queen entertains the President of Botswana – The Queen Mother has fishbone removed from her throat

1983
February Queen and Duke visit Jamaica, Cayman Islands, Mexico, USA and Canada

March Queen opens Henry Cole Wing at Victoria & Albert Museum – Queen receives members of the Arab League led by King Husain – Prince and Princess of Wales, with Prince William, visit Australia and New Zealand

April Queen entertains the Sultan of Oman at Windsor – The Queen Mother visits Brixton – Queen opens National Horseracing Museum at Newmarket

May State Visit to Sweden

June Prince and Princess of Wales visit Canada

July Queen Mother attends King Olav of Norway's 80th birthday celebration – Queen entertains the President of the Ivory Coast at Buckingham Palace – Prince and Princess Michael of Kent's marriage receives blessing of the Roman Catholic Church

September Princess Margaret represents the Queen at independence celebrations of St Christopher and Nevis

October Queen entertains the King of Tonga, and the Presidents of France and Mozambique at Buckingham Palace – The Duke of Edinburgh visits Hong Kong, Thailand and Malaysia

November The Queen unveils statue of Lord Mountbatten on Foreign Office Green – The Queen's State Visits to Kenya, Bangladesh and India

December Queen entertains the President of Lebanon at Buckingham Palace – Prince and Princess of Wales visit victims of Harrods IRA bomb

1984

February Princess Anne tours Africa on behalf of SCF – Queen entertains the President of Zimbabwe at Buckingham Palace – Bank of England's 250th anniversary lunch

March Queen entertains the Crown Prince of Japan and the President of the Gambia at Buckingham Palace – Queen's State Visit to Jordan – 500th anniversary of College of Arms

April Prince Andrew visits St Helena – Queen entertains the President of Israel at Windsor – The Queen Mother opens new paddock complex at Kempton Park – State Visit of Emir of Bahrain

May Queen opens International Garden Festival in Liverpool – Queen opens Thames barrier – Queen visits Army on the Rhine

June Queen entertains the Presidents of USA, Sri Lanka and Costa Rica at Buckingham Palace – 40th anniversary commemoration of D-Day landings in Normandy – Prince of Wales attends memorial service for Sir John Betjeman

July Princess Anne visits USA – Queen Mother "tops out" new Lloyd's building

August Queen opens Queen Elizabeth bridge over Dee

September Queen and Duke visit Canada

October Queen takes bloodstock holiday in USA

November NSPCC Centenary Thanksgiving Service in St Paul's Cathedral

December Queen visits RIBA 150th anniversary exhibition

1985

February Queen visits *The Times* on its 200th anniversary

March Queen's State Visit to Portugal – The Queen Mother opens Museum of Eton Life

April Duke and Duchess of Gloucester visits New Zealand – Prince and Princess of Wales tour Italy – Queen's 59th birthday

Acknowledgements

The author's chief debt of gratitude is to his old friend and collaborator Hugo Vickers for expert guidance and for the run of his unique royal archive of books, papers, press-cuttings albums and videos. Among others who kindly provided practical help or advice were: Gillon Aitken, Mark Bence-Jones, Alexandra Clayton, Charles Kidd, Patrick Montague-Smith, and David Williamson. The manuscript was admirably typed by Cynthia Lewis. The author's parents, John and Marsali Montgomery-Massingberd, read the proofs and made many useful suggestions. It was also a pleasure to collaborate with the designer of the book, Paul Watkins.

Even a very select "bibliography" on this subject would be somewhat overwhelming, but the following publications (many of which are alluded to, or quoted from, in the text) must be mentioned: *Thatched with Gold* Mabell Countess of Airlie (1962); *Memoirs* Princess Alice, Duchess of Gloucester (1983); *Is the Monarchy Perfect?* edited by Lord Altrincham (John Grigg) (1957); *The English Constitution* Walter Bagehot (1867); *Self-Portrait with Friends: The Selected Diaries of Cecil Beaton* edited by Richard Buckle (1979); *Philip* Basil Boothroyd (1971); *Royal Ceremonies of State* John Brooke-Little (1979); *The Castle Diaries* Barbara Castle (1984); *Her Majesty* Helen Cathcart (1962); *Memoirs* Viscount Chandos (1962); *Chips: The Diaries of Sir Henry Channon* edited by Robert Rhodes James (1967); *They Serve the Queen* Randolph Churchill (1953); *Crowded Life* Lady Cynthia Colville (1963); *Sporting Royals* Nicholas Courtney (1984); *The Little Princesses* Marion Crawford (1950); *The Diaries of a Cabinet Minister* Richard Crossman (2 Vols, 1975/76); *The Reality of Monarchy* Andrew Duncan (1970); *The Court at Windsor* (1964) & *The Court of St James's* (1979) Christopher Hibbert; *Select Committee on the Civil List* HMSO (1971); *Charles, Prince of Wales* Anthony Holden (1979); *Royal Palaces* (1970) & *The British Monarchy* (1977) Philip Howard; *Prince Philip* Denis Judd (1980); *Majesty* Robert Lacey (1977); *How the Queen Reigns* Dorothy Laird (1959); *The Royal House of Windsor* (1974), *The Queen Mother* (1981) & *Elizabeth R* (1983) Elizabeth Longford; *The Country Life Book of the Royal Silver Jubilee* Patrick Montague-Smith (1976); *The Country Life Book of Royal Palaces, Castles & Homes* Patrick Montague-Smith and Hugh Montgomery-Massingberd (1981); *Burke's Guide to The Royal Family* (1973) & *Burke's Royal Families of the World, Vol I* (1977) edited by Hugh Montgomery-Massingberd (1982); *The Queen* Ann Morrow (1983); *The Princes of Wales* Alan Palmer (1979); *Royal Heritage* J.H. Plumb and Huw Wheldon (1981); *Queen Mary* James Pope-Hennessy (1959); *Royal Residences* John Martin Robinson (1982); *George V* Kenneth Rose (1983); *Walter Bagehot* Norman St John Stevas (1959); *Debrett's Book of the Royal Wedding* (1981) & *We Want The Queen!* (1977) Hugo Vickers; *Two Centuries of Royal Weddings* (1980) & *Princess Margaret* (1983) Christopher Warwick; *King George VI* Sir John Wheeler-Bennett (1958); *Victoria & Albert At Home* Tyler Whittle (1980); *A King's Story* Duke of Windsor (1951); and *The Heart Has Its Reasons* Duchess of Windsor (1956)

Finally, the author would like to thank John Stidolph and Robert Dudley of Antler Books, the begetters of this illustrated volume, for their great patience, forbearance and understanding during its gestation.

In their turn, Antler Books wish to express appreciation for the help received in the production of this book from Gillon Aitken, Marcus Bishop (Lord Chamberlain's Office), Jennifer Damrel (Private Secretary's Office, Buckingham Palace), Frances Dimond (Curator, Photographic Collection, Royal Archives), Bridget Hayward (Palace Theatre), Sir Robin Mackworth-Young (The Librarian, Windsor Castle), Michael Shea (Press Secretary to The Queen), Alan Smith, Kate Truman and Caroline White (Willow Books).

Picture Acknowledgements

Antler Books acknowledges the help received from many photographers, agencies and libraries. The following is a list of the sources from which pictures were obtained and the pages on which they are published:-

Reproduced by gracious permission of H.M. The Queen: 59, 174, 178, 181 bottom, 187 top, 210, 230, 250
Reproduced by permission of H.R.H. The Prince of Wales: 231
Royal Archives copyright reserved, reproduced by gracious permission of H.M. The Queen: pp 10, 13, 14/15, 16, 28

Alpha: 9 *Godfrey Argent*: 212 *Associated Newspapers*: 233 *Steve Back*: 243 bottom *Barry Batchelor*: 152 bottom left *BBC*: 21 *Camera Press*: 46, 51 bottom, 55, 42, 116/117, 147 bottom, 160, 172, 179, 181 top, 205 centre top, 205 top right, 206 top left, 209, 59 *Central Press*: 52, 88 top left, 88 bottom, 96, 104, 132 bottom right, 158 top, 206 top right, 225 top, 228 bottom *Lionel Cherruault*: 111 bottom, 150 bottom, 215 top right *Martin Cleaver*: 148 bottom right *Bryn Colton*: 124 *Clive Cooksey*: 164 *Fritz Curzon*: 153 *Alan Davidson* 125 bottom *Reginald Davis*: 50/51, 54, 67, 74, 79, 83, 86, 87, 110 top, 114, 119, 131, 146, 154, 219, 226 *Mark Ellidge*: 220 top left *Rex Features*: 222 *Jayne Fincher*: 102, 152 top left, 186, 243 top right *Fox Photos*: 2, 20, 22/23, 24 inset, 25, 26, 27, 29, 30, 32, 33, 37, 43, 44, 48, 53, 56, 57, 60, 61, 72, 76, 77, 80, 84, 105, 108, 109, 110 bottom, 112, 120, 125 top left, 157, 166 bottom, 167 top, 169, 177, 185, 188, 190 top right, 192 top, 193, 196, 213, 214, 215 bottom, 232 top *Kent Gavin*: 93, 100, 133 left below, 136, 144, 149 bottom, 205 bottom, 220 top right *Tim Graham*: 158 bottom, 201 *Peter Grugeon*: 183 *Hamlyn Picture Library*: 17, 164, 184 *Glenn Harvey*: 163 *Jon Hoffman*: 71, 126, 162 bottom, 238 top right *Derek Hudson*: 220 bottom *Jarrold*: 191 *Colin Jones/The Field*: 216 *David Jones*: 125 top right *Edward Jones*: 141 *Dmitri Kasterine*: 170 *Margaret Lavender*: 243 top left *Roy Letkey*: 229 *Lichfield*: 122 *Mike Lloyd*: 65, 140 *Mike Maloney*: 202 *Anthony Marshall*: 148 top, 204, 232 bottom *Paul Montgomery*: 8 *Mike Moore*: 221 *National Portrait Gallery*: 19 *Richard Parker*: 235 *Norman Parkinson*: 156, 161, 242 *The Photo Source*: 31, 35, 40/41, 51 top, 78, 82, 98 top, 106, 107 bottom, 130, 134, 138 bottom, 139, 145, 147 top, 166 top, 171, 176, 182, 189, 190 top left, 198, 199, 205 top left, 224, 225 bottom, *Photographers International*: 115 top, 118, 127, 142, 150 top, 151, 159 right, 162 top left, 203 top right, 219, 234, 238 top left, 238 bottom left and bottom right, 239 *Photographic Records*: 206 bottom *Press Association*: 88 top right, 92, 121, 128 right, 133 top left, 137, 138 top, 203 bottom, 228 top *Press Photo Combine*: 81 *Harry Prosser*: 132 bottom left *Mike Roberts*: 6 *Phil Rudge*: 180 *John Shelley*: 90, 91, 98 bottom, 99, 111 top, 155, 159 left, 162 top right, 163 top left and bottom, 203 top left, 207, 215 top left, 246 *Snowdon*: 143, 167 *Sothebys/The Palace Theatre, London*: 94 *Syndication International*: 45, 68, 89, 97, 113, 128 left, 129, 132 top, 148 bottom left, 149 top, 152 top and bottom right, 165, 200 *Dennis Waugh*: 175

Index

Abel Smith, Colonel Sir Henry, 170
Abel Smith, Lady May, 170
Abel Smith, Lady, 207
Abergavenny, Marquess of, 204
Abergavenny, Marchioness of, 204
Adeane, Edward, 209
Adeane, Lord (formerly Sir Michael, 65, 69, 71, 75, 105, 109, 209
Adenauer, Dr, 49
Aga Khan, 211
Agnew, Sir Godfrey, 65
Aguiyi-Ironso, Major, 79
Airlie, 13th Earl of, 165, 201, 202
Airlie, Mabell Countess of, 11, 26, 29, 165, 202
Airlie, Countess of, 202, 204
Airlie, Lord, 165, 202
Alanbrooke, Viscount, 197
Albert, Prince, 38, 44, 173, 175, 182, 186, 188, 194
Alexandra, Princess, 73, 112, 164, 165, 168, 202, 208, 221
Alexandra Princess, Duchess of Fife, 168
Alexandra, Queen, 11, 12, 15, 78, 168, 173, 188
Alexandra of Yugoslavia, Queen, 34
Alice, Princess, Duchess of Gloucester, 21, 73, 112, 157, 159, 168, 208, 221
Alice, Princess, Countess of Athlone, 112, 165, 170
Allison, Ronald, 156
Altrincham, Lord, 58, 60, 76, 207
Althorp, Lord (see Spencer)
Amin, Idi, 47, 101
Ancaster, Earl and Countess of, 197
Anderson, Mabel, 39
Andrew, Prince, 66, 69, 70, 73, 78, 83, 85, 112, 113, 141, 145, 147, 150, 168, 175, 221
Andrew of Greece, Prince, 33, 34
Andrew of Greece, Princess, 33, 34
Andrew, Elizabeth, 177
Anne, Princess, 38, 39, 66, 67, 70, 73, 76, 78, 85, 103, 104, 112, 113, 145, 150, 152, 153, 155, 157, 164, 165, 168, 201, 208, 216
Annenberg, Walter, 185
Argyll, Duke of, 58
Armstrong-Jones, Antony (see Snowdon)
Armstrong-Jones, Lady Sarah, 103, 156, 157, 221, 234
Arthur of Connaught, Prince, 168
Ashley, Edwina (see Mountbatten)
Ashmore, Vice-Admiral Sir Peter, 202
Asquith, Lady Cynthia, 18
Astor, Jane, 197
Astor, Nancy, Lady, 197
Astor, 2nd Viscount, 197
Athlone, Earl of, 170
Auchincloss, Louis, 185

Bagehot, Walter, 63, 65, 71, 103, 123
Bailey, Lilian, 56
Balding, Ian, 213
Banda, Dr, 97
Beaconsfield, Earl of (see Disraeli)
Beaton, Sir Cecil, 29, 53, 123
Beatrix, Queen, 105
Beaufort, 9th Duke of, 202

Beaufort, 10th Duke of, 170, 202
Beaverbrook, Lord, 66
Bellaigue, Vicomtesse de, 29
Benn, Tony, 69
Benson, A.C., 78
Bernhard, Prince, 85
Birendra, King, 105
Blunt, (Sir) Anthony, 223
Boothroyd, Basil, 34, 38, 66
Bowes-Lyon, David, 15
Bowes-Lyon, Elizabeth (see Elizabeth, Queen Mother)
Boxer, Mark, 157
Boyd-Rochfort, Captain Sir Cecil, 211, 213
Brabourne, Doreen Lady, 223
Brabourne, Lord, 157
Bridges, Sir Edward, 69
Brooke-Little, John, 117
Buccleuch, 7th Duke of, 21
Bulganin, Marshall, 75, 105
Burghersh, Lord, 202
Butler, R.A. 'Rab', 63, 64
Buttle, Mr, 75

Callaghan, James, 63, 68
Cambridge, Marchioness of, 170
Cambridge, George, Marquess of, 170
Carl XVI Gustaf, King, 105
Carrington, Lord, 97, 197
Carnarvon, Earl of, 213
Carson, Willie, 216
Casson, Sir Hugh, 185, 186, 188
Castle, Barbara, 68, 69
Castle, Lord, 69
Cavendish-Bentinck, Cecilia (see Strathmore)
Cawston, Richard, 103, 104
Cazalet, Peter, 127, 211
Cecil, Lord David, 123
Cecil, Henry, 211
Chandos, Viscount, 7, 40, 44
Channon, Sir Henry 'Chips', 21
Charles, Prince, The Prince of Wales, 38, 39, 56, 58, 66, 69, 73, 76, 78, 85, 103, 105, 112, 113, 127, 128, 129, 130, 134, 135, 140, 141, 145, 147, 150, 155, 164, 168, 170, 186, 194, 197, 201, 208, 209, 216, 221, 223, 224, 228, 229, 233, 234
Charteris, Lord (formerly Sir Martin), 47, 65
Chesterton, G.K., 71
Cholmondeley, Marquess of, 197
Cholmondeley, Sybil, Marchioness of, 197
Christian, John, 75
Churchill, Sir Winston, 7, 29, 47, 49, 58, 63, 66, 70, 159, 197
Clark, Ronald, 194
Clynes, J.R., 18
Colville, Commander Richard, 208
Colville, Lady Cynthia, 20
Connaught, Alastair, 2nd Duke of, 168
Connaught, Prince Arthur, Duke of, 11, 26, 39, 79, 168
Constantine I, King, 33
Coward, Sir Noel, 29, 53, 66, 123
Crawford, Marion ('Crawfie'), 18, 20, 23, 25, 26, 29, 33, 34
Crawley, Canon, 26
Crossman, Richard, 68, 69

Dalhousie, 13th Earl of, 168

Davies, Donald, 156
de Gaulle, President, 75, 85, 105, 108
Dewar, Caroline, 168
Diana, Princess of Wales (see Wales)
Diefenbaker, John, 82
Dimbleby, Richard, 53
Disraeli, Benjamin, 123
Douglas-Home, Sir Alec (see Home)
Dugdale, Mrs John, 207
Dulles, Mr, 82
Duncan, Andrew, 44

Eden, Sir Anthony, 57, 63, 70
Edinburgh, Alfred, Duke of, 168
Edinburgh, Philip, Duke of (see Philip)
Edward VII, King, 11, 17, 63, 66, 78, 105, 168, 173, 175, 186, 188, 194
Edward VIII, King, 11, 18, 21, 49, 65, 76, 85, 129, 157, 170, 188, 201, 202
Eisenhower, President, 82, 83
Elizabeth II, Queen, *passim*
Elizabeth, Queen, The Queen Mother, 11, 12, 15, 16, 17, 18, 21, 23, 25, 26, 29, 30, 34, 40, 49, 53, 56, 73, 82, 112, 113, 123, 127, 134, 140, 155, 168, 177, 185, 186, 194, 202, 208, 211, 221, 223, 233
Elphinstone, Lady, 11
Esher, Viscount, 63

Fagan, Michael, 117, 176, 177, 204, 207, 223
Fellowes, Lady Jane, 208
Fellowes, Robert, 208
Fellowes, Sir William, 208
Fermoy, Frances (see Shand Kydd)
Fermoy, 4th Lord, 134
Fermoy, Ruth Lady, 134, 194
Fife, James, 3rd Duke of, 168
Fife, Caroline, Duchess of, 168
Fitzalan-Howard, Miles (see Norfolk)
Fitzalan, Marsha, 199
Foot, Michael, 70
Forster, E.M., 123
Fraser, Malcolm, 64, 233
Frederik of Denmark, King, 81
Frost, David, 145, 199

Gandhi, Mrs Indira, 89, 101, 104
George II of Greece, King, 38
George V, King, 11, 12, 15, 17, 18, 21, 34, 49, 58, 65, 66, 70, 123, 150, 157, 161, 168, 173, 188, 191, 194, 200, 202, 209, 223
George VI, King, 11, 12, 15, 16, 17, 18, 21, 23, 26, 29, 30, 34, 37, 38, 40, 44, 49, 56, 64, 70, 75, 123, 134, 145, 150, 170, 186, 194, 197, 202, 209, 213
George of Teck, Prince (see Cambridge)
Giscard d'Estaing, President, 105
Gloucester, Princess Richard, Duchess of, 112, 140, 159, 168, 186, 208
Gloucester, Henry, Duke of, 21, 47, 53, 73, 157, 159, 160, 168, 170
Gloucester, Prince Richard, Duke of, 140, 159, 186, 208, 221

Granville, Countess, 18
Grafton, Duchess of, 204
Grafton, Duke of, 204
Grigg, John (see Altrincham)
Gustav VI Adolf, King, 79, 81, 105
Haakon VII, King, 78, 168
Hahn, Kurt, 34, 127
Haile Selassie, Emperor, 75, 85, 105
Hailsham, Lord, 63
Hamilton, William, 44, 71, 73, 155, 228
Harewood, 6th Earl of, 11
Harewood, 7th Earl of, 168, 170
Hartnell, Sir Norman, 12, 37, 81
Hassan, King, 87
Heath, Edward, 63, 64, 68, 165
Henry 'Harry' of Wales, Prince, 113, 141, 145, 153, 157, 207, 234
Hern, Major Dick, 213
Heseltine, Sir William, 208
Heuss, Dr Theodor, 105
Hicks, Lady Pamela, 47
Hirohito, Emperor, 75, 105, 108
Holland, Mr, 76
Home, Lord, 63, 64, 194
Howard, Philip, 65, 120, 130, 233
Husain, King, 89
Hussey, 'Duke', 207
Hussey, James, 207
Hussey, Lady Susan, 207
Huston, John, 197

Ingrid, Queen, 81
Jaipur, Maharajah of, 221
Jones, Colin, 221
John, Prince, 21, 188
John XXIII, Pope, 83
Johnston, Sir 'Johnny', 202
Joynson-Hicks, Sir William, 11
Juan Carlos, King, 228
Juliana, Queen, 82, 83, 105

Kaunda, Kenneth, 97
Kelantan, Sultan of, 53
Kent, Prince Edward, Duke of, 73, 112, 160, 168, 170, 186, 208, 221
Kent, Prince George, Duke of, 20, 23, 26, 34, 53, 147
Kent, Princess Edward, Duchess of, 112, 160, 168, 208, 221
Kenyatta, Jomo, 85
Kerr, Sir John, 64, 86, 233
Kinnock, Neil, 224
Knatchbull, Nicholas, 223
Knight, Clara ('Allah'), 11, 15, 17, 18
Kosygin, Alexei, 108
Krushchev, Nikita, 75, 105, 108
Kuwait, Emir of, 87

Lang, Archbishop Cosmo, 11, 21
Lascelles, Sir Alan ('Tommy'), 49, 58, 64, 65
Lascelles, George (see Harewood)
Lascelles, Gerald, 11, 168
Lascelles, Henry, Viscount, 11
Laski, Professor Harold, 64
Lash, Professor Nicholas, 123
Lean, David, 157
Lebrun, President, 25
Leveson-Gower, Lady Rose (see Granville)
Levesque, René, 87, 93
Levin, Bernard, 70
Lewes, Earl of, 204
Lightbody, Helen, 39
Lillee, Dennis, 87

Lindsay-Hogg, Michael, 156
Linley, David, Viscount, 156, 164, 221, 234
Lloyd George, David, 129
Longford, Earl of, 12
Longford, Elizabeth, Countess of 12, 17, 29, 66
Louis of Battenberg, Prince, 33, 34, 37
Louise, Princess, Duchess of Fife, 168
Louise, Queen, 79
Lutyens, Sir Edwin, 18, 173, 185
Lyttelton, Oliver (see Chandos)
McCulloch, Derek, 26
McConnell, Brian, 153
Macdonald, James, 47
MacDonald, Margaret ('Bobo'), 17, 18
MacDonald, Ramsay, 200
MacDonald, Ruby, 18
Maclean, Lord ('Chips'), 165, 201, 202
Macleod, Iain, 64
Macmillan, Harold, Earl of Stockton, 57, 63, 64, 66, 70, 83, 95
Mahendra, King, 105
Makepeace, John, 156
Margadale, Lord, 207
Margaret, Princess, 17, 18, 20, 21, 23, 26, 34, 49, 56, 57, 73, 79, 112, 113, 123, 155, 156, 157, 168, 185, 208, 216, 221
Margrethe, Queen, 79, 81
Marie Louise, Princess, 20, 37, 53, 78
Marina, Princess, 20, 34, 164, 221
Marten, George, 209
Marten, Sir Henry, 25, 49
Mary, Princess, The Princess Royal, 11, 58, 150, 168
Mary, Queen, 7, 11, 12, 15, 16, 17, 18, 20, 26, 38, 47, 49, 66, 69, 165, 170, 173, 175, 185, 186, 191, 202
Mary Adelaide, Princess, 170
Maud, Princess, 168
Melbourne, Lord, 66, 70, 200
Meldrum, W., 216
Menzies, Sir Robert, 208
Mercer, Joe, 213
Michael of Kent, Prince, 161, 164, 168, 208
Michael of Kent, Princess, 161, 164, 168, 208, 221
Mildmay of Flete, Lord, 211
Milford Haven, 1st Marquess of (see Louis of Battenberg)
Milford Haven, George, 2nd Marquess of, 34
Miller, Sir John, 202
Mitterand, President, 105
Montagu of Beaulieu, Lord, 159
Moore, Captain Charles, 211, 213
Moore, Sir Philip, 65, 207, 208
Morrah, Dermot, 49, 66
Morrell, Lady Ottoline, 12
Morrison, Mary ('Mossy'), 207
Mountbatten of Burma, Earl, 25,

34, 44, 47, 56, 66, 78, 79, 95, 108, 129, 135, 157, 161, 170, 223, 228
Mountbatten, Edwina Countess of, 47, 78
Mountbatten, Lady Pamela (see Hicks)
Muggeridge, Malcolm, 53, 58
Murless, Sir Noel, 211, 213
Muzorewa, Bishop, 97

Nagako, Empress, 105
Nevill, Lord Rupert, 204, 207
Nicolson, Sir Harold, 17, 47, 191
Nixon, President, 85
Nixon, Tricia, 85
Nkrumah, Kwame, 83, 95
Norfolk, Bernard, Duke of, 53, 199
Norfolk, Miles, Duke of, 199
Northumberland, Hugh, Duke of, 199
Nyerere, President, 97

O'Donovan, Timothy, 112, 113
Ogilvy, Angus, 165, 202
Ogilvy, James, 103, 165, 221
Ogilvy, Lord, 202
Ogilvy, Marina, 165, 221
Olav, King, 78, 168
Oliver, Alan, 152
Oliver, Ann, 152
Osborne, John, 58
Owen, Dr David, 97
Palmer, Alan, 21
Palmerston, Lord, 186
Parker, Commander Michael, 38, 47
Parkinson, Norman, 147
Patricia, Princess (see Ramsay)
Paul VI, Pope, 161
Peel, Sir Robert, 200
Pembroke, Earl of, 145
Philip, Prince, Duke of Edinburgh, 25, 26, 30, 33, 34, 37, 38, 40, 44, 47, 49, 53, 60, 71, 75, 76, 78, 79, 81, 82, 82, 85, 87, 89, 103, 108, 112, 113, 123, 128, 134, 135, 147, 150, 152, 165, 168, 180, 186, 202, 204, 208, 216, 221, 233, 234
Phillips, Captain Mark, 66, 70, 104, 150, 152, 153, 208
Phillips, Peter, 70, 150, 185
Phillips, Zara, 150
Piggott, Lester, 213
Pius XII, Pope, 123
Porchester, Henry, Lord, 213
Powell, Enoch, 70, 101
Powell, Lady Violet, 12

Ramphal, Sir Shridath ('Sonny'), 97
Ramsay, Admiral Sir Alexander, 168
Ramsay of Mar, Captain Alexander, 170
Ramsay, Lady Patricia, 168, 170
Reagan, President, 89, 197
Richards, Sir Gordon, 211

Roberts, David, 186
Rocksavage, Earl of, 197
Roosevelt, President F.D., 161
Rothermere, Viscount, 202
Roland, ('Tiny'), 165
Ryan, Virginia (see Airlie)
Ryecart, Patrick, 199

St Andrews, George, Earl of, 103, 160, 221
St John-Stevas, Norman, 71, 204
Salisbury, 'Bobbety', Marquess of, 57, 63
Saltoun, Lady, 170
Sassoon, Sybil (see Cholmondeley)
Secombe, Sir Harry, 130
Selote, Queen, 53, 75, 86
Shand Kydd, Frances, 134
Shea, Michael, 208
Simpson, Mrs (see Windsor)
Sitwell, Dame Edith, 56
Sitwell, Sir Osbert, 186
Smith, Ian, 96
Smith, Sybil, 216
Smuts, Field-Marshal Earl of, 7, 30, 37
Snowdon, Lord, 103, 130, 155, 156, 157, 168
Snowdon, Countess of, 156
Sobers, Sir Garfield, 87
Somerset, David, 170
Southesk, 11th Earl of, 168
Spence, Sir Basil, 86
Spencer, Charles, 135
Spencer, Lady Diana (see Wales)
Spencer, Lady Jane (see Fellowes)
Spencer, 7th Earl, 134, 140
Stansgate, 2nd Viscount (see Benn)
Stamfordham, Lord, 65, 209
Stanhope, Earl, 233
Stanley, Oliver, 207
Stark, Kathleen 'Koo', 145
Stein, Mrion, 168
Stockton, Earl of (see Macmillan)
Strathmore and Kinghorne, Countess of, 11, 12, 15, 16, 18
Strathmore and Kinghorne, 14th Earl of, 11, 12, 15, 16, 18
Strathmore and Kinghorne, 15th Earl, 58
Strong, Sir Roy, 103

Taufa'ahau Tupou IV, King, 86
te Kanawa, Dame Kiri, 140
Teck, Prince of, 170
Teresa, Mother, 89
Thatcher, Margaret, 7, 63, 64, 68, 70, 95
Thomas, George, Viscount Tonypandy, 70
Thomas, Hugh, 150
Thorpe, Jeremy, 64, 168
Tiarks, Brigadier John, 150
Toms, Carl, 130
Townsend, Group-Captain Peter, 56, 57, 58, 80, 155
Trestrail, Michael, 204, 207, 223
Trudeau, Pierre, 85, 87, 96, 101

Truman, President, 40
Tuckwell, Patricia, 168
Tynan, Kenneth, 58

Ulster, Alexander, Earl of, 140, 160

van Deurs, Birgitte (see Gloucester)
Verwoerd, Dr, 95
Victoria, Princess, 168
Victoria, Queen, 11, 33, 58, 65, 66, 75, 79, 112, 113, 120, 168, 173, 175, 182, 194, 200, 209, 216, 229
von Reibnitz, Baroness Marie-Christine (see Michael of Kent)

Waldegrave, Earl, 207
Waldegrave, William, 207
Wales, Charles, Prince of (see Charles)
Wales, Diana, Princess of, 15, 73, 81, 112, 113, 130, 134, 135, 140, 141, 157, 168, 194, 202, 208, 209, 221, 223, 229, 233, 234
Wales, Edward, Prince of, (see Edward VIII)
Walker, Lady Bettie, 47
Walker, Captain Eric Sherbrooke, 47
Wallop, Jean, 213
Walwyn, Fulke, 127
Waugh, Auberon, 95, 108, 153
Waugh, Evelyn, 209
Wellington, Duke of, 11
Wells, H.G., 12
Wemyss, Earl of, 65
Westmorland, Countess of, 202
Westmorland, Earl of, 202
Wheeler-Bennett, Sir John, 18
Wheldon, Sir Huw, 185
Whitelaw, Viscount, 70
Whitlam, Gough, 64, 86, 101, 233
William of Gloucester, Prince, 159
William of Wales, Prince, 15, 141, 145, 153, 233
Wilson of Rievaulx, Lord, 63, 64, 68, 69, 70, 96
Windsor, Duchess of, 21, 57, 170, 201
Windsor, Duke of (see Edward VIII)
Windsor, Lady Davina, 160
Windsor, Lady Gabriella, 161
Windsor, Lady Helen, 103, 160, 221
Windsor, Lady Rose, 160
Windsor, Lord Frederick, 161
Windsor, Lord Nicholas, 160
Wodehouse, Sir P.G., 123, 127, 297
Worsthorne, Peregrine, 223, 224
Wyatt, Sir Woodrow, 123

York, Peter, 134
York, Duchess of (see Elizabeth, Queen Mother)
York, Duke of (see George VI)

256